Somatic Healing for the Modest Goddess

An Anthology of Love and Guidance for the Jewish Woman

Praise for

Miriam Racquel's Work

"These have been the most freeing and life-changing sessions I've ever had! Miriam is magic!" **— A.H., Colorado**

"Miriam Racquel has helped me tremendously release childhood trauma using her somatic healing skills." **— Gail, New York**

"My recommendation to anyone who is reading this, and perhaps looking to increase their quality of life, quality of relationships, and quality of personal wellbeing, is to be in direct touch with Miriam Racquel Feldman.... The quality of every aspect of my life has increased and I finally feel happiness and freedom." **— Aviva, Israel**

"There is hope! Miriam has shown me that it's possible to release trauma, even if it's been there for a very long time. The antidote to trauma/triggers is found in listening to your body. No matter how difficult, Miriam is one of those women who can hold your story, and guide you to a new beautiful 'what if?. If you allow it, the solutions will surprise and delight you."

— Chana, Baltimore

"I am floored every time I enter a session feeling tied up in knots, and come out the other side with clarity and calm. It often becomes clear that the reason I was stuck in my decision-making process was an underlying issue that only became apparent through the work I was doing with Miriam Racquel. She is gifted at helping women get in touch with their own wisdom. I wish every woman could have such a coach, and feel blessed to call her mine!" **— Sharon, Chicago, Illinois**

"I looked forward to Miriam's sessions. She is genuine and caring and I highly recommend Miriam and her somatic method!" **— S.B., Texas**

"Within just a few sessions I began feeling so empowered to make positive, lasting changes in my marriage that I had control over, and the wisdom I have accessed through Miriam Racquel's help has truly transformed my marriage into the playful, passionate one that I have always desired."

— N.C.G., Atlanta, Georgia

"I began working with Miriam after several years of extreme stress and trauma. The grief, stress, and other toxic emotions were keeping me from moving forward in my business. In addition, the frustration of feeling so deeply stuck was affecting my relationships, my energy levels, and sense of well-being, and more. The sessions Miriam and I did together were healing and illuminating, interesting and uplifting. They took me deep into my intuition, gave me profound insights into some of the underlying limiting emotions and beliefs that were holding me back, allowed me to reframe many of the things that were in my way and in some cases to actually energetically move them aside. After our work together, I was able to create an extremely successful program, and with far more ease than I would have expected. I have since recommended several people to Miriam, and would unequivocally do so for anyone who is interested in Mindbody coaching." **— Shifra Hendrie, Israel**

"I began working with Miriam not only to resolve the back pain I was experiencing but also to do deep emotional releasing that had built up over a period of time for me, especially in relation to working with highly difficult individuals. I now feel so much more empowered in making choices that align with what my soul and body needs. Without her support, I would have had a very hard time making changes and letting go of toxic relationships and situations that weren't serving me anymore."

— K.W., Manchester, UK

"Miriam's work is amazing! She is a Healer. Miriam operates with laser-like focus using tools to remove trauma long held in the body. She has helped me access my inner wisdom for guidance and recommended numerous resources for me to pursue between sessions. The results have provided me with clarity, motivation, and deep self compassion." **— G.T., New York**

"After almost a decade in a toxic relationship with a narcissist, I knew I needed more healing and resolution than standard talk therapy could provide. Miriam provided a somatic approach to mind and body coaching that really helped me turn my life around. I learned the importance of trusting my intuition again to make the decisions that were right for me. Thank you so much Miriam for the incredible difference you've made in my life!"

— Nicole T., Canada

"Each session with Miriam I become more deeply acquainted with my inner being both past and present. I am feeling an "at home" feeling in my body that I have never known. I have opened a beautiful space for my voice to be heard and for me to be seen as the kind sensitive soul that I am. Miriam's intuitive wisdom and fail-proof techniques have allowed me to release deeply held feelings through my body and my voice creating space for my intuition and creativity to come through. I have tools to stay grounded. Thank you for your beautiful and compassionate work, Miriam!"

— L.A., Boston

"I came to Miriam looking for help recovering from a painful breakup with a covert narcissist that I'd been suffering over for far too long. I realized that I'd not only been struggling from my most recent relationship but also from my childhood relationship with my father, which I thought I'd dealt with years ago. I learned that I had energy stuck in my body from real traumas I'd experienced, which talk alone was just not able to process. Miriam helped me with real-time processing in my body and clearing the immediate pain, as well as healing the source of my unhealthy relationship choices, and gave me tools for compassionately helping myself when difficult emotions arise in the future, leaving me feeling stable and self assured about myself and my future."

— T.H., Colorado

"I had been a follower of Miriam's on Facebook and was attracted to her approach to healing, and the beauty she shared through her photos and words. I reached out to her and in my first session felt the shift of energy

in my body that I had been longing for. Miriam uses somatic healing techniques that have been extremely effective for me. It is my great pleasure and honor to work with her." **— T.C., Kentucky**

"I was losing confidence in myself and starting to lose all hope in what's ahead of me. I now gained all of it back and feel even more hopeful and confident. I am very grateful to Miriam. She helped me go through one of the toughest periods of my life. She taught me how nothing can stop me if I believe in myself, if there is hope inside, and if I follow the hidden signals coming from my own body." **— S.M., Jordan**

"Miriam Racquel has the unique ability to invite you to HEAL. Releasing pain, dismantling mental distortions and replacing those with truths, and gaining new perspectives improved my emotional well-being, physical health, and personal/family relationships. She is a pleasure to work with: I leave smiling and encouraged! She has breadth of training & resources, which I'm grateful to continue to learn from. Thank you, Miriam Racquel!"

— L.H., Utah

"I was referred to Miriam by a friend to help me gain clarity, wisdom, and understanding after exiting an abusive relationship with a narcissist. Miriam's approach encompasses connecting the mind, body, and soul through a modality of techniques including discussions, deep thinking, and engaging the senses in a cathartic way. After each session, I feel revitalized, and I have a sense of calmness and peace." **— L.P., Connecticut**

"The sessions were probably the most impactful self-help I have ever received. Miriam's skill in understanding and connecting to my emotional struggles were very comforting and was what helped me grow exponentially from our time together. I am so grateful for the clarity I gained through our work together and most importantly the strong connection I now have with my intuitive wisdom which I know will help me overcome any challenge life brings my way." **— C.S., New York**

Also By Miriam Racquel

BOOK

God Said What?! #MyOrthodoxLife

E-GUIDES

The ROAR! Process for Somatic/Mindbody Wellness

3 Secrets to Solve Burnout and Get Energized the Mindbody Wellness Way

6 Simple Tips to Up the Vibe of Your Marriage Today!

Escape from the Borderline/ Narcissist's Web

Empowered Dating for the Enlightened Woman: A Mindbody Wellness Guide

The Mindbody Wellness Dating Guide For Frum Women

Soul Speak Guide

Somatic Healing for the Modest Goddess

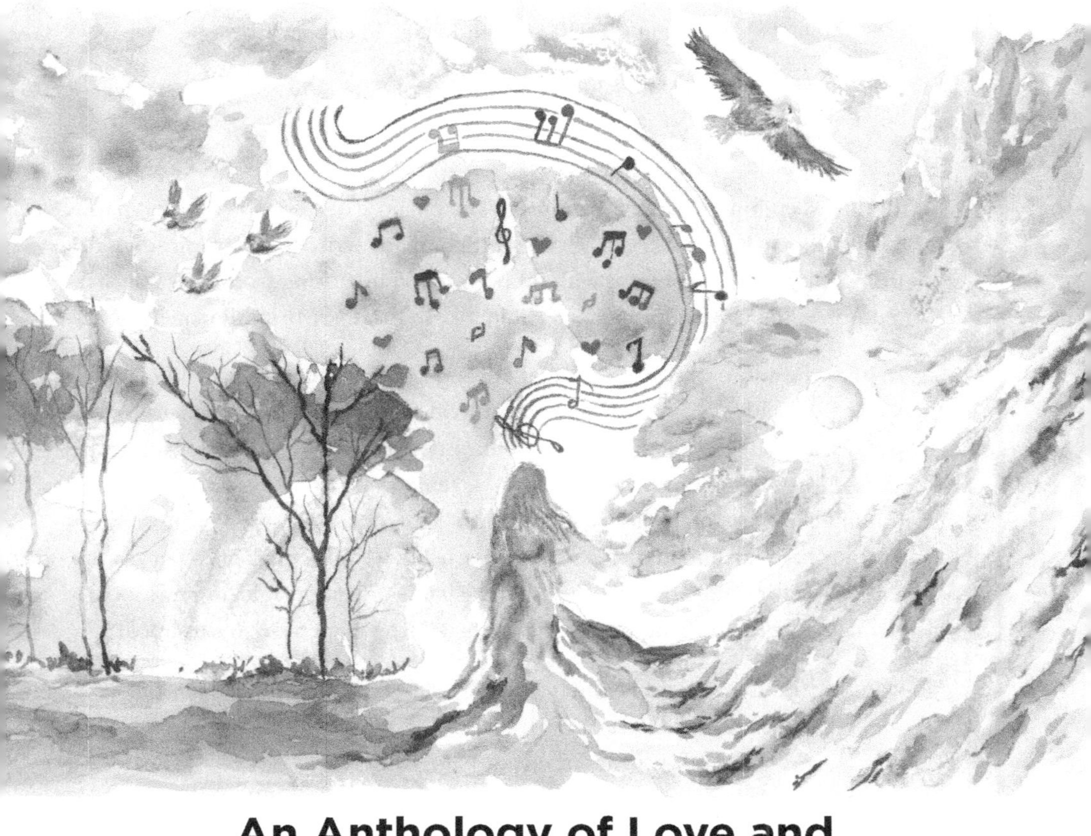

An Anthology of Love and Guidance for the Jewish Woman

Miriam Racquel (Meryl) Feldman

Somatic Healing for the Modest Goddess
An Anthology of Love and Wisdom for the Jewish Woman

ROAR! Process created by Miriam Racquel Feldman

Editors: Dovid Feldman, Deb Meister, Emma Danbury
Cover art: Chaya (Hazan) Carlebach; ChayaFineArt@gmail.com; www.instagram.com/ChayaFineArt/
Interior design: Rebecca Finkel, F + P Graphic Design, FPGD.com

Library of Congress Control Number: 2024911751
ISBN trade paper: 978-1-7377454-2-6
ISBN eBook: 978-1-7377454-3-3

Women & Judaism | Jewish Marriage | Emotional Self-Help

For all the Modest Goddesses out there—this book is for you!

May you shine your light for the world to see.

May you be blessed with health, joy, and love.

May you feel Hashem's smile in your lives.

May you feel like who you truly are—a gift to humanity.

~

For all the hostages—

I pray that by the time this book

reaches the hands of my readers,

you will all be home, safe and sound.

May Hashem heal your pain and

may the world know suffering no more. Amen!

~

A special thank you to all brave soldiers

who put their lives on the line to protect their people.

May the Jewish prophesied Geulah be revealed

and free you from your posts because there will only be peace.

Author's Note

Dear Awesome Reader,

While I wrote this book to address the concerns of my Jewish Orthodox community, the ideas, values, and practical advice within are universal. I coach women of all faiths and find that we are more similar than different, all facing the same challenges.

Because many Jewish ideas, words, and phrases are stated in their original language, I have provided a glossary in the back for easy reference.

Contents

Preface
Why I Wrote This Guide

I entered the frum community in my early twenties. The story of my baalas teshuvah journey is unique, and I share it in my memoir, *God Said What?! #MyOrthodoxLife.* Once observant, I felt an excitement in living a life of Torah values. Such new territory is filled with hope, emunah, and joy.

However, there were potholes. In my early 40s, I was in terrible physical pain from aches all over my body. I faced emotional burnout that I didn't recognize even though an expert did. Finally realizing that I was running on empty, I began a healing journey that led to becoming a somatic healer, marriage coach, and trauma & anxiety specialist.

When I look back on the road that I have traveled as a frum woman, I wish that I had had the wisdom that I am presenting to you here. I was often confused and encountered many challenges. As much Torah as I studied and knew, I still had many misconceptions. I ignored my body, suppressed my emotions, and didn't listen to the G-d given intuition that lay inside me.

And though I often reached out to mentors, friends, rabbis, and rebbetzins, most of whom were very helpful, I still felt I was missing something fundamental in my healthy and joyful service to Hashem.

With this book, I hope to reveal somatic awareness of your body, teach you how to process your emotions, help you reconnect to your feminine intuition, and share somatic wellness techniques and professional advice so you don't stumble into some of the potholes that I did. I'd love for you to have emotional, spiritual, and physical wholeness to serve Hashem b'simcha.

I believe that great health is Hashem's desire for the Jewish woman —the Modest Goddess. In today's world, there is a tremendous shadow that not only tries to snuff out the light but reprimands the light for being light. Traditional values are being attacked. You, the Modest Goddess, are holding the torch to bring forward a wisdom that the world desperately needs. According to the Lubavitcher Rebbe:

> "The Arizal explains that the generation of the geula is the gilgul of the generation that went out of Mitzrayim. Just as Chazal tell us about yetzi'as Mitzrayim, that 'the Jewish people went out of Mitzrayim in the merit of the righteous women of that generation,' so it is in regard to our geula: it will come in the merit of the righteous women of our generation (who are the [gilgul of] the very same righteous women of the generation [of yetzi'as Mitzrayim])."
>
> *—The Rebbe, Parshas Beshalach 5752*

Most of the content of this book is in the form of letters asking advice regarding personal situations, many of which I've addressed for my clients. I have been blessed to have several of these letters and articles published for The Jewish Woman on *Chabad.org* and various other wonderful women's magazines such as *Bodies and Souls, Nashim,* and *N'shei Chabad Newsletter.*

The wisdom I share has been gained over thirty-plus years. I've integrated the Torah that I live every day as a Jewish woman and what I've learned as a master somatic healer and life coach. I have also incorporated wisdom from relationship training, mentors, books, and life experience.

My hope in sharing this wisdom is that you feel pride as Hashem smiles at you and that we greet Moshiach together in health, wholeness, and joy.

Blessings,
Miriam Racquel (Meryl) Feldman

Introduction
Keeping the Goal in Mind

This book gives you a powerful opportunity to rewire yourself and create a life of greater positivity, joy, peace, and expansiveness. I've arranged the content in such a way that you can go to the chapters that feel most relevant and interesting to you or you can start from the beginning and work your way through.

Maybe you will see yourself in the questions being asked. Perhaps you have experienced a similar situation. I don't address all the complexities of life. Instead, I've chosen to focus on the ones I've navigated personally and others I've helped my clients navigate as well.

A Note on the exercises:

One of my goals in writing this book is to help minimize your self-pressure and your self-judgment, which are tricks of the *yetzer hara,* the evil inclination. Therefore, in the exercises, I use the word "Homeplay" because the word "work" (as in homework) evokes a response in the body that may cause tension, put pressure on the self, and may result in self-judgment if the exercise isn't completed or if it is judged as "not done right." Some things in our lives (many, really) will require tremendous effort, but striving to live as some of our wise sages have advised— with joy of heart—is the key. This includes being kind to our bodies. If the word "homework" brings on tension and pressure, then I don't want to use that word. I'll be using "Homeplay" instead.

Let this book be a source of inspiration for you—a welcoming home to your true self, to the genuine beauty within. It can bring you enlightened awareness of what is working in your life and what is not. It can help you shift negative patterns and unproductive habits. What I don't intend is for this book to be another source of negative messaging. As women, we are naturally hard on ourselves, always trying to do the right thing while at the same time pleasing others. If you, like me, struggle at times, you may need some help and guidance. My ultimate intent is to teach and inspire you to make changes and bring greater health and well-being into your life. This book brings you an awareness of how you treat yourself and how you take action in the world. It's especially effective if you take a few minutes during your busy day to sit down with a pen and paper and do an exercise or two. I also invite you to practice the tools. Knowledge (daas) and tiny turtle-step actions are key to making positive shifts.

When I was making changes in my life, moving from drained to joy, I took time to focus on my personal development. After sending my youngest to school, I would go to the library with my self-help books and training manuals and with curiosity, dive into the exercises. I gave myself the space to go within and take a quiet journey to explore my feelings, my thoughts, my childhood history. Taking time for these exercises was worth it.

Please make yourself worth it, because you are. So, my suggestion to you is this: do some exercises, take the tools seriously, and evolve into the woman you are meant to be—one who is kind and honors herself. One who serves Hashem with greater joy and health. One who is a great representative of her Jewish faith, nurturing her beauty within.

Somatic Wellness

For the later the generation, the closer the time to Moshiach's imminent arrival; a time when the latent spirituality found within the body will come to the fore, nurturing and sustaining its soul. As such, special care must be given to the body and it should be accorded an additional measure of respect.

—*The Lubavitcher Rebbe,*
Likkutei Sichos, Vol. II, pp. 530-532

For many years, I suffered from aches and pains all over my body, running to chiropractors, massage therapists, physical therapists, and doctors to try to find answers and relief. I had my spine adjusted, my body massaged, my blood taken. My youngest child was about two, my oldest about sixteen, and I was in my early forties.

One day, as the massage therapist treated me, pushing and prodding my body in the soft comfort of her dimmed room, aromatic smells of lavender wafting in the air, I asked her what she thought was causing my pain.

She rested her hand near my collarbone and sighed. Looking at me gently with kind eyes, she said, "You are empty. There is nothing here."

I was puzzled by her words. "What do you mean?"

"You are completely drained."

The massage therapist did me a great favor that day. She took my focus off of the pain in my body, and focused me in the direction of what was really asking for healing. It was my life.

Something had gone terribly awry during the many years of caretaking, of focusing outside of myself so completely that there was little vitality left inside me. The pain in my body reflected that. Though my hips hurt, my legs ached, and my back felt fragile, these were just symptoms of a greater problem, not the source of the pain.

My family, my friends, my religion, and my community were the most important things to me, but parts of myself had been neglected. What were they?

I left her office saddened and understood something needed to change.

Maybe you have had an experience like this. Perhaps you have tried over the years to conform to certain expectations of yourself or your community, but in the process have hurt yourself trying.

Now is the time to explore whether you have been living from a set of false expectations (we'll be uncovering that in this book). Perhaps you have lived in your head so much that you forgot it was attached to a body with limits; you pushed yourself too hard trying to complete your "very important" to-do list. Maybe your body is rebelling like mine did.

As Modest Goddesses, we are always guided by halacha, but we waste precious energy confusing halacha with what we believe are our community's expectations of us. We may prod our husbands and children to also live up to expectations that are not wise to pursue. We each have our own G-d-given path, purpose, and destiny. We each have our own body and our own nature that G-d has blessed us with. Yes, we can go beyond our nature in serving Hashem, but *what* does Hashem truly desire from us?

Perhaps you are familiar with the famous anecdote of the chassid Reb Zusha of Anipoli. On his deathbed, he explained to his students that he wasn't afraid of being asked why he wasn't Moshe because G-d already had a Moshe. He was terrified of being asked, "Zusha, why weren't you Zusha?"

It is not for us to be another, but for us to be our best selves with all the wonder and all the imperfections. Within these challenges, we bring light into our being and into the world. This is how we do our bit of tikkun for our individual souls for who knows what our challenges were in a past life? It is up to us to heal, and by doing so we elevate ourselves and the world with us.

On a psychological level, most of us have pitfalls from our past—bad experiences, loss, or unhealed childhood wounds. We experienced trauma which generated false beliefs that we have mistakenly folded into our adult selves. It is not wise to ignore these—those wounds need to be healed and the false beliefs revised.

Each of us has a purpose, a divine mission, a unique way of serving Hashem.

Let us steer by divine light, not ego shadow, trauma wounds, false beliefs, and harmful expectations.

As we'll explore in this book, the mind is a tricky thing. While halacha puts our heads in the right direction, for Torah is the blueprint for our journey as souls in bodies, our minds convince us of falsity. It may tell us many stories about who we should be and the way we should do things.

The yetzer hara dresses in all kinds of clothing—sometimes taking on the appearance of piety or self-pressure. It lies to us causing us to doubt our own self-worth. The yetzer hara's "shoulds" can lead to tremendous tension in the body, causing pain and unhappiness. Communities may put societal expectations on us that are based on the desire for conformity but are not good for our wellbeing.

Your well-being is a precious commodity. It is not a mitzvah to ignore your body, to get burnt out (as I did), and to feel like a schmatta. It is not a mitzvah to overexert yourself to get your to-do list done, or to listen to the inner slave driver's voice telling you that you're not "good enough." It's not a mitzvah to compare yourself to other women, noticing that they're more organized than you, dealing with more children than you ("And look, their house is so clean!") or working and accomplishing so much. It's great to learn from others, but not to expect yourself *to be* others. I came to realize on a first-hand basis that "compare and despair" did not bring joy and neither did pushing myself so hard.

The Lubavitcher Rebbe shares:

> "... the Rambam goes so far as to say that maintaining 'a healthy and whole body is part of Divine service.' Thus, not only is self-mortification prohibited, we are also to take measures—as part of our spiritual service—to ensure that our bodies are 'healthy and whole.'"
>
> —*Likkutei Sichos, Vol. II, pp. 530-532.*

Well, isn't it a type of self-mortification if you drive your health into the ground by listening to that inner slave driver that says you're not doing enough, being enough, giving enough? Hashem gives women gevurah for a reason. It means setting limits for ourselves, what we do with our precious time, and who we surround ourselves with. Hashem also gives us smarts and wits to understand who we are and what we need in order to be our best selves.

Along my journey, I discovered an important Wellness key:

You've Got to Feel to Heal.

When you have aches, pains, autoimmune symptoms, migraines—by all means, go to massage therapists, physical therapists, doctors, homeopaths, or nutritionists. Hashem is the true source of healing and determines the best path for recovery. Your healing can come from a doctor, a pill, or a chiropractic adjustment. However, in my coaching/healing practice and my own experience, I've come to learn that without delving into the underlying emotions, our relief is often short lived. Pain brought on by emotional distress, *even unconscious* emotional distress, will hop around, as a headache today and plantar fasciitis tomorrow.

The somatic approach to healing asks that you take a good look within your emotional realm. Notice your thought patterns, your work patterns, and your relationship patterns.

Some of the somatic approach I was trained in is grounded on the incredible work of Dr. John Sarno, a back doctor who revolutionized the medical field with his radical approaches to healing back pain and other physical ailments. He coined the term TMS, *tension myositis syndrome,* to describe a circulatory constriction in blood vessels that results in pain in the body. These pain symptoms are also known as mindbody pain syndrome. To sum up what Dr. Sarno has written in one of his many books, *The Mindbody Prescription* and taught for over 30-plus years, the brain will cut off blood and oxygen flow to different parts of the body in order to distract the individual from recognizing and feeling emotions that they are trying to avoid. This lack of blood and oxygen flow is the direct cause of pain. In order to get relief from the pain, a person will go running around to different doctors and scour the internet to get answers and diagnoses for help with pain relief, when the healing is within their reach and within their own body. They just need to feel to heal.

This is not to say AT ALL that the pain is only in the mind. The pain is real and the symptoms are real. But the healing comes from turning inward, getting honest about our emotions—especially our very human emotions of anger, fear, sadness, and grief. Most of us have the very normal habit of ignoring, repressing, or suppressing our emotions.

The good news: according to Dr. Sarno, when we give the message to our brain that we are not afraid of our emotions, it won't try to distract us by constricting blood and oxygen flow and causing pain or dysfunction. We are freeing ourselves from the suppression-pain cycle and are able to live a more vibrant, healthy life.

As my training continued and as I researched more into the "feel to heal" basis of good health, I collected tools for processing emotions. As I used these techniques on myself and with my clients, not only did my health improve and my vitality strengthen, but theirs did as well.

Emotions are "energy in motion." This is crucial to understand. They show up as physical sensations in the body, starting out very quiet and subtle, almost vibrational. When ignored, the tension in the body gets louder and louder until it "screams" as a migraine, backache, or some other pain or weakness in the body. The key here is to notice what our emotions and bodies are communicating to us, and this means being honest with ourselves. Now the healing can begin.

What Is Your Body Trying to Tell You?

By way of physical sensations, your body speaks to you. Your emotions *are* those physical sensations—before your mind grabs a label, like sadness, fear, or anger. For example, sadness may be felt as the physical sensation of heaviness in your chest. When you put your attention on that heavy feeling in your chest, even putting a hand to rest there, the energy of that emotion of sadness will flow. Your body has registered that you received the message that it was giving you. Each emotion has a message, and each person's body has their own way of expressing that energy.

One of the reasons that I love the opening quote from the Lubavitcher Rebbe is that the Rebbe is speaking about the spirituality of the body. The coming revelation of geulah is the refinement of the body to the extent that we can hear its wisdom and guidance. That is somatic wellness. We will be tuning into the wisdom of our bodies. The messages our bodies have for us, now in this time of Moshiach, can help guide us into more aligned action with our souls.

By starting on this journey for yourself, you are owning your G-d-given beauty and light.

Love and blessings,
Miriam Racquel

2

Self-Care

If I am not for myself,

then who will be for me?

And if I am only for myself,

then what am I?

And if not now, when?

—*Hillel,* Ethics of the Fathers, 1:14

Letter 1

Relieving the Pressures, Pain, and Drain of the Yetzer Hara

Dear Miriam Racquel,

I became a baalas teshuvah a few years ago. At first it was so exciting—I loved being part of a community, I loved doing chesed for others, I loved getting married and having a family. And I still do love all those things, but I'm feeling drained and irritated a lot. Sometimes I feel if another person asks me to do them a carpool favor or watch their kids, I'm going to snap.

It seems like in Yiddishkeit that "I" is a bad word and that everything has to be done for others or else you're judged for not being a good person or doing enough. I'm sure that I have this wrong because I know the quote from Hillel that clearly says I have to be for myself, yet the pressure is so intense to do more and more. Where do balance and self-care fit in?

Dear Awesome Woman,

I'm sorry that you're so drained and irritated. I get it!

That quote from Hillel enlightens us about being there for ourselves as well as for others. But how do we find that sweet spot?

Self-care is a necessary component of Yiddishkeit. If we are burnt out and drained, then how can we serve Hashem with joy?

We must be able to combine a joyful service to Hashem and Hashem's Torah, which *includes* staying in alignment with our health—mental and physical. Somatic wellness helps us do this because it brings about an integration of our emotions, our body, and our mind, as well as soul. Halacha puts our head on straight; and from there we do the dance with recognizing what is yetzer hara and what is kedusha.

We can do our best to fulfill what the Lubavitcher Rebbe says in Igros Kodesh, Vol. XI: "The point stressed in Chassidus that service of G-d in general is to be performed with a maximum of joy, for only then is one's spiritual service in the greatest possible manner...."

And, also in the words of the Lubavitcher Rebbe, know that, "When G-d gives every one of us something as precious as the body, we are to make every effort and truly exert ourselves to ensure that the body be healthy. In so doing, we make it possible to fulfill's G-d's will [of performing Torah and mitzvos, which is specifically performed with the body]."

Keeping our bodies healthy is not just about eating well and exercising, but about clearing out childhood wounds and trauma, dissolving false expectations and limitations, being kind to ourselves, and seeing ourselves for who we are truly—souls in bodies with distinct personalities and missions here on this planet.

Self-care is about honoring, respecting, and cherishing the person you are so that you can be at your best functioning capacity. It's about honoring your time, your energy, your spirit, your body, your desires, your space, and your authentic personal self so that you can show up for Hashem and do your particular services in the world. Through self-care, you can get to know what lights you up and what nurtures your body, mind, and heart.

Essential to self-care is setting boundaries, dropping limiting ideas, being receptive to help, dropping "shoulds," and tapping into your creativity. Taking responsibility for your own self-care is empowering and takes the burden off of others—your family, friends, community, rabbis, rebbetzins, and husband. This does not mean being an island and not reaching out for help when you need it. In fact, quite the opposite. Taking responsibility for your self-care includes knowing when you need assistance, acquiring it from kind sources, and receiving it with humility.

You're feeling burnt out, drained, and irritated. Let's start with dropping some of the lies of your yetzer hara that have been leading you down this unhealthy path. Much of the pressure that you feel may be coming from these lies. The Alter Rebbe says that the yetzer hara can dress up in very frum clothes and trick us into believing that we "should" do something, when actually it is taking us in the wrong direction. That wrong direction can be overwhelming, an inner slave driver telling us to do more community service at the expense of ignoring our families and our health.

So, what are the lies of your yetzer hara that are causing tension and stress for you? We won't be able to unravel all of them here. Even if we did, the yetzer hara will remain a trickster, attempting to stop you from your incredible missions here on earth, until Moshiach is fully revealed. The yetzer hara can confuse, drain, and play games. Awareness is key, and getting assistance from a coach, healer, or therapist can always be helpful. Being accountable for your self-care means making your mental, emotional, and physical health a top priority.

Homeplay Exercise

Uncovering and Dissolving the Lies of the Ego-self (a.k.a. Yetzer Hara)

On paper, finish these sentences with your own words. Don't censor, just quickly jot down what comes up in your mind. This is a first step in revealing the lies your yetzer hara is telling you:

A good Orthodox/Chassidische woman should feel ...; should think ...; should do ....

I should always ...

A good friend should ...

A good wife should ...

A good daughter should...

A great parent should ...

This exercise helps you recognize the rules that you have in your head about the way you "should be." You may have gotten these rules from your family, from society, from community, from friends—and your body has a reaction to each answer that you've given.

Let's see what's going on inside your body. Feel the physical sensations that arise when you read your statements. Does your chest expand or constrict? Do your shoulders feel heavy or light? Does your jaw tighten? Does your stomach clench?

Do the statements you jotted down cause inner tension and stress or do they protect your energy and bring you joy?

continued

When you read through them, do you feel light, expanded, and optimistic? Or do you feel constricted and burdened?

Now, rip that paper up and try replacing those "should" statements with these affirmations instead. Pay particular attention to your body when you read them.

This first one is based off of the work of Dr. Harriet Braiker, clinical psychologist and author of The Disease To Please:

> *I am not obligated to the expectations, desires, or demands of others. I can choose who to give to, as well as when and how. I get to decide.*

Here are a few others:

> *G-d gives me permission to say no when I need to.*
>
> *I can be kind and yet say no. People may feel disappointed.*
>
> *It is human to disappoint people and let them down sometimes.*
>
> *I give myself the freedom to discern wisely by asking myself these questions:*
>
> 1. *Will this drain me?*
> 2. *Will saying yes overstress me to the point where I get irritated at my loved ones?*
> 3. *Am I afraid to say no because the person will get mad or distance himself/herself from me?*

How does it feel in your body to read these affirmations and questions as replacements for the "shoulds?" Is there a release of pressure or tension in your body?

Please hang these up in your closet, on a mirror, or the fridge to empower yourself and give yourself that release of tension every time you read it, especially if you're someone who tends to "people please," or stretch yourself too thin.

Your energy is a precious commodity. If you don't take care of it and choose how to use it wisely, who will? Taking accountability for your self-care means that Hashem expects you to fear Him, not other people or their judgments. Taking accountability for your self-care means saying yes and no wisely.

Homeplay Exercise

Sticker Breathing

Relax Your Mind, Body and Soul

Another lie the yetzer hara tells us is that we haven't done enough. Hyperfocusing on your to-do list will cause tension and stress in the body. Rushing through life not taking time to breathe, relax, and enjoy is not serving Hashem with joy.

Many women falsely believe that if they can just get this and that done, then they'll be happy. Life is such that we won't get everything done before we die, so let's stop living the lie that we can. Your body and soul will thank you.

Sticker Breathing—Put some stickers around the house and a few times a day, when you come across them, pause, take an expanding belly breath in and release. Take another conscious breath and relax the muscles in your body that you notice are clenched or tight. You can even raise your arms above your head—yes, you may look weird (it doesn't faze my kids anymore)—but you'll get a great stretch in the shoulders and chest area. Your health matters!

Homeplay Exercise

Sense Spot Meditation—Get Present

If possible, go outside for this one. Do Sense Spot a few times weekly, for many minutes at a time. Feel your feet on the ground, close your eyes and just tune into your senses: what do you hear, smell, feel, taste? Bird song, cricket music, the wind in the trees, fresh-cut grass?

Then open your eyes and take in the sights.

Homeplay Exercise

Receive From Hashem and Others

Accept help, compliments, and gifts (unless the person is not emotionally or physically safe, then use boundaries). Receive help and revealed goodness—all of which comes from Hashem: that person holding the door open for you, that person helping you lift your heavy carry-on luggage into the above storage space, your husband bringing you flowers, your friend caring for you. You can't do it all yourself, so it's time to stop trying.

May these suggestions and exercises help relieve you of drain and irritation, and may you befuddle your yetzer hara by taking care of yourself as well as being there in a healthy capacity for others!

Blessings!

Letter 2

Stop the Compare and Despair and Appreciate You!

Dear Miriam Racquel,

I know that I should be happy with who I am, but I'm finding that I look at other women in the community and online and see how organized they are, or how fun they are with their kids, or even how confident they are, and compare myself to them. My childhood home was very critical and it never seemed okay the way I was, so I'm assuming my negative feelings towards myself come from there. I know that story about Zusha—him being afraid that Hashem will ask him, "Why weren't you more like Zusha?"—and that I shouldn't wish I was like someone else, but the truth is, I do.

Dear Awesome Woman,

Thank you for being so honest and vulnerable with me. Many people were raised in critical homes—older generations didn't necessarily have the awareness that we have today about the dangers of criticism. And previous generations were often victims of antisemitism, poverty, and the difficulties of immigration. There was tremendous trauma they faced and needed to rely heavily on a survival attitude, with lots of fight-or-flight response-filled hormones for their nervous systems. Untold stress and anxiety filled their beings.

Instead of creating a loving and accepting home, these suffering individuals created homes filled with expectations, fear, anger, and criticism. I'm sorry that you experienced that in your childhood home.

The good news is that at any age, we can get to know, accept, and love ourselves more than we did before. And this will lower our stress levels, which is not only wonderfully healthy for our bodies, but will help us serve Hashem to our highest potential.

When you pitch yourself against others and fail in your own eyes, this is called "compare and despair." All day long you are bombarded with images and blurbs from social media, advertisements, Hollywood, workplaces, and WhatsApp groups, as people announce their achievements with constant snapshots in time.

Take a moment to feel into your body to see whether you feel uplifted or drained by all this coming at you. As a start, know that it is up to you to make empowering decisions about closing your personal gates to the amount of exposure you have.

At the same time, you can also fortify and ground yourself in awareness of what makes you tick. Knowing who you are and what you love helps dissolve the compare and despair monster.

Let's look in particular at the feelings you get when you see all the things others are doing. You might be thinking, "Gosh, if I only did it their way, then I'd be … or I'd have …"

Since you know the Zusha story, then you know that G-d created you uniquely, and there is no way that you can do something someone else's way. It's impossible. Sure, you can learn some things from others, but it's only by tapping into your individual style and nature that will align you on your path.

Whether you're socializing, working, parenting, choosing a career, having downtime, exercising, eating, traveling, or doing whatever you're doing, recognize your own awesome way of being. Honor your own flare and style.

I love the work of Kathy Kolbe and Carol Tuttle in getting to know ourselves better. Please take some time to explore their work and see how the information resonates with you. I've learned so much about myself and my children by doing this. We'll start by looking at two of their ideas, Conative Styles and Energy Profiles, and then I'll share my "Recipe for an Introvert" and ideas for getting to know yourself through simple creativity.

Homeplay Exercise

Distinguish Your Conative Style

We all take action differently. According to Kathy Kolbe, if a car with four people in it were to break down in Alaska, each one would pile out of the car and attempt to handle the situation differently.

Person 1, the **Quick Start,** would run to the hood, open it up, and wiggle some wires around, even if they are completely ignorant of how a car works.

Person 2, the **Fact Finder,** would Google the problem and try to gather all the information they could before taking action.

Person 3, the **Implementer,** would look under the hood and fix the problem. They are a person who understands engines and is good with their hands.

continued

Person 4, the **Follow Thru,** would have Triple AAA as a contact and dial them up for assistance. They're super organized and tend to place their dirty silverware in the dishwasher by grouping together the knives, spoons, and forks.

Which one are you? There's one problem—in this case, a broken car—and four different approaches to handling it.

These four different approaches are referred to as a person's **conative style** or "typical action pattern." And of course, most of us are a mixture of all the styles, but there is probably a style that is more dominant for you.

Conative styles are instinctual—meaning a person is born with these patterns. Neither style is better or worse than the other. What is important to understand is what our individual conative approach to taking action is. When we get this, we can stop criticizing ourselves for the way we do things. And we can stop hitting our heads against the wall in comparing ourselves to others.

We stop beating ourselves up for not being as organized as Person 4, not as handy as Person 3, not as informative as Person 2 and not as spontaneous as Person 1.

Recognize your dominant style and respect yourself for it.

"It is funny: We ask G-d to to change our situation not knowing G-d put us in the situation to change us."

—Unknown

Homeplay Exercise

Distinguish Your Energy Profile

Energy Profiling is the work of Carol Tuttle, and she has a lot of podcasts, books (It's Just My Nature and The Child Whisperer are my favorites), and free videos for you to check out online. Her work is extremely helpful in understanding not only your own uniqueness but that of your loved ones as well. She believes that we have a dominant and secondary profile type, which is just how we were created. As you read about the four types below, think about which category aligns best with your personality. When I share this information with my clients, they immediately sense a truth about themselves that resonates at their core. What I share here is focused on personality descriptions. I encourage you to explore Tuttle's work which includes some fascinating connections with our physical features and structures as part of the Energy Profile.

Type 1: Air. Characterized by upward energy. Extroverted, spontaneous, fun, upbeat, unstructured. May have difficulty with being on time.

Type 2: Water. Characterized by gentle energy. Introverted, steady, subtle. Likes to feel comfortable, even when it comes to clothes. May have challenges making decisions; becomes stuck in self-doubt.

Type 3: Fire. Characterized by swift, dynamic energy. Extroverted, action-oriented, confident, irregular. "Let's get the show on the road." May be considered pushy at times.

Type 4: Earth. Characterized by still energy. Introverted, bold, structured, precise, organized, exact. Wants to be their own authority, even from a young age. May be considered stubborn or blunt at times.

continued

Distinguish your primary and secondary types and soar with accepting yourself as well as shifting your weaknesses.

Homeplay Exercise

Recipe for an Introvert (and Extroverts Needing a Break)

If you are an introvert or an extrovert needing a break, then try this recipe on for size. Inward processing is an introvert's best friend. In this day and age, the fast pace of life is even more of a challenge than it used to be. Self-care is a must in maintaining grace and health.

I have found that I am more energized, grateful, and productive when I have a continuous pattern throughout the day of inward energy, outward energy, inward energy, and outward energy, etc.

Downtime is the essential ingredient for staying centered and kind to myself and others, but to get things done, I intersperse that downtime with chunks of action.

Here is my **Recipe for an Introvert**—something I learned the hard way. I hope that it will benefit you and help keep your energy in check:

1. **Wake up and do inward energy things** like meditation, prayer, contemplation, inner processing, conscious breathing, or walking in nature.
2. **Do a chunk of outward energy activities.** Work, parent, clean up, declutter, exercise, socialize, talk, or interact on social media.

3. **Take time for inward energy.** Do breathing exercises, journal, process emotions, spend time in nature, collage, paint, crochet, or close your eyes and rest.

4. **Back to outward energy activities.** Parent, work, talk, run errands, clean, work on your to-do list.

5. **Return to inward energy** with conscious breaths, meditation, prayer, reading something feel-good, sitting and doing nothing for 5 minutes, or enjoying simple creativity.

All of the above can be mixed around, but always with the continued pattern of inward energy, outward energy, inward energy, and outward energy, etc. For an introvert, sprinkling inward energy breaks throughout your day will help preserve your sanity and health.

Homeplay Exercise

Simple Creativity

As we open our creative channel to the Creator,
many gentle but powerful changes are to be expected.
—Julia Cameron, *The Artist's Way*

Simple creativity is a great way to get to know yourself better and bring more joy and kindness into your life.

Many years ago, feeling drained and empty, I started to collage. From magazines that I had lying around the house, I cut out pictures and words that felt good to me, gluing them on paper using a simple glue stick. Pictures of oceans, flowers, paths, and words that caught my attention went on these papers, sometimes in a pretty way, and sometimes in a random way.

continued

Once I started, I couldn't stop—I collaged on cardboard, hardcovers from used books, and blank sheets of paper from scrapbook albums. I went to used bookstores and got inexpensive magazines, I clipped images from advertising fliers and store catalogs. Anything with pictures or words was put to good use.

This simple creativity started to fill a void that had been missing in all the caretaking roles that I had fulfilled over the years. I decorated my closet and later my office space with these collages. I surrounded myself with beauty and with images of things that brought me pleasure.

When I collaged, I didn't let the word "should" get in the way. I never "shoulded" myself with what I put on my boards. If I felt a little inner spark of uplift in my body, a subtle delight from a picture or word, it went on my board.

This action of collaging set me on the right track of increasing joy in my world. And guess what? Things on my board started showing up in my life. Call it synchronicity, or divine providence, but a lot of what I collaged came alive in real-world time.

And I did too—I came alive again—knowing what I wanted in my life, what lit me up and what gave me energy. I encourage you to give collaging a try. The key is to choose whatever images or words uplift you. There is no need to be artistic—just cut out words and images and glue them on paper to release your creative inner muse. Maybe you've heard this before *whatever you turn your attention to, more energy flows there.* Increasing your attention on feel-good words and pictures will cause energy to flow in that direction and enhance your spirit and life.

If collaging doesn't do it for you, then use a different creative outlet. Try watercolor pencils, charcoal drawing, weaving, rock painting, dancing, gardening, writing poetry, playing an instrument —whatever lights you up. You will start shifting your vibration and your happiness factor by creating something from nothing, that nothing being a space inside you that is open, vulnerable, available.

Simple creativity can be done in small chunks of time. I started doing this when some of my children were young, and so when I felt the need for some private time—a desire to disappear from the chaos of life—I locked my bedroom door and gave myself 10 minutes to collage. Of course, I only did this when I knew the kids would be safe or supervised. The goal wasn't to complete anything—it was just to enjoy the experience of creating.

I also brought this light of healing to a small group of kind friends. We gather every Rosh Chodesh to collage, paint, shmooze, and share thoughts on Torah, empowering and supporting each other through trying times as well as celebrating each other's successes. This has added tremendous joy to my life as well as the lives of the women who gather with me. Women lifting each other up helps heal the world.

Getting simply creative will increase your self-esteem and bring more happiness into your life. And as such, your negative feelings towards yourself may just disappear!

I hope that these suggestions and exercises help you discover just how awesome you are! Getting to know yourself dissolves a great deal of the "compare and despair" cycle because you begin to see and fully appreciate your uniqueness. Your body and soul will thank you for nurturing yourself in the way Hashem created you.

Blessings!

Letter 3

Releasing Tension with the ROAR! Process

Dear Miriam Racquel,

Thank you so much for your help—I've gotten to know myself much better and am taking care of my energy and health. My family and friends really appreciate these changes in me because I am more calm and relaxed. I do have a question though—what can I do with the regular frustrations of life? Or if I get annoyed with a family member? I know that you mention getting honest with yourself and not suppressing emotions—but how do I do that? What do you suggest?

Dear Awesome Woman,

So glad that you've gotten to know yourself better and are taking good care of your health. And you're asking a great question! You're absolutely right. There will be things that come up in life—situations or relationships—that frustrate, annoy, and scare us. Sometimes every day. If you've done some of the Homeplay exercises to dissolve the lies of your yetzer hara and gotten to know yourself better, then you're on your way to increasing joy in your life and decreasing your body's tension. Let's explore an emotional release technique to further your mental, emotional, physical, and spiritual health to prevent pent-up negative energy.

I created the **ROAR! Process** which is a somatic technique and can also be called **Miriam's Somatic Temper Tantrum Release** (what a mouthful!). It is my star signature and favorite exercise I do with my clients (and with myself). Through this exercise we feel our emotions in a bodily sense, allowing energy to be released instead of suppressed. Since we are not taught as children nor as adults how to listen to the wisdom of our bodies, layers of anger, anxiety, trauma, fear, frustration, grief, and resentment can remain stuck for years in the cells of our bodies, G-d forbid. What society has taught us is that we should hold in what we're feeling lest we hurt others, or that we should do the opposite and let it all hang out. Neither of these teachings will have a lasting effect if any.

We don't want the energy to stay stuck, and we don't want to ruin relationships by letting loose on others. The **ROAR! Process** helps us positively release our emotions instead of suppressing them or unleashing them onto others, while at the same time helping us to process trauma that may have gotten stuck in the cells for decades.

Emotions are "energy in motion" and need to be felt in your body as physical sensations. A furrowing between your brows, a desire to run, a desire to push forward, a constriction in your chest, a clenched jaw, a fluttering stomach—all these are physical sensations. You have a natural desire to fight or take flight to confront the source of pain or escape it. Good manners or fear of retaliation that could escalate the situation inhibits such a response. The result is to freeze which serves only to increase the anxiety and resulting tension.

Placing attention on these sensations allows for a flow of energy, a release of tension, and brings wisdom. Also, your body *wants* to complete the action it was not able to take. The **ROAR! Process** helps unlock freeze, allowing frustration, anger, and annoyance to dissipate in a particular and safe way—you're not leaking your messy emotions all over the ones you love. Instead, you're giving yourself the ability to release the freeze and activate the fight and flight response that has arisen from difficult interactions. Since you are not in the situation at the time you are doing the **ROAR! Process,** you can activate both the fight and flight at the same time (in real situations you do either or). You are making motions and getting movement (in private) to regulate your nervous system. The **ROAR! Process** is an excellent way to relieve pent-up anxiety, stress, and tension.

To develop the **ROAR! Process,** I integrated what I have learned through education, training, and intuition after years of practice.

The many benefits of using this tool:

1. **Physical Health.** To sit and steam about something your friend, partner, child, co-worker, boss, parent, or even stranger did, didn't, or should do is not healthy. It's also not healthy to rationalize away their behavior, because a change may need to be made. Being honest with yourself and getting present with your feelings will provide wisdom and discernment in your relationships.

   Using somatic wellness techniques means getting out of your head, into your body, and discharging energy. It means allowing flow.

   Since emotions are "energy in motion," if you're angry at someone, your jaw may unknowingly clench. This small shift in the body will most likely lead to a headache a few hours later. You may have tried rationalizing away the negative thoughts about that person, but your body will hold onto the emotion. And fighting what you are feeling leads directly to pain.

If you're criticized by your boss, then your stomach may sink and your chest may tighten leading to all kinds of ailments, G-d forbid.

If you're taking on too much responsibility, then you may be holding your shoulders up to your ears, trying to carry the weight of the world.

And if you're being stubborn about something, then in the morning you may wake up with a stiff neck.

This is your body talking to you. You can use **ROAR!** to listen to your body and give it emotional release, which can help prevent illness.

2. **Emotional Health.** You'll feel saner. By releasing the intensity of feelings inside, your emotions won't rule over you. Like a pressure cooker releasing steam, so are you—privately and safely.

3. **You'll Get in Touch with the Wisdom of Your Emotions.** All emotions carry messages for us. Since emotions are energetic and presented in the body as physical sensations, you can look at them as "words that your body is speaking to you." The **ROAR! Process** helps you to hear them because instead of judging your reaction to a person or situation, you are honestly being human. Angels don't have emotions. Humans do. Venting on paper, spilling out what is in your mind, heart, and throat allows you to identify what emotions you are feeling and what message they are carrying. Each is felt in the body—a constriction, a trembling, a heaviness, etc.—and the **ROAR! Process** release helps the energy flow.

   For example:
   Fear = focused awareness. What is happening around you? Is there a threat? How can you make yourself safe?

Anger = a boundary has been crossed by someone, either purposely or unintentionally. What action do you need to take to restore a healthy, respectful boundary for yourself? How can you protect yourself? Do you need to change the subject, get distance, deflect, etc.

Shame = you have uncovered a childhood wound. What wound have you uncovered?

Frustration = taking an ineffective action. What can you do differently?

Sadness = wishing something were different. Is there a release you need to do? What can be renewed?

Disappointment = something didn't match your expectations or work out as planned. What can you adjust?

Guilt = you have crossed your own boundaries. What value of yours have you disrespected? What was the motivation? How can you repair the damage? How can you get the help you need in a healthy way?

Envy = desiring a character trait, lifestyle, or possession that someone else has. If it's a character trait, are you sure that you don't have it? How can you develop it more? If it's a possession or lifestyle, what do you believe they have that you don't? What healthy changes can you make to acquire that?

Grief = a person or significant belief has been removed from your life. How can you mourn or let go? How can you celebrate or move on from what was?

Joy = an uplift of the spirit. How can you bring more of this light into your life?

4. **Space is created for positive change in your life and relationships.** This starts with getting honest with yourself. Changes can be made in very gentle ways, but awareness does need to happen for you to even make the changes in the first place. If you don't know what you want or if you don't know what's hurting you, then what can change? It's essential to get in touch with your feelings. Honesty with yourself is the best policy.

5. **It helps you tune into your intuition (your soul wisdom) and to be guided by actionable steps.** When you release trapped energy by getting out of your head and thoughts, you are able to hear your intuition more clearly—either in the way of an image, a thought, or a word.

6. **It helps release trauma by allowing your body to use survival responses.** These are the fight, flight, or freeze responses. When we've been criticized, hurt, humiliated, angered, our bodies want to respond. It's not usually the best action to hit someone or go running and screaming from a room, but our bodies may want to do just that. **The ROAR! Process** allows your body to release energy so that the energy doesn't get stuck as trauma.

7. **ROAR! helps prevent lashing out with words that cannot be taken back once said.** Yes, sticks and stones do hurt, and so do words. This tool can help keep relationships safe because honesty is not always the best policy with another person.

Homeplay Exercise

The ROAR! Process

Miriam's Somatic Temper Tantrum Release — the ROAR! Process for short! is meant to be done in a private space. You can do **ROAR!** anywhere—in a bathroom, in a car, in the privacy of your bedroom or office. The key is to feel uninhibited in your temper tantrum release. It's good to have paper and a writing utensil handy. I have inexpensive spiral notebooks in my drawer by my bed, in my office, and in my large pocketbook so that I can **ROAR!** anytime, anywhere. That way, if I catch myself ruminating about a situation or feeling freshly triggered by a situation, I can **ROAR!** on the spot before the negative energy gets stuck in my cells. However, if it's not the right time or place or if there is no privacy, I just take a moment to recognize that I'm feeling triggered and know that I will deal with it later when time permits. Until then, take a few minutes, or as much time as you have in that instance, to imagine your **ROAR!**

How to **ROAR!**

1. Rip: Rip starts with scribbling or writing (you can even draw) your anger, frustration, annoyance, or disappointment towards a person or situation onto paper. The writing does not need to be legible. Just pour out anything that is ruminating in your mind, heart, and throat area about what the person did, didn't do, or should be doing that is causing you to feel triggered emotionally. You can even do it as a letter to that person ("Dear ..."). They are never going to see it because you won't be showing it to them. Say anything that you want. On paper. If the situation is causing you grief, then write down all the "shoulds" and "shouldn'ts" of that situation. Scream on paper. You are emptying your mind of all the toxic thoughts rolling around in there. Again, **ROAR!** can be used for any situation and any relationship where you feel emotionally triggered.

After the writing, rip the paper up. Listen to the ripping sound as you rip and exaggerate the motion. The act of destruction makes way for new space and creation.

If you do not have paper or it's Shabbos, then air-write and pretend to rip. That works too. Imagination is a powerful tool in healing.

***For those who feel uncomfortable expressing angry words on paper (especially towards someone you love), please know that the emotion of anger signals that a boundary has been crossed. There is a reason why this emotion has surfaced. Though everything Hashem does is "for the good, " your job is to get insight from the emotions (physical sensations) that are coming up for you in a situation. Rabbi Zelig Pliskin in his book, Anger—The Inner Teacher, also recommends writing an angry letter and ripping it up.

2. Open (note: combine this with Action in part 3): Open your mouth in a silent scream. Yes, I know—it may look weird and you may feel weird doing it, but no one has to see you (except G-d, and G-d has seen weirder things than you doing a silent scream). Do this in the privacy of your room, bathroom, or car. What you're doing is releasing pent-up frustration from your throat area, where energy can sometimes get stuck. Words left unsaid block energy, stifle creativity, prevent hearing intuition, and are a health hazard.

You can also grumble or roar quietly, as well as do a dragon breath out: imagine blowing out a dragon fire breath—and do it for real by way of blowing outward—which pushes away or burns up whatever was frustrating or angering you. Don't worry, no one will get hurt, but you've released tension from your body and are creating a boundaried space for yourself.

continued

After you've opened your mouth to release the energy there, take a belly breath in and out.

How many people do you know who are walking around with thyroid issues? That's it—the throat area. Expression. Speaking up for oneself. Does that mean that if you have a thyroid or throat problem, you haven't been expressing yourself? No, not necessarily. Diseases have different causes. But I do know and have experienced myself that there can be a connection between body parts and their kabbalistic energies (such as the right and left side) and emotional representations. You may find helpful information in the reference section of Louse Hay's book, *You Can Heal Your Life*. In the back of the book she links body parts and ailments to probable causes. She also provides affirmations to create new thought patterns of healing. I have used Hay's methods successfully (along with somatic techniques) in my practice with my clients and for myself.

3. Action *(combine with part 2—opening of the mouth):* For this part, you're giving your body action. Run with your legs (either in a sitting down position or actually running around the room), punch out with your fists or hit out with a flattened palm. It's like having a temper tantrum, grown-up style (and with a silent scream instead of a toddler scream).

If you need more gentle movements, try walking around—you're giving your body movement. And you can punch with little motions—like a kangaroo with arms held closely up to the chest area. You can also push out in all directions instead of punching.

You're using your body's flight response by running and the fight response by punching the air. You are getting bigger with your energy instead of suppressing it. You're angry, mad, humiliated, and hurt. Instead of being frozen, you're letting loose. And no one is getting hurt by your release.

4. Released: Congratulations! You've just released pent up energy. Also, take a moment to gesture with your palms upward and imagine sending all this released and difficult energy to Hashem to recycle into love and light away from you, your body, and your home. Bring down energy, clarity, and strength from Hashem.

If your heart is pounding, rest your hand on it. Just notice the pounding. Give it love.

Listen to the sounds in your environment. What do you hear? The fan humming, an airplane outside? Birds singing? Feel your feet on the floor for grounding. Be present with your senses.

Also, notice any brief thought (intuition) or image that pops into your mind. You may hear, "They had a bad day," or "You do need to speak up." If you don't feel freedom or relief in the body, then it's not intuition. Intuition feels neutral and is kind, though sometimes blunt. You may hear that someone was being a bully or being cruel. The truth can be disconcerting to the mind. However, in my experience, I have found that intuitive soul wisdom is not afraid to call a spade a spade.

Another way to access intuition after the **ROAR! Process** is to imagine a compassionate angel or compassionate friend, relative, Tzaddik, or even part of you that can give you insight. What do they say or do when you visualize them? Offer a hug, a loving word, a compassionate insight?

You can also grab a gratitude as well — what about this situation has revealed something good that you don't take for granted?

Good for you for using **ROAR!** This is a great way to release resentment, preserve and protect your very precious health, and tap into inner wisdom. **ROAR!** can also help maintain relationships that you'd like to keep because it will prevent you from lashing out and saying things that you won't be able to take back.

Please use the **ROAR! Process** anytime in your life when you're feeling anxious, angry, frustrated, fearful, or annoyed with anyone or any situation. The **ROAR! Process** is the perfect somatic release for our bodies and emotions.

Blessings!

Letter 4

"I'm So Overwhelmed!"

Ways to Release Self-Criticism and Choose Kindness

Dear Miriam Racquel,

I am so overwhelmed! My life is filled with so much rushing and work and hecticness, and a "To Do" list a mile long. I have so much on my plate; my body is filled with aches and pains. I'm constantly criticizing myself for not being as organized, patient or accomplished as some of my friends. I also find myself snapping at my kids and husband. I feel like a mess! Any helpful suggestions would be greatly appreciated.

Dear Awesome Woman,

I'm so sorry that life is overwhelming and you're in pain. Even reading your words and how you signed your letter puts me in pain. And I remember feeling very similar to you. But I changed and so can you. Life can be busy, yet we can choose to be kind and nurturing to ourselves.

The Rebbe teaches that we have an obligation to go out of Mitzrayim, "Egypt," every day. What does this mean?

The word Mitzrayim also means "limitations." Each time we push past our limitations and tap into our soul's infinite power to touch the Divine and traverse difficulties, we are performing miracles, akin to those did during the Exodus.

When you beat yourself up inside—when you compare yourself to others and continuously fall short—you are living in a straitjacket of limitations.

It's time to set yourself free.

Many years ago, I came across a quote from the Rebbe that rocked my world. "Judaism is, essentially, a 'feminine' religion. As a religious and ethical system, it seeks to change the world into a better place, but its approach to achieving this goal is a uniquely feminine one."[1]

The feminine approach to change is through nurturing, as opposed to a masculine approach of conquering by force.[2] In this way, women are able to bring the underlying qualities of a person to the surface and help them grow at their own pace.

And so, I asked myself if the methods I was using to grow as a Jewish woman were those of conquering and subduing or gentleness and nurturing. I certainly didn't feel nurturing or gentle to myself. And that lack of gentle energy sometimes spilled over onto others.

I became aware that similar to you, I spent a lot of time criticizing myself, pushing myself and comparing myself to other women. I believed that if I worked harder on my "weaknesses," then I could conquer them.

Years have passed, and I have made a few simple shifts. I encourage you to try them too, to lessen the tension and stress that you're feeling in your daily life. This is you going out of your Mitzrayim, your

---

[1] Kol Menachem Haggadah, p. 85, quoting from *Likkutei Sichot,* vol. 20, p. 218.

[2] Yevamot 65b.

limitations, and choosing health, joy, nurturing and kindness—your birthright as a Jewish woman.

Our thoughts can affect the actual physical state of the body. As part of our autonomic nervous system, G-d created two primary modes: sympathetic (fight, flight and freeze) and parasympathetic (peace and patience). Like a hunting lioness—ears forward, eyes focused and body ready to attack—our sympathetic nervous system enables us to hyper-focus on the task at hand. However, operating from this model also creates a surplus of stress hormones and puts us in a controlled mindset, closing off our ability to recognize other responses available to us.

To maintain balance in our lives, G-d designed the parasympathetic nervous system, giving us the ability to rest, digest and recuperate after the body experiences stress. Reacting from this more peaceful space puts us in a more relaxed state of being. And, importantly, new and creative ideas and options become available to us for—we are no longer hyper-focused on trying to control the outcome.

Here are four ways to bring in more feminine, nurturing energy, while cutting down on the conquering/criticism:

1. Choose kinder words when speaking to yourself.

By using the word "choose to" in lieu of "have to," you'll notice an immediate softening effect on your body, emotions and behavior.

For example, when your mind begins to race in the morning with your "To Do" list, worrying how you will get everything done, feel the effect on your body. It is most likely a sense of dread and heaviness. If your kids enter your room with smiling faces (they have "play" on their list), you may start acting like a drill sergeant: "Did you do this? Are you almost ready for school? Did you … ?"

Now tweak it: Take a conscious breath and substitute the thought that "I have to get all this done today" with the thought "I am choosing to get some things done today." You'll feel your body soften, and your face and shoulders relax. Your chest will feel less constricted. From this gentler state, your mind will open to what you can realistically accomplish. You'll also be kinder to your children and husband—that vibration of feminine nurturing will radiate out.

You may be thinking "choose to" sounds nice, but there are things that you "have to get done." Yes, things have to get done, but technically, everything is a choice. You are choosing to do things because you want a certain positive outcome or are avoiding a negative one. You are choosing to do laundry because you want clean clothes to wear, and you choose to pay bills to avoid late fees. But does everything have to get done today? Are these emergencies? "Have to" feels forceful (conquering!) versus "choose to," which is more gentle.

Here are a few other word changes:

"Could" in lieu of "should."

"Notice" instead of "focus on."

"Play with" to replace "work on."

2. Celebrate yourself for your efforts.

Put your hands above your head and say "Yay me!" just like you would cheer on a child who did well on a test. Cheering someone on is kind, supportive and nurturing. Do this for yourself, and you'll slowly be able to release the need to compare yourself with others. You'll be noticing the good that you do in your life instead.

3. 'Tracht gut, vet zein gut.'

This is a Chassidic teaching: "Think good, and it will be good." Use positive affirmations to ease tension in your body and put your mind in a positive place. Focusing on the idea that we have an unlimited G-d Who is responsible for our care and will provide a good outcome will help your nervous system drop into the gentle parasympathetic state, rather than operating from the sympathetic state of sharp focus and intense control.

Here's one to try on: "G-d is good to me and gives me time to do what needs to be done." Breathe.

4. Never take anything for granted.

There are some very difficult things going on in the world today. Things are changing quite quickly and dramatically. Many of us may feel unsure and have trouble feeling grounded. Make a practice to grab for gratitude with the phrase "never take anything for granted." You'll find a whole list of things to appreciate that if they weren't in your life now (eyesight, ability to take action, family, breath, etc.), you would feel a loss.

Every day we have the opportunity to leave the inner exile of our previous place of limitations and enter into one that contains more presence, trust, calmness and kindness. Your calmer state will open you up to different possibilities of how and when to get things done, and even which tasks need to be done if at all. This is a more freeing way to live your life. Your mind, body, and soul, as well as those of your loved ones, will appreciate this new gentle, feminine energy of yours.

I'll leave you with a statement from the Zohar:

"If down here (people live their lives) with joy and with light, then the world Above reciprocates in kind, with light and joy."

Blessings! 

(Originally published at *TheJewishWoman.org*)

Letter 5
Addressing October 7th

Dear Miriam Racquel,

I see the news daily, and it's frightening. Since October 7th, antisemitism has reared its ugly head and the world appears to be falling apart. I feel overwhelmed by my emotions and am still in shock and grief over what happened. I don't know if I should look at the news or not look at the news; say tehillim all day or just go about coping with my life as regular and say tehillim when I can. My nerves are frayed, and I regret to admit that sometimes I take out my anxiety on those closest to me—my children and my spouse. I know that I should have more faith, but as much as I try, I'm still scared and getting more scared by the day.

Dear Awesome Woman,

I hear you. I believe that we are all in the same boat when it comes to feeling nervous about the world. You are not alone.

What happened on October 7th in Israel and to the Jewish nation as a whole is beyond words and comprehension. It is a testimony to our faith and resilience as a people that we rise in the morning and keep moving through our days when the pain is so deep, when hostages are still in captivity, soldiers' lives are at risk, and the world burns with antisemitism.

And where is G-d in all of this? We know that He's running the show, but it seems that everything has run amok.

The issues feel enormous, and we feel so small. Powerless.

But the Torah tells us that we are *not* powerless. In fact, the Torah consistently empowers us.

As Jews, we cannot live only in the world of nature and what appears before our eyes. We need to go beyond the physical. The world is made up of the energy of Divine letters. Right now, our eyes are not privy to see it that way, but it is G-d's truth.

The spies that were sent to report about the Land of Canaan returned with this statement:

> “We are unable to go up against the people, for they are stronger than us. … We appeared like grasshoppers in our eyes, and that's how we were in their eyes.”
>
> —*Numbers 13:31–33*

To sum it up in one word: powerlessness. But the spies were punished for this report, and the Jews were punished for believing them. G-d wants us to know that He is limitless. He can do anything, no matter what the world looks like.

And we need to know that that same G-d empowers us. It is our job not to believe what the world is telling us, but to believe in this limitless G-d and believe ourselves to have the power to make positive changes in this world. But we can't do this if we are frozen in fear and see ourselves as negligible to make change.

To share my personal experience—when I first heard the news of that horrible day, shock and fear overtook my body. And continued for many days after. The freeze effect was in full force and I needed to continually use my somatic knowledge and do my **ROAR! Process** to allow emotional energy to flow. I knew I could not allow myself to get stuck in the trauma response that my mind and body kept returning to.

Now, months later, I find it necessary to continuously pull myself up by the bootstraps and move forward, along with saying extra tehillim, giving extra charity, and posting on social media my thoughts and feelings about Eretz Yisrael and the state of the world. I still use my somatic processes in relation to the continued sadness, fear, grief, and anger, and I know that Moshiach is the only answer to this pain and chaos.

I'd like to help you move forward in this world that can feel so unstable and make us feel small, overwhelmed, and powerless. And since stress is harmful to your nervous system and to others around you, let's see if we can dial down some of that anxiety.

Here are some suggestions:

1. A Breath for Me, A Breath for You

As souls in bodies, we each have our own journeys on this very complicated planet. Our paths intersect with others and oftentimes, we can be helpful with acts of kindness, words of tehillim, and lending a hand. But what can you do if after all this, the person you care about is still in a place of suffering? What do you do then?

When someone we care for is suffering, there is intense emotionality around the situation. Breathing consciously can help prevent our nervous systems from shutting down. When your hands are tied to help someone more than you already have, your deep love and compassion for the other can be transmitted into breath.

This technique is simple and I learned it in a self-compassion healing class. I do this for the hostages, for the families of the hostages, for anyone who has lost loved ones in this terrible war, as well as for anyone else I feel compassion for. It goes like this: **take a conscious breath in and release as you think quietly to yourself:** ***A breath for me, a breath for you.***

You can even think a hundred breaths for me and a thousand breaths for the other. You can be creative with the number of breaths—whatever pops to mind. But you're basically breathing in deeply and consciously with the intention of breaths for you and breaths for the other. This has a very big calming effect on the body and I believe, a spiritual effect (like a prayer) for the other. You are sending compassionate energy through the big internet waves of life.

2. Do the ROAR! Process

Anxiety is generally made up of three emotions: anger, fear, and sadness.

- Clenched jaw, constricted breath and tight chest?
  Who are you angry with?
- Dropped stomach? What are you afraid of?
- Heaviness in your chest? Listen to your body and acknowledge that sadness.

You can process all of this emotional energy using the **ROAR! Process** (Letter 3 of this chapter) as often as needed to get unstuck and to release anxiety. Pour out ruminating thoughts on paper and rip it up with gusto. Are you angry at evil people? Are you angry at Hashem? Are you grieving the loss of families, the loss of dreams of a better world? Get it out on paper. And after the ripping, silent scream and temper tantrum.

If you need more gentle energy, notice which physical sensations are coming up for you and put your hand on that part. Or just bow your head and cry. Comfort yourself with compassion.

Let that emotional energy flow. Then send all that energy to Hashem to recycle into love and light and for it to be removed from your body, your soul, your being.

***A note about true fear. Please be aware that the message of the emotion of fear is asking you to have external awareness of your environment. Are you safe? How can you make yourself safe? Get present. If you're sitting in your bedroom processing emotions, then you are in a safe environment to do that. Otherwise you'd be fleeing or fighting. All this being said, in the dangerous times of today, we do need to be aware when our physical environments have become unsafe because of vicious antisemitism. Protests in your area can turn violent in a second, mob mentality can result. Know when it is time to leave or move to keep you and your loved ones as safe as possible.

3. Strengthen Your Bitachon

Jewish teachings explain that everything that G-d does is for our good, even if it doesn't look or feel that way. We must practice leaning into our natural bitachon—after all, we are called "believers, the children of believers." *(Shabbat 97a)*

We don't know everything. In fact, because of the infinite world we live in and the spiritual concealment that exists, we understand very little about life.

Clinical Psychologist Gabriel Strenger spoke of a nisayon as an opportunity to learn who we are and to develop powers within ourselves that we were not aware of before. We have an inner container that is stronger than we thought; Hashem does not need our tests, but we do.

He also shared that his definition of faith is "what I am not" and emphasized that we can cry and feel and be shaken, but Hashem has the key. We do not have the key nor the answers to these painful situations.

The Lubavitcher Rebbe also encouraged us to focus on our belief in Moshiach and the imminent Redemption. This not only strengthens us, but has the added benefit of hastening the coming of this peaceful time.

4. Limit Your Exposure

The Torah tells us to protect our gates. Those can be external property gates or our eyes and ears—the gates to our mind and soul.

There is good happening in the world. This is rarely shared in the media, which is often alarmist and doomsday-oriented. As philosopher Alain de Botton said, "Always remember that the news is always trying to make you scared. It's bad for us, but very good for news organizations: the easiest way to get an audience is through frightening people."

Choose carefully what you expose yourself to. You can listen to music that is soothing and Torah classes that are enlightening. You can engage with others, perhaps leading the conversation to topics that are uplifting and connecting. Your friends and colleagues may feel very grateful to hear of the abundance of kindness and unity that is also happening in the world. This will help lessen your anxious state of stress.

5. Take Action, However Small

Take small steps to help the causes you care about. Charity or volunteering with organizations that you feel make a difference is a great plan. Don't overwhelm your nervous system with big tasks; understand that tiny steps can lead to big changes.

The Rebbe always encouraged action. The Torah tells us how to take that action—by performing acts of kindness, smiling at people, giving charity, praying, saying Psalms, and exchanging inspirational words with others. G-d is in you and empowers you to make a difference in this world. Keep adding light and bring uplifting, soothing energy to a world that is broken, yet yearning to be fixed.

6. Reach Out for Support

The events of October 7th can trigger secondary trauma symptoms for people. Even if a person wasn't physically present at the site of the attacks, they can *feel* that they were and have symptoms of such. Please get help to release those trauma symptoms from your nervous system. Some symptoms may be layered on top of past traumas and there are release techniques for this.

7. Understand the Security of Eretz Yisrael

Jewish people need to understand that the safety and security of Eretz Yisrael relies on our inherent Jewish values and in particular, following halacha.

The Lubavitcher Rebbe stresses that the custom of the Jewish nation has been that a five year old begins studying the Five Books of Moses. This means that Rashi's following words are directed to the Children of Israel beginning at age five:

> "If the nations of the world should say to the Jews 'You are thieves, for you have conquered the land of the seven nations,' the Children of Israel should answer them: 'The whole world belongs to the Holy One; at will He gave it to them, and at will He took it from them and gave it to us.'"

So you see, the Rebbe does not encourage political or rational arguments. The Rebbe encourages the direct words of the Torah.

The Rebbe also stresses that according to Torah law, it is mandatory to have strong military on the borders of Eretz Yisrael and that it is dangerous for Jews everywhere, G-d forbid, to even discuss giving parts of the land away. The land of Israel was gifted to us from the Creator and we cannot give a gift from Hashem away. There can be no more misjudgments. Gaza was unfortunately given to people who hate Jews with a passion. They used the gift Hashem had given to **us** to slaughter our people.

With our rage, we can cry out: NEVER AGAIN and follow the rulings of our holy Torah. This will keep Jews everywhere safe (and non-Jews as well) until the coming of Moshiach in which:

"There will be neither famine nor war, neither envy nor strife, because goodness will flow in abundance and all delightful things will be as available as dust. The occupation of the entire world will be solely to know Hashem (G-d, spirituality)."

—the Rambam

Blessings!

3

Transitions for the Baalas Teshuvah

Don't give up you—just integrate you.

Remain creative and be kind to yourself

and others on your journey.

Become an even better version of you.

—Miriam Racquel Feldman

Letter 1
Retaining Friendships

Dear Miriam Racquel,

I've been becoming frum for a while, hanging out and learning with a rebbetzin at the college I attend. The problem is that when I go home for breaks, I feel so different from my childhood friends. I feel like I can't relate to them anymore and yet we share such a deep past together. Should I just let go of these relationships?

Dear Awesome Woman,

I would say no—do not let go of these precious relationships. If these childhood friendships rest on a foundation of kindness, then by all means, they are rare treasures and you'll benefit by maintaining them as best you can. Just because your values are changing to align more with Torah values does not mean that your personality is changing. I remember over 30 years ago, a very wise rabbi, Rabbi Yitzchak Berkowitz, said to the baalas teshuvah girls who were learning with him that we take our personalities with us when we become frum. You may not want to join them in going to the nightclubs anymore or to the non-kosher restaurants, but you can join them on hikes, shopping outings, and just pure, plain hanging out together.

And by all means, do not try to mekarev these childhood friends—they will wind up feeling judged and perhaps even missionized. I know that your intention is to share what is newly passionate in your heart, but they would most likely experience that passion as intrusive and not appreciate it. I offer the insight of the Lubavitcher Rebbe who did not like the word "mekarev," which means to draw close: the Rebbe asked, who knows who is close and who is far?

Instead, you can look at the people nearest and dearest to you with a good eye and with kindness, respect, love, and appreciation. This is the way you would also like to be treated. You can also share with them what you love about the Torah that you are learning and share how much their friendship means to you. Let them know that you are in the midst of a major life change, but that their friendship is very precious to you. Let the love flow. Your friends and family will feel your sincerity and they will see your changes as positive instead of as negative and contradictory. Your transition can be a kiddush Hashem, where they can see that Torah is making you an even kinder, more compassionate person than you already are.

Blessings!

Letter 2

Straddling Two Worlds While Becoming More Observant

Dear Miriam Racquel,

I feel like I'm very unsettled between two worlds—that of the Torah world and that of the non-religious world. Yes, I know what I should be doing. I'm learning all this stuff that I didn't know before, and yet I feel like I'll break if I try to do everything at once. My rabbis and rebbetzins are kind and wonderful and tell me to go slow, but it feels so weird to be straddling two worlds.

I'm still wearing pants (and not skirts) because I'm not ready to give those up yet. I'm still going to non-kosher restaurants with my secular family (though not eating the food) because I haven't told them that I don't want to go anymore. Help! It feels crazy and scary.

Dear Awesome Woman,

I'm right there with you! You're making some really hefty changes in your life, your paradigm is shifting, and if you move too fast, it won't be healthy for you. I'm so glad that your rabbis and rebbetzins are telling you to go slow. Your keli, or "vessel" (which is your body and being), is stretching to receive all these changes that you are making.

We don't want that vessel to break. Please continue to ask your mentors (or if you haven't, then begin now) what is the best mitzvah to take on and when. This way, you know that you are moving forward on your Torah journey but not overwhelming yourself. Slow and steady is better than fast and breaking.

I also have three other suggestions for you to help ease your journey:

1. Remove the "shoulds."

Say this: "I *should* be wearing skirts." Notice what that feels like in your body. Do you feel a constriction in your head or chest? Do you feel like your body wants to turn and run? This is the fight/flight or freeze reaction being triggered in your body. This is not great for your health unless you're in physical danger.

Now say this: "I *could* be wearing skirts." Notice what this sentence feels like in your body. Less tightening? A more neutral feeling? Do other thoughts flow, like: "I could be wearing skirts, but the rebbetzin said it's best if I wait and take it slow." Or, "I could be telling my family that I don't eat at those restaurants anymore, but the rabbi said it's not time to stop yet because my family is already feeling my distancing from them in so many ways, and adding this extra distance between us won't help. They don't seem ready to switch to going to only kosher restaurants for me but this may come in time."

The journey that you are on is very courageous. When you lessen the internal judgment and pressure by using the word "could" instead of "should," you will feel safer moving forward.

Toggle between the two words in your thoughts and even jot them down in sentences. You'll experience a sense of kindness to your body and being. This kindness is not only a healthier choice but opens up your mind to hearing your intuition, your "soul speak," as I call it. It can help lead you forward on your journey, making wise decisions in interactions with others as you are guided by your mentors.

When you have this kindness within you, it also radiates outwards to others. It is a felt energy, and will make your loved ones feel less threatened by the changes that you are making.

2. Feel the vulnerability and fear in your body.

Feel your feet solidly resting on the floor and wiggle your toes. Put your attention on your feet and toes wiggling. Exhale all the way out and count to four before breathing in. Do this a few times.

Now take a look inward—where do you feel the vulnerability and fear of change in your body? Is it in your chest, a tight feeling? Or maybe it feels like a bunch of rocks or a single boulder sitting in your stomach. Wherever that sensation sits, put a hand or two on that area and just breathe gently while noticing. The energy will flow. Maybe an image will come to mind or you'll get an intuitive thought.

You can also bring a *tzaddik* into your imagination or a compassionate mentor to sit by your side. Imagination is very helpful in calming down your nervous system.

Recognize that you are very vulnerable now in the midst of all the changes that you are making. You are like a caterpillar that is losing its identity and forming a new one, that of a butterfly. This is exciting, as well as new and scary. Witnessing the somatic sensations of your body and allowing that emotional energy to flow helps you step forward with more ease and health on your journey.

3. Know (and do) what brings you joy.

Stay creative, fun and playful on your journey to becoming observant. Don't let your devotion to religion knock that out of you; be you and even a better version of you with Torah. You may have already let go of the playful, creative side of you once you became an adult, but we all need to embrace some parts of being a child in order to stay healthy and joyful in our lives.

Fun and play means different things for everyone. Some people are introverted and some extroverted; some love art and some gardening; some love cooking, and others love nature. What do you love?

Know your "body compass." This exercise is based off the tool from author and coach mentor Martha Beck. Draw a straight line on a piece of paper. On the left side of the line, draw a sad face and write –10. On the right side of the line, draw a smiley face and write +10. In the center of the line, put the word neutral and write the number zero.

Conjure up activities in your mind and place them hypothetically on this chart according to what you feel in your body. If you feel an uplift in your body, a lightness in your chest, a smile on your face, then rate them close to the +10.

Other activities that may feel like a drain or tightness in your chest—tension in your body—place those closer to the –10. You can even rate them; I have found that my clients intuitively know whether certain activities are a +7, +5, -4, -2, etc. It's unexplainable, but very cool to see how instinctively we know ourselves.

The point is to notice what things you love to do and to do more of them. Of course, they need to be in line with Judaism because that is where the Jewish soul wants to be. If you love to sing, gather friends and make a *farbrengen*. Make time to do what brings you joy.

You may notice that there are things that may bring a negative, constricting feeling in your body, but you still choose to do them, such as laundry or chores when they don't feel uplifting. Not everything we choose to do will bring us joy—doctor's appointments don't bring me joy, for example, but I believe that they are necessary for maintaining good health. Using the body compass is just a great way to remember to bring joy into our lives—to do fun things that activate a feeling of vitality in our souls.

Living a Torah life doesn't mean losing yourself or your individuality. It means channeling those unique things that make you who you are into living a life aligned with G-d's will, to live your best life.

Blessings! 

(Originally published at *TheJewishWoman.org*)

Letter 3

Criticized by Family Members for Becoming Religious

Dear Miriam Racquel,

My family is giving me a hard time about the changes I'm making in my efforts to become more religious. They don't understand why I won't eat at their favorite restaurant anymore, why it's so important for me to wear modest clothes, or why I won't drive with them to Aunt Marsha's on Saturday. They think that the laws are stupid and separate me from them. And sometimes, I think that they're right! I feel so alone and it makes me question the journey that I am on.

But I want to do things according to the Torah. What they refer to as "archaic," I see as timeless wisdom. My journey would be so much easier if my family would let up and be more respectful and understanding. How can I navigate this?

Dear Awesome Woman,

I hear you, and I'm sorry that you're experiencing this. Your journey is difficult as it is, without being ridiculed. How much more difficult it is when others are acting unkind.

And I'm so sorry that you're feeling alone. Know that you are truly not. There are so many of us who have taken similar journeys with our own share of difficulties and loneliness, too. We have come to understand that G-d is right there with us and yet on this physical plane we can't necessarily feel the support or hear the answers in each of these difficult moments. For each grimace and snide comment that our families make, there is pain.

So, let's take it slow. Here are a few suggestions:

1. You are not the rabbi for your family and friends.

You do not need to explain each law or Torah teaching to your family; that's not your job. While you can briefly explain what you do and why you do it, it's not your responsibility to convince them of anything. Your job is to try and maintain a loving connection despite the changes that you are making. I don't know what your relationship has been with your family until now. Usually, the same patterns that existed before are there after you become observant, too.

2. Be as independent as you can be.

Can you work, earn money and not live in your family home if they are not keeping kashrut and observing mitzvahs like you are? Or if you must live at home, can you pay for your own food and needs?

Try not to rely on your family for sustenance. They have boundaries as well, and if they don't understand what you're doing, then they also don't need to support it financially or even emotionally. Sure, we'd love them to, but that is not a requirement of a family member.

To treat you kindly and respectfully is a requirement—just like they would a stranger—but to financially or emotionally support you is not. As painful as it is, they do not need to understand you. Your rabbi or rebbetzin or friends and community who share your journey with you will understand you. Make sure to spend time developing those relationships (even connecting online will help you feel supported and understood).

3. Check your energy; how are you showing up?

People can sense our energy. If you're feeling insecure and defensive, your family will sense that. If you're confident in what you are doing and believing, they will feel that energy from you.

Are you being too critical of yourself? The kinder you are to yourself, the kinder others will be to you, too.

Are you being ornery? Entitled? Uncompromising? Are you being wishy-washy? Or the opposite—are you being "holier than thou" and judgmental?

If you're judging others—"They're not religious enough," "They're not doing what they're supposed to do," and even, "They should understand me"—that will be felt. People respond to the energy behind your words, not necessarily to the words themselves. Speak to your mentors, rabbis and rebbetzins, or enlist the help of a safe coach to guide you through this transition so you can be as respectful as possible to yourself as well as others.

4. Set boundaries to maintain your mental and emotional health.

If you're showing up with kindness, and your family is being critical, pressuring and unkind (probably patterns from before you took the journey to religious observance), you may be feeling shame, hurt, sadness and anger. That anger may be letting you know that there is a "boundary violation" going on, and it is very important to assess for healthy boundary setting. It's not OK to be treated with disdain. This is where you can practice speaking up for yourself, distancing when you need to and treating yourself with the respect and kindness you deserve.

It's also important to only share what feels safe to you. Your vulnerability is very important. If family members have the past pattern of trampling on that preciousness, then it is wise to stop sharing your thoughts and feelings. This is setting boundaries for yourself: Have respectful interactions, but don't share your innards.

If you don't live with your family, then you can be respectful by making brief phone calls or visits. And even if you do live with them, interact wisely. Spend the time focusing on them and their welfare. You don't need to share what you are doing or learning.

By setting up boundaries, you'll avoid resentment and you'll also be taking accountability for your life. You need energy for embracing this new path towards a Torah life, as well as energy for your creative endeavors. Having limits allows you to say yes to beautiful things on your soul's path.

If your family members are the type (and you would know this by now since you have grown up with them) where it is possible to have open conversations, then do so using "I" statements. For example, you could say: *"I feel misunderstood, and that makes sense considering that I am taking a different path than I used to. Maybe there is fear and worry on your part. I do love you and I am being as cautious as possible on my journey. I'd love to be close to you during this time of transition. What I need is love, kindness and acceptance as I am making my choices and decisions, as kooky as they may be to others. I will also try to be kind and respectful to you, though I won't be choosing to do some of the things that I used to do—like eating non-kosher food or driving on Shabbat."*

5. Celebrate you!

You are on an incredibly brave journey, leaving a familiar past and entering into the unknown. Put your arms up in the air and say, "Yay, me!" What a beautiful statement of courage. The Torah life is a beautiful one—one where you choose to cherish your soul. Good for you!

Blessings! 

(Originally published at *TheJewishWoman.org*)

Letter 4

Feeling Rejected by My Former Shabbat Hosts

Dear Miriam Racquel,

During my journey of becoming more observant, I've been very close to a certain family—always sleeping there for Shabbat, staying up late talking with them, calling them when I have questions. Now I feel like they don't have as much time for me anymore. I feel rejected and lonely.

Dear Awesome Woman,

The teshuvah journey is complex and can be lonely. When we meet people whom we connect with closely, it makes the path so much easier. Here are some ideas that can help you with your feelings of loneliness and rejection.

Look to Broaden Your Scope

Keep in mind that people go through things and you are not always privy to the details. For myself, there are times when I am able to engage a lot with others, and times when I need more privacy because of what G-d is bringing into my life.

Can you broaden the range of people who can be your mentors and Shabbat hosts? That way, if one is not available, you can turn to another.

Also, keep in mind that during different times in your life, different mentors will be needed. Life and relationships change, and the more that we are aware of that, the better we will flow with the ups and downs.

Turn to Your Source to Ask for Help

Remember that G-d is the true Source of everything, and just as He has provided you with one family that you have been close to, He can provide you with more. Practice turning to G-d when you need something and ask for His help.

When I was looking for a new doctor, I did my research and called around, but I also said, "G-d, I know that you are the one who provides me with what I need, and now I need to find a doctor who is kind, has good energy, and most importantly, great skill. Thank you!"

You can do the same in this situation.

Self-Care and Joyful Activities

It's important to make yourself happy. Though we need other people in our lives—friends, family, mentors—the joy we can create on our own is crucial for our mental, emotional and physical wellbeing. Make sure that you are doing things you love and sprinkle those throughout your week.

Walks in nature, going to the gym or the pool, and even dancing to music are options to uplift your energy. When your mood is lighter, loneliness has fewer opportunities to sneak in.

Are there ways to bring more kind people into your life? Perhaps joining classes will help. Even if they are on Zoom, you could easily meet others on a similar life journey.

Acknowledge Your Disappointment and Step Into Gratitude

When we don't get what we ask for, it can mean that even though we feel we "need" something, G-d has a different plan or different timing. This can be disappointing and frustrating to our very human selves.

Take time to feel that disappointment in your body; these are very real emotions. Putting your hands on your chest and bowing forward into the grief for a few seconds acknowledges the physical sensation of the loss. It is OK to mourn the loss and distance of this family. Then stretch upwards and bring your arms out to the sides. Take up space and feel your empowerment to move on with G-d's help. Step into gratitude that you found this family in the first place and be appreciative to the family for that as well.

Open Up to Your Mentors

Once you've tried these suggestions, you may feel less lonely. Hopefully, this will be felt as an energetic shift in your body. At this point, you may choose to open up to them about the distance you're feeling.

Sometimes, these kinds of conversations are worth having because the feedback we get can be life-changing. Perhaps you were leaning a bit too much on this family. Perhaps they are going through something that is difficult for them. If you approach with soft and gentle energy, this conversation may bring awareness as well as a closer connection.

A conversation could go like this:

You: "Thank you so much for all you've done for me. I really appreciate the talks that we've had and the many Shabbats that I've spent by you. You've been so giving of your time and energy. I've loved the warmth and connection that I have felt here, and I hope one day to have my own family and do the same for others on their journey. I'm just wondering if you felt that I leaned on you too much, or if I took too much of your time and energy? I'm feeling a slight distance between us, and I apologize if I've done anything that has been disrespectful or draining to you. If there has been anything that I did, I'd like to understand and make amends."

Life and relationships are a series of changes, and so are your feelings and actions. Keep in mind that you are resilient and strong, making a very powerful transition. Give yourself kindness, hugs, and high fives—yes, literally—along the way.

Blessings! 

(Originally published at *TheJewishWoman.org*)

Letter 5

Why Date Orthodox Style?

Dear Miriam Racquel,

Meeting men through a matchmaking system seems so strange compared to meeting them on my own. I'd like your perspective since you dated the secular way in college and then became more observant and dated Orthodox style.

Dear Awesome Woman,

I'd like to share my perspective shift through a story I originally published at *TheJewishWoman.org: G-d Said What?! A Conversation About the Jewish Way in Dating and Marriage.* Enjoy!

> I glanced at the teacher in front. Referred to as 'rebbetzin,' she had her hair covered by a blue floral scarf, legs covered by a long cotton skirt and elbows covered by sleeves rolled to just below that part of her arm. She looked to be in her early 30s, and her long, Bohemian skirt was similar to the ones I wore in California sometimes. If it weren't for all the talk, I could imagine hanging out at a coffee shop with her back home.
>
> I tuned into what she was saying. Today, she wasn't discussing codes; she was talking about dating the Torah way. My ears perked up.

"And so, there's no touching while the couple dates, no hand-holding, no hugs. This is out of respect and honor for each other's bodies. The dating period doesn't last that long; that would be physically and emotionally difficult for the couple. And they're not dating for fun. It wouldn't be much fun to date and not touch, would it?" The rebbetzin opened her palms to us. "They're dating to determine whether they want to marry and spend the rest of their lives together." I leaned forward and placed my bare elbows on the table, eyes glued on the rebbetzin.

"They're dating for the sole purpose of seeing if they want to build a home together. Physical intimacy is a very holy act in Judaism, and it's not supposed to only involve the body. There's a very strong emotional and spiritual aspect as well. And with the heart and soul involved by way of a structured commitment in the form of marriage, the couple unites on all levels."

"But hand-holding and hugging aren't really intimate," said a woman sitting behind me.

The rebbetzin took a few steps forward. "Oh, but they are. When one is sensitized to the physicality of the body, then there is a natural attraction between men and women. Touching, even a handshake, can feel arousing." She paused. An astonished silence filled the room.

"In fact, even when a couple is married, there are about two weeks during the month when they don't touch or even pass things to each other. They sleep in separate beds. Orthodox Jewish homes have two beds in the master bedroom just for this reason."

My mouth fell open.

A woman from the other side of the room called out, "You mean not being together, like … together *together?*" I realized that we were all being a bit careful with our language in the presence of a religious person.

The teacher replied with an understanding smile, "Yup, that means not being 'together together'—no touching whatsoever."

I had to make sure I was understanding this. "Are you serious? You mean even when the couple is married, they purposely aren't together or even hug, kiss or anything for weeks?"

"Yes," she replied. "It's the secret of the Jewish marriage. It keeps the flame of attraction alive. One of the reasons the sages give for why G-d put these marriage laws in the Torah is to keep the couple desiring each other instead of taking each other's bodies for granted. Once a month, the wife goes to a special body of water called a mikvah, and immerses herself in order to reunite with her husband, body and soul. It's like a built-in marriage honeymoon for the couple."

I shut my mouth. Wow. No wonder religious Jews believed that G-d wrote the Torah; there's no way a man would have written these kinds of rules. I knew that in Christianity, there are monks and nuns who commit to celibacy. But in Judaism, men and women were dating and marrying, yet abstaining during certain times. Huh. Maybe there was a G-d who came up with these strange laws. Certainly, none of the guys I knew would have come up with no touching while dating and marrying.

"Look around, ladies," the rebbetzin continued. "Don't you see the divorce rate in the secular world skyrocketing? In the Torah world, divorce happens, but is more rare, and adhering to these laws of separation and reunification within the marriage helps keep those rates down. G-d created human beings to want what they can't have. The couple remains wanting each other because for a few weeks during the month, they can't have each other. These marriage laws are a built-in system of the natural ebb and flow of desire and attraction. The couple yearns to touch each other during those 'forbidden' weeks, desire builds, and then, voilà! They get to reunite in physical, emotional and spiritual intimacy, all in one, until they separate again a few weeks later."

The rebbetzin continued, but I had stopped listening. A trip down memory lane brought me to all the pain I had had when David and I broke up after college. In the secular way of life, it made sense to David not to be "tied down" to me as a girlfriend back home while he studied abroad. But I had been terribly hurt, and had wasted so much time and energy trying to get over him and move my heart on.

The rebbetzin had introduced a whole new way of explaining things—a different perspective on men, women, relationships, intimacy, dating and marriage. A paradigm shift that sounded odd, restrictive and a bit crazy, but maybe a bit easier on the heart and emotions. Dating only for the purpose of marriage? Maybe it lessened that confusion of, "Where is this relationship going? What do we mean to each other?"

And from where I sat—having found myself on a journey to heal the past year's heartache and muck of an open-ended relationship—dating the way the rebbetzin proposed suddenly sounded like a great idea.

Blessings! 

Letter 6
Modesty? What's in a Button?

Dear Miriam Racquel,

I grew up in Hollywood, California and as you can guess, the pressure to dress immodest was immense. The more skin you show, the better. As a baalas teshuvah, what was your turning point in making the decision to button up?

Dear Awesome Woman,

Great question! It really does come down to a decision. My turning point happened on a street corner in Israel after having perused through some fashion magazines in a bookstore. I'd been learning Torah Judaism, but nothing is like choosing to live it. Enjoy *To Button or Not Button? Hitting the Reset Button and Becoming a Modest Goddess,* an article I previously published *at TheJewish Woman.org.*

> **To button or not to button?** That was the question I asked myself as my fingers paused on the ivory button of my blouse.
>
> Button. *I'll try buttoning my blouse one inch closer to my neckline.*
>
> *There. Not so terrible.*
>
> *I can still breathe. In fact, it feels kind of good. No strap peeking out, less skin showing. Not my usual look, but I'm not doing*

this for life—just trying it out. Like on a trial basis. I can always go back to the way I've dressed for the past 20-plus years. My rules, my code of law and no one else's.

This argument in my head took place many years ago on a street corner in Jerusalem.

I had come to Israel in the summer of 1989 to rescue my previously agnostic Jewish boyfriend from the clutches of Orthodox Judaism. With my hopes to draw him back into secular sanity, I enrolled in classes myself in order to arm myself with what he was learning and become the enemy from within. I thought I would argue with him regarding the restrictive traditional Torah dress codes, and yet, here I was arguing with myself.

I was a graduate of Grinnell College, a small Midwestern school amid the cornfields of Iowa. There, I had honed my liberal philosophy of life—truth is relative, dream big, save the world and challenge the status quo.

And I had been doing that since finishing college and living in Berkeley, Calif., working in the resource library of UCB and enjoying weekend trips exploring the vast coast of the West. Up until landing in Israel and attempting to free my boyfriend's mind and heart from religious Judaism, I was convinced that my dress codes were independently decided upon by me.

On this street corner, I was challenging that. Wasn't it only me who decided how to dress my body?

As a hippie and somewhat of a rebel, I certainly didn't believe that society or Hollywood dictated how I should dress. I was my own woman. An independent and free thinker. An individual down to the last drop.

Fashion Whim Changed With the Times

But the rebbetzins—the women teachers of the classes I was enrolled in—were encouraging me to explore my present identity.

Where did my fashion style and way of dressing come from? Was it truly my own, independent of others?

Or was it dictated to me based on the values of others whose fashion whim changed with the times, like the wind that blew in different directions based on always changing Hollywood values or lack thereof. Wasn't I just a puppet of the media and of people who either worshiped women's bodies or degraded them based on how they saw fit? Didn't they shame and disgrace, didn't they use and abuse the female from the beginning of time, dictating to the women of the world how they "should" dress to attract the male species?

I didn't know the answer to those questions, but I was in the midst of exploring hitting the reset button on my life. Stepping into the Orthodox shtetls of Israel was not on my bucket list as a 23-year-old. But when a strange letter from that boyfriend arrived at my funky Berkeley rental one morning, my life turned upside down.

I took myself and the letter to a rabbi whose name I found in the Berkeley yellow pages. He took one look at the return address on the envelope—the Jerusalem yeshivah's address—and told me the alarming news.

“Your boyfriend is in a cult.”

“What? He’s in a cult?” my mouth dropped open in shock and response from the other side of the rabbi’s large wooden desk.

As far as I had known, my boyfriend was traveling around Europe after his junior-year-abroad studies had finished. The letter showed differently. He had gone to Israel and winded up enrolling in some yeshivah, learning ancient biblical texts. Not just learning, but doing things that were outside the realm of the secular, liberal upbringing he had. In the letter, he spoke of observing the Jewish Sabbath, eating a kosher diet and dressing differently.

The Yellow Pages rabbi responded back, “Yes, he’s in a cult. Those schools that they call yeshivahs? They’re actually places where they teach secular Jewish youths all about religious Judaism in hopes that they’ll choose to live according to the biblical commandments that many Jews like you and me find outdated and restrictive.“

“But you’re a rabbi,” I said. “Don’t you live that way?”

“No, I don’t. I like the teachings of the Torah, the Old Testament as the Christians call it, but I don’t believe it comes from G-d. I believe it was written by man. But those rabbis who are teaching your boyfriend will probably convince him that the biblical customs are from G-d. That’s why I call it a cult. Your boyfriend will change in ways that you won’t be able to recognize him. If I were you, I’d hop on a plane and get him out.”

I told the rabbi that I had plans to go to Guatemala and do volunteer work with refugees. The rabbi’s words convinced me that my boyfriend was a much greater cause.

Which Was More Oppressive?

I was actually a bit familiar with Torah Judaism—in a superficial, disdainful way. Growing up in a suburb of New York on the outskirts of a very religious, quickly expanding Orthodox/Chassidic neighborhood, I had seen religious Jews. But growing up secular and liberal, worshiping no higher power, I was not impressed by what I saw. Especially the way the religious women folks dressed. Long sleeves in the summer, socks and tights underneath long skirts. All I could think of was how oppressed they were to cover themselves up that way.

And yet there I stood on a street corner in Jerusalem arguing with myself about a button.

What was in that button? A lot.

Which was more oppressive? To button or not to button?

I had hopped on a plane six weeks earlier to convince my boyfriend to come back to the States and leave this crazy notion of biblical Judaism behind. I hadn't been too successful battling him with our liberal ideas from college. I didn't understand his side of the battle and so enrolling in classes seemed like a good idea. And a safe one—this cult wouldn't get me because I was too smart to be convinced of a who cared about what someone ate and how they dressed.

And yet that was at the core of my battle with my boyfriend. If man wrote the Bible, then who cares what they said about dress codes. But if G-d had dictated the Torah to Moses, then a paradigm shift needed to take place in my mind.

And that's what was happening on that street corner over the decision of a little button. A paradigm shift. All my values were being questioned—not just the way I dressed. But the dressing was a biggie to me and represented a lot.

I had sat in my seat in class staring up at the rebbetzin. Her hair was decoratively covered by a floral scarf. Her elbows covered by sleeves and her long, billowy skirt brushed her ankles. I would say the style was bohemian hippy. And yet the words coming out of her mouth were unlike any hippy talk that I'd ever heard.

"In the Torah, anything that is precious and sacred remains private. This is completely opposite to what society teaches which is 'let it all hang out' and 'expose it all.' The secular social values that we were raised with, for I was also raised just like you," she gestured to me and the other women in the class, "tell us that if we cover certain parts of our body it is because we are ashamed of our bodies. But according to the Torah, just as a Sefer Torah, which is one of the most holy and precious things in the Jewish faith, is wrapped lovingly in velvet and not to be shown off, so is a woman's body wrapped lovingly in clothes and not meant to be on display. Her body is holy, and it is a matter of honor to treat it as such. These women don't hide their bodies out of shame. They cover them out of love. They dress attractive, yet not attracting."

"Whoa. What's the difference between attractive and attracting?" I called out from the back of the room.

"Dressing attractive is representative of your dignity and worth. Dressing attracting is just as it sounds—wanting to dress in a manner that attracts attention. Unfortunately, the attention would be on the external rather than the internal. If someone is trying to attract attention by showing off something external, then what does that say about their self-worth? If all a woman wants to be is body parts rather than a person with ideas, personality, values and integrity, then what does that say about how she views herself? Who is she truly dressing for? Others or herself?"

"Well, I don't really care what others think about my clothes, I just want to be comfortable. If it's hot out, I want to wear shorts and tanks. If I'm hiking, I want to wear pants."

"Yup, that makes sense in a human centered world—to dress as you please. But in a G-d-centered world, with a belief that G-d is the architect of our modern world, dressing as you wish is like building a home in contradiction to the architect's plans. And then you've got a rocky foundation. Something will be off-kilter."

Willing to Question My Values

Often during those weeks in Jerusalem, my mind replayed the image of Charlton Heston holding the tablets on the mountain, Hollywood-style. Could it be true? Was there really an infinite Being who created the world and us humans? Was there really a grand architect? My college educated boyfriend had come to believe that. And the people I was meeting in yeshivah? Many of them had grown up secular and open-minded like myself and then had immersed themselves in the words of the living Torah, coming out the other end dressing and living as the religious neighbors who I had so disdained and distanced myself from growing up.

During my classes, I struggled greatly with having been raised too rational to entertain the existence of an Infinite Being who was invisible to my eyes yet had created the world. When I slowly came to realize that my boyfriend was not in a cult, I made a commitment to myself. With a youthful and open mind, I was willing to at least take a leap and consider a different reality than the way I was raised. I was willing to look again at the effects that secular media had on me as a woman. I was willing to question my values.

I explored the values of the Torah—teachings that may have come from an Infinite Being who had created and continues to create my body. And I played with that. On that street corner, I played with the notion of dressing according to the values of this Infinite Being. An Infinite Being who created my body as holy and desired for me to treat it as such by dressing with less exposure.

Kind of like a science experiment with nothing to lose, I played with buttons and skirts. I played with elbows, knees and necklines covered. And what I discovered was something that I never had touched on before.

Dignity. Dignity of my body. A dignity touched upon by exposing less skin. Not from shame, but from boundaries. G-dly boundaries, not human boundaries. What's mine is mine and not "yours" (the outside world). Not yours to see, not yours to dictate fashion to, not yours to dress.

Unlike secular society trying to smoosh the gender lines to be the same, Torah Judaism makes distinctions between men and women -centered rather than human-centered distinctions.

I was willing to explore that men and women had been created with different biologies and different spiritual makeups as well.

Male and female come from different aspects of the Divine. Testosterone and estrogen make a difference. Not one better than the other, but different and distinct. Again, a paradigm shift of non-defensive exploring led to eye-opening revelations of the world around me.

Both men and women are expected to show up in their Divine image. No one—not men or women—is a body without a soul. A woman's beauty is not on display for men nor should a man's be. To be honored, recognized, respected, yes. To be objectified, degraded, stared at, no.

And that is what I came to with that little button. Eventually, over time and much learning and exploring in both Israel and in America, I became more observant of a G-d-centered Judaism. I came to observe what I have come to believe are G-d's values regarding my dress. I have many beautiful parts of my body—some meant for the public eye and others only meant to be shared with my husband, my partner in life. G-d has also become my partner in life. A G-d that cares for the dignity of my body.

I reset my button many years ago, choosing different values than the way I had been raised.

I chose a more modest path. I am the modest goddess.

Blessings! 

Letter 7

The Opposite of Blending In:
Were My Wealthy Hosts Fugitive Nazis?

Dear Miriam Racquel,

I'm learning more Torah and very happy on my path of becoming a Baalas Teshuvah. I do feel funny about one thing though. I used to really believe in the blending together of Jews and non-Jews. I thought that this was the way to world peace. And now, getting more in touch with my Jewish soul, I know that blending isn't the answer, Geulah is. And Jews being more unified and whole as a people and practicing more Torah and mitzvahs as individuals. It's just such a different concept than what I used to understand about the world. Any thoughts?

Dear Awesome Woman,

Thank you for sharing! I understand where you are coming from. I grew up believing as you did about world peace and it was quite a shocker for me to discover along my Torah path that the key to world peace really rests on the Jewish people's shoulders. Becoming more deeply connected to each other and recognizing our soul's roots and oneness to Hashem will bring Heaven down to Earth.

I share my soul's journey in my memoir, *God Said What?! #MyOrthodoxLife,* and I invite you to read it. It's full of humor, love, and mysticism as I take readers on my path as a 23-year-old atheist hippy trying to rescue my college boyfriend from the "cult" that I thought he was in. It was actually Orthodox Judaism and the journey has so many twists and turns that if I hadn't lived it I wouldn't believe it!

Returning back to what you wrote about, I'd like to share a little piece of my journey with you through an article I wrote for the *TheJewishWoman.org:*

Were My Wealthy Hosts Fugitive Nazis? The Holocaust Menorah

Before I became more observant of my Jewish heritage, I often had interesting encounters of the strange kind that kept reminding me of my Jewishness. You see, I grew up not only unobservant of my faith, but I rejected it and was ashamed of it. I rejected religion in general because as a very free-spirited liberal college grad, I loved being able to do, think and behave by the rules that I decided. I was ashamed of my Jewish roots because that thing that seemed to make Jews different and therefore selected us out for antisemitism, persecution and prejudice frightened me terribly. If only we could blend in and be like others, no one would single us out. Perhaps that was the protection we needed.

And so I did the best I could to blend in with the world at large, have fun, explore different cultures and make purpose out of causes that interested me.

But what was odd was that no matter how much I tried to forget about my Jewish roots, the universe kept bringing it front and center into my life. And sometimes in frightening ways.

After graduating college, I took a month-long trip to Brazil with a friend. Marie was half German and half Spanish, and was raised in Canada. I had met her in Germany during my junior year studies abroad. She was employed as a scientist at the German university where I was studying. As an extrovert, she easily befriended the many German Brazilians who, as a result of their dual citizenship, were able to study at the university. They warmly welcomed her to visit them upon their return back to South America and she generously included me in that invite.

In the course of our travels around that very large country, we visited many of her German-South American friends and oftentimes, I would be met with a question—"What are you?"

Though I would try to get away with replying that I was just American, they would question further and not be satisfied until I said I was Jewish. It was almost like they sensed it—hence the deeper questioning. And then I was surprised how often I would hear back: "Oh, my grandfather was Jewish!" or, "My great aunt was Jewish." I remembered learning in my Holocaust studies course that as the winds of antisemitism blew in before Hitler started World War II, many German Jews made their way to South American countries to seek refuge. I felt an odd but familiar connection to these new friends, ones who shared a piece of Jewish ancestral lineage with me. They were curious to know more about Judaism, but I didn't have much knowledge to share, and so the topic was dropped.

One evening, Marie borrowed a sedan and I found myself being bumped along a dark road, on a visit to the German-South American parents of a coworker of Marie's who had recently settled in Germany. Huge metal gates and a guard greeted us upon our arrival to this very wealthy suburb outside of Sao Paulo. After sharing the name of the family we came to visit, we were allowed to enter. The looming gates parted and we continued along the road, large street lamps illuminating the finely manicured lawns of each stately home.

Pulling up to one, we parked and rang the bell of the impressive doorway, white marbled lions perched on either side. If this was the outside, I wondered what the inside would look like. I hugged Marie and said, "It's so amazing to get such an insider's tour of Brazil. This is like the 'behind the scenes' version that I never would have seen if I traveled here by myself. Thank you."

"No problem." She hugged me back warmly. "Gretchen will be so excited that we visited her mom and dad."

Suddenly the humongous wooden door opened. A gray-haired couple stood on the other side: a short, stout woman and a tall, erect man.

The woman said, "Hallo, please come in." She waved us in.

Marie's face lit up and she grasped the hands of the hostess. "Hallo! I'm Marie and this is my good friend, Meryl. We're so glad to visit you—Gretchen is such a dear friend of mine.

The hostess turned and put her hand out towards me, "Nice to meet…."

I didn't hear the end of her sentence. My eyes were glued to a huge silver Menorah that sat on a platform in the center of the sunken living room. Nine branches stared at me, four level on each side of an elevated branch in the middle. A Jewish candelabra placed barren on display, like in a museum, except we were not in a museum. Why did this German couple have a Jewish article on display in their home? Either they were Jewish, or, like the Holocaust stories that flashed through my mind, they were Nazis who had ransacked Jewish homes.

I froze in place. I believed it was the latter.

I ignored the hostess's outstretched hand and looked to the man, so straight was his stance, like a soldier. I pointed to the gleaming silver structure and asked clearly in English, "Where did you get that Jewish menorah?"

He walked over to it and stood behind it. With the platform, its largeness reached up to the top of his chest.

"I'm a collector of things and I brought this with me when I left Germany." The floor dropped out from under me as I nodded and stared. I had no words for his simple explanation and I didn't have the guts to confront him on my suspicions.

He paused and then asked, "Are you Jewish?"

"I'm American, but my family is Jewish."

I was chilled as an awkward silence filled the room like a heavy fog.

This couple had been on one side of the war, my Jewish ancestors on the other.

Lost in my thoughts, I barely heard our hostess's invitation to the table, "Come let's sit and eat. The food is getting cold and we want to hear about your travels around Brazil."

She beckoned us forward and we sat ourselves around the elegant table laden with food. The seductive steamy waft of schnitzel filled the air as the host removed the hot cover of the china dish. Doling out warm portions of food, the couple was the epitome of politeness. I picked at what was on my plate, having left my appetite behind at the doorway to this grand manor. The hosts and Marie babbled in German and I sat quietly, alone in my thoughts.

History had become present for me; all those stories from my high school Holocaust class flooded my mind, stories of Nazis who had run to South America to escape trial and accountability for their horrible war crimes against Jews. I had such sympathy for the few Jewish survivors who, having slipped from death's hands, survived and returned to their homes only to find them looted by antisemitic neighbors. I paid no attention to the flow of conversation. Instead, I put two and two together: some Nazis must have taken their looted treasure abroad to decorate their new homes, bringing something of the people they had persecuted with them. My stomach turned; my travels had led me to one.

I politely nodded as we took our leave. The fog of silence followed me into the car as we rode back to the city.

"Are you ok?" Marie asked.

"Yeah, sure," I said.

Marie rambled on excitedly about her German friend's home and parents. "They were so nice and their home was so beautiful and huge. I loved the artwork they had; it was like being in a museum." Her words droned on.

A museum alright. A collection of the artifacts of dead people—people they may have even killed. And if I had lived in Europe during that time, I would have been one of their victims.

It was only later in time that I embraced my Jewish heritage and became more observant of my faith. I came to study about the Jewish soul and how deeply connected it is to G-d—even to the degree of being a piece of G-d. It wasn't something that a Jew could escape from. No matter where they traveled, their Jewish soul came with. And it prodded them to seek. To seek and find that connection. To dust off the falsities that may have covered it and to reveal its essence. There was truly nothing to be ashamed of but only light to proudly embrace.

The memory of the Holocaust Menorah remained seared in my brain. It showed me that the G-d I thought I didn't believe in had taken me on a journey. I could travel to a far away place, one decorated with beautiful things, but my connection to my people would be right in front of me. I would always stand apart, but the more I learned about my G-dly connection, the less alone I would be. I had deep roots that connected me to this world, but a soul that connected me on high.

Blessings! 

4

Friendship and Community

Friendships are not for

drama and trauma.

If the relationship doesn't feel kind,

then it's not.

—Miriam Racquel Feldman

Letter 1

Taking Good Care of Your Energy

Dear Miriam Racquel,

I have a very good friend who drains me and I don't know what to do about it. We've been friends for years and I'm noticing that she tells the same "stories" over and over again. I spend hours listening to her and offer tons of compassion. I sometimes give her a little advice which she is open to hearing. She even thinks the advice is helpful, but afterwards doesn't do anything different. And then when she gets the same results, she uses me to vent some more. She is also an extrovert and I'm an introvert so all that talking makes my head spin.

And it's not like I don't talk to her about my stuff too—I don't mean to sound ungrateful. But I also have a coach I go to for professional advice and help. I wish she would do that as well—go to professionals so she could really get the help she needs.

I'm growing tired of the pattern. When the phone rings and it's her caller ID, I don't feel like answering. I'm avoiding talking to her, which is awkward since we live in the same community. What should I do?

Dear Awesome Woman,

I'm so sorry you're having difficulty with your friend. I totally get it! And I love your awareness! Noticing our energy levels around situations and people is so important.

I'd like to break down your letter into a few distinct issues so we can deal with them one piece at a time:

1. **The Change-Averse Friend**
2. **Making Discerning Choices**
3. **Introverts and Extroverts**
4. **Changing or Leaving a Friendship**

Let's look at each of these points.

1. The Change-Averse Friend

All of us for sure go through difficult times in life. I wish there was a way to avoid that. When the complete geulah comes, we will be finished with suffering, but until then Hashem will challenge us. And we need people to speak to, to vent to, to complain to—people we can share our troubles and pain with. We rely on the compassion of others because we are relationship beings. It is not healthy or wise to brave life alone.

That being said, we all know that we get to choose who we share our woes with. Usually the pick is friends, spouses, siblings, and parents. (*Under no circumstances should it ever be a child.* They are not our best friends. Clear boundaries with children are so important for the health of the child, who should not be carrying the burden of our worries. When a parent shares their personal issues with a child, it is called "emotional incest" and is very damaging to the child).

However, when something weighs heavily on our hearts and minds, a situation that is complicated, serious (like marriage issues and children's issues) and/or chronic, then choosing to hire a professional is a necessity. Not a luxury, but a necessity. We can't expect a friend, spouse or family member to be our constant sounding board.

Quality professionals, whether they are coaches, somatic healers, therapists, psychologists, or psychiatrists, can help us make important changes and even grieve properly. They can help us see our blind spots in difficult situations and process the emotions and wounds that rise up. We can be vulnerable with them without judgment and they are trained to guide us. The correct professional help is a life-saving investment for your mental, emotional, physical, and spiritual health as well as protecting the health of your relationships and loved ones.

Story Fondling

To return back to your complains-but-takes-no-action friend, if someone just loves to vent about a certain subject over and over again—their marriage, their job, their boss, their spouse, their difficulties with their children—then they are avoiding the hard work of making changes. They are avoiding dealing with what Hashem is bringing to them and doing something that life coach Martha Beck calls "story fondling" in her book *Steering by Starlight*:

> "Story fondlers are chockablock full of disappointment and anger about the bad things that are present in their lives and the good things that are absent. By talking about this constantly, they get help and sympathy from others. This

> affords them just enough well-being to endure life, as long as they keep complaining (thereby venting their emotions and getting people to do things for them). ”
>
> —*Beck, 91*

You do not have to play victim to a story fondler. It's for sure a mitzvah to help others and give compassion—I'm sure that most women do this a lot of the time because nurturing seems to be part of our DNA—but when it starts affecting our health and zaps us of energy, it needs to be recognized as such. We can't take care of ourselves or our families if listening to a friend over and over again is harming us. And it doesn't do the other person any good, either. It just enables them to stay stuck in a pattern that doesn't serve their highest good.

So, what can you do about it? Perhaps simply say, "I'm so sorry that you're having such a difficult time. My heart aches for you. I really think that this situation requires a professional who can give guidance."

Then try changing the topic and see what happens. Again, this is for the venting, constantly complaining friend who takes little if any action to make changes. This is not for a grieving friend whose heart is breaking over a loss, who just wants a shoulder to cry on. This is for the friend who isn't being aware and respectful that venting about her dead-end job to you all the time is harming your health. This is you setting limits for yourself—you're in charge of who you give your time and energy to. The friend is in charge of whether they get professional help or not. You're just trying to conserve your energy (and keep the friendship). By changing subjects, you're avoiding the drain that you've noticed you feel when listening to the non-stop venting over and over again.

If they say, "I am getting help and so-and-so (the professional they are seeing) just isn't getting the full picture...," and you notice a pattern of these kinds of excuses, then your friend may be choosing victimhood over empowerment—even the help they hire isn't helping them! You can suggest to them to hire someone else but then switch subjects. If they look at you in shock and awe, or if there is silence on the phone, then it may feel awkward, but you've established boundaries for yourself in a very kind way.

Or you can try being honest: "My heart goes out to you that you are dealing with this difficult situation. I love you and I want to be there for you in the way that I can. I do find that I'm feeling drained after our calls, though, and then I can't be there for my family. What do you think we can do about that?" You know your friend enough by now to know if she'll be able to handle your honesty and take accountability or not.

Now at this point, you might be thinking that at times in your life, you could have done just what your friend is doing. You may have "story-fondled," and that's ok. You're human, and as a soul in a body, you're experimenting a lot on this planet, on this journey through life. You may not always show up as your best self. You can even apologize to a friend if that's been the case. This is you taking accountability for past mistakes.

And as Maya Angelou says,

> "Do the best you can until you know better.
> Then when you know better, do better."

2. Making Discerning Choices

Women are relationship beings and tend to love sharing, being compassionate, being nurturers, and connecting with others with their heart and spirit. That being said, there is a risk in this way of being; if we don't use our G-d-given gevurah to discern who we are connecting to, are we seeing them for who they are showing us to be or are we trying to make them into someone that we want them to be? To judge someone positively is fine, but to ignore behavior is not fine.

> "Are we seeing them for who they are showing us to be or are we trying to make them into someone that we want them to be?"

Homeplay Exercise

Circles of Trust

A basic foundation for life that many don't recognize because of their dysfunctional childhoods is the importance of surrounding oneself with kind people. This exercise, based on a concept I learned from life coach Martha Beck, will help you figure out how to do just that.

Draw a dot in the center of a page. This represents you. Then draw widening circles around the dot. Those are your "Circles of Trust," which can also be called "Discerning Choices of Connection." You get to decide who is close and who is far.

Place dots on those circles to establish where you want others to be in proximity to you. The closer to the center dot (you) a

continued

person is, the more vulnerable you can be with them because they exude kindness and compassion and are safe in holding your heart.

Some people you may move around the circles—bringing them closer or moving them further away, depending on life changing situations—you may move to a different state or community or make lifestyle changes—or on their behavior.

Some dots (people) you may choose to remove from the circles altogether. Perhaps they are continually unkind, critical, or are a Borderline/Narcissist. Just a note: you may feel this way about your spouse or children at times, but these relationships are very different from friendships or extended family relationships. Wisdom and different tools are needed for marriage and parenting.

You get to discern your Circles of Trust and judge the distance of friends (and family, co-workers, etc.) based on the wisdom of your body and mind.

Homeplay Exercise

Messages from Your Body

Listen to your body—it does bring wisdom. When interacting with a friend, a co-worker, a relative, or even a stranger, notice how your body speaks to you.

Do you feel an uplift in your chest, an expansion? Do you have a warm, safe feeling inside—a comfort? Positive interactions feel like this. There is emotional safety and kindness.

What is the opposite interaction? Do you feel drained, or notice an energy drop? Is there a clenching in your jaw, a tightness in your chest, a sinking in your stomach? Do you feel like shrinking or caving inwards? Do you feel smaller? Or do you cringe and want to run away? This is your body conveying an aversive feeling.

Now what if you've already been friends with someone for a while, but then they get critical, cynical, or hot/cold? Your mind might be confused, but your body won't be. Your body knows the score and will feel an aversion to the person. Like an amoeba recoils from negative stimulus, so does your body. It will recoil from hurt. Can you mention something to the person? Of course. And then notice how your body reacts to their response. It can sense honesty and it can sense dishonesty.

If you notice that you are afraid of a friend (or anyone for that matter), then this is very serious business. People with Borderline/ Narcissist traits instill fear in friends as a "power-over" dynamic. They try to establish control and can be very manipulative about it. Run for the hills from these kinds of friends!

In the specific case you've brought to the table, a friend has started to overburden you with things that seem serious enough for a professional. And your body feels that burden. The avoidance you're doing is actually a protective measure.

Hashem has created our bodies to register effect. The body either feels safe in an interaction, with a desire to come closer, or the opposite which signals a lack of safety and a desire to avoid, to move away from the threat. Our responsibility is to discern what is happening, hear the wisdom, and make choices.

Homeplay Exercise

Limiting Belief Exercise

Please be careful if your mind ignores, justifies, or rationalizes any friend's behavior. If you have beliefs like, "a good friend always listens," "a good friend always picks up the phone," "a good friend is always there and is always supportive," "a good friend never ends a relationship," etc. then you will be apt to ignore your body's wisdom, your intuition and your discerning inner voice. With those beliefs, which are called "limiting beliefs," you will ignore the instinctual signals from your body that the friendship is not a healthy one.

Get present with your body when the phone rings. Does your chest constrict? Does your stomach drop? Do you feel a desire to pick up the phone or do you cringe? Maybe you're thinking, "Oh no, her again—I just can't listen to how her husband isn't treating her well for the umpteenth time and how the therapist just doesn't get it." Do not ignore your body's signals.

Let's do an exercise to uncover some of your "limiting beliefs" that are lurking under the surface:

On a piece of paper, complete the sentences below, making sure to jot down all of what comes to mind—just list them down on the paper.

A good friend should ...

A good friend is ....

A good friend does ...

A good friend never ...

A good friend always ...

These are the rules in your head for how a good friend "should" be. What's wrong with having these kinds of rules for yourself? One reason is that you may be paying more attention to the rules than you are to the situation you are in with your friend and the impact this relationship is having on you.

As a rule (pun intended!), rules with "always" or "never" are harmful to your health. Life is ever-changing and Hashem wants you to be discerning according to situations and people.

Here are 3 examples of how limiting beliefs can be just that — limiting:

Example 1: You are friends with someone who suddenly turns cold and critical. What does your mind tell you in this situation? If you've got the belief system that "A good friend always judges positively," then you may ignore that your stomach is sinking, and your torso wants to turn and run during your interaction with this friend. Maybe you ignore your body and rationalize her behavior by saying, "Huh, that was weird. But they've always been nice so maybe they're having some bad days. I'll judge them positively."

It is fine to judge someone positively, but it is not fine to ignore the behavior. There may be a pattern of hot and cold, kindness and meanness. And listening to your body will bring that wisdom. You may need to say something to bring light to the situation—you can do this with curiosity and kindness—or you may need to take some distance if your body is telling you that something isn't safe here. You may then choose to speak with a professional if you have fear in this relationship—either fear of confronting the unkind behavior of the friend or fear of leaving a situation that is not healthy for you.

continued

Example 2: Let's look at the limiting beliefs in the case of your situation—the "leaning too heavily" friend. You keep listening and listening because your mind has the rule, "A good friend is always there for the other person. She needs my help, and I have to be there for her or I'm being selfish."

It is okay to be selfish and take care of your needs. Your health—emotional, physical, spiritual, and mental—is top priority. You need your health in your service to Hashem and to your loved ones. If you are not careful with your energy then you have none to give. Try this thought instead: "A good friend could be there if it doesn't drain or overburden. If it does, I'll take direct action to do something different."

Example 3: What happens if you develop a new friendship but have the limiting belief, "a good friend should listen"? If the person you're listening to is respectful and kind, great! But if over time, you notice they're a person who only talks about themselves or talks very negatively about others, should you be listening? If you're following your rule and ignoring your body's wisdom, then you'll rationalize away the feeling of constriction in your chest when this person drones on and on about the latest sheitel (wig) they have or how so and so isn't wearing the latest style. You'll ignore the clenching of your jaw that is trying to tell you enough is enough. Your body wants to run away from them yet you stand in place listening.

For years, I had aches and pains all over my body, suffering terribly. The pressuring thoughts and rules that I had for myself were causing havoc in my body. These were not just about friendships, but about a lot of areas of my life.

The war between what your mind is telling you ("A good friend always listens.") and what your body is telling you ("Run!" or "I don't like this!") creates tremendous internal pressure. This can result in headaches, migraines, autoimmune disorders, muscle aches and pains, and disease, G-d forbid.

Healthy limits and boundaries—that well-discerning gevurah that Hashem has given you—is just as important as the chesed Hashem has given you. Give when and where you can and allow Hashem to do the rest. Your friend **can** choose other resources —you are not the only one. Hashem is the true resource and provides multiple channels for healing. Do not overdo you.

Homeplay Exercise

The BRAKES Method

With friendships, it's best to move slowly. You do want to tread carefully and not trust or be too vulnerable right away. It's appropriate and wise to take your time in getting to know others.

I wrote **BRAKES** as a checklist based off of Brené Brown's *Braving the Wilderness* to determine how near or far you want someone in your Circle of Trust.

People have so many different facets to them and it's much easier to bring people into your inner circles rather than push people from inner circles to outer ones. People get hurt and confused, and not all decisions can be explained when distancing oneself or leaving a relationship. Honesty with others is not always the best policy. But self-care is. Remember Hashem is the one who is empowering you. Since it is a mitzvah to take care of your health, you are empowered to be discerning in your choices of connection with others.

continued

Using **BRAKES** doesn't mean that you won't be friendly or friends with a person, but it does mean that your expectations will be based more on the reality of the person you are with rather than a fantasy of who you want them to be.

BRAKES

Ask yourself these questions:

1. BOUNDARIES—Does this person honor your boundaries? What happens when you say no to them? Are you afraid to say no because when you have said no, they get mean and nasty, threatening, manipulative or have a temper tantrum claiming that you don't like them? Some people use "emotional blackmail" to try to get what they want. They will call you selfish, greedy, cold, rigid, and other nasty things in order to make you feel really bad about saying no. Please watch out for this kind of labeling of your character. Not only are they put downs, but they are also manipulative lies in order for the other person to get you to do what they want. In your body, it is felt as pressure, discomfort, and shame.

2. RESPONSIBILITY—How responsible and reliable is this person? Do they follow through and do what they say they'll do? Or are they like a chicken with their head cut off, committing themselves to a whole lot of stuff that they can't possibly do, and then backing out at the last minute? That could leave you feeling resentful because there has been a boundary violation — your energy and time has not been respected. How self-aware are they about what they can do and can't do?

3. ACCOUNTABILITY—Does this person take accountability? Have you experienced them owning up to their mistakes? Do they apologize and make changes? Some people are great at apologizing, but then do not follow through with making changes. If this is unsatisfactory to you, then take note and make changes yourself. Don't be a victim. As Maya Angelou so wisely says,

> *When someone shows you who they are,*
> *believe them the first time. People know*
> *themselves much better than you do.*
> *That's why it's important to stop expecting them*
> *to be something other than who they are.*

It is so important to open our eyes to what people are showing us about themselves. And decide if you like it or not.

4. KEEPERS—How reliable is this person in keeping what you share with them private? If you share something with them, do you feel confident that they won't share it with others, including their spouses, siblings, children, parents? Or maybe you're okay that they share it with their spouse and family members? It depends on what the two of you decide as friends. Also, how reliable are they in keeping other people's confidences? Do they share things with you about other people that may have been meant to be private? If they talk behind others' backs—meaning if they share with you a lot of stuff from others—then they just may share with others a lot of stuff about you. It's important in regards to feeling emotionally safe in a relationship to know that what you do share is kept confidential and that your vulnerability is honored.

5. ENERGY EXCHANGE—What is the energy exchange between the two of you? Are you a priority for them? Are you a low priority for them? Either is fine as long as you know where you stand so that you're not constantly getting hurt from false expectations.

continued

Never make someone a priority

when all you are to them is an option.

—Maya Angelou

6. SYNC—Is this person in sync with your values and their own values? Do you respect them? Do they make choices in line with your values? Do they even make choices that are in sync with their own values or do they just talk about them? Actions speak louder than words. Pick people who are in sync with your values and ones who are in sync with their own values.

These questions are not only great for deciding where to put people on your circles, but also in managing your expectations of others.

For example, if you know that someone is not great in the "Keepers" area—meaning they tend to share things w th others —then you're going to be careful what you share about yourself with them.

Or, if they have a weakness in the "Responsibility" area in terms of time—meaning that they say they'll be somewhere at a certain time and they rarely are—then know this abcut them. If you want to meet them for a lunch date, figure out how to do it without expecting them to be on time. Choose when you'll show up and what you'll do if they're late.

Or if they are a safe friend who you can speak your feelings to, then try telling them that you'd love to meet them for lunch, but you don't feel comfortable sitting by yourself or waiting if they're late. Tell them that you're arranging your busy schedule around meeting them. Ask them if they're able to get there at the time that you both have chosen. See how this friend reacts to this soft way of making a request. Their response to your request will tell you a lot about them.

> If they follow through on your request, then that's a win-win for both of you. If not, then this is important information to have moving forward. You can set your expectations properly or take a deeper look at this friendship.
>
> Life is always changing and so are relationships and people. There is a flow, and when we allow the wisdom of our bodies to guide us as well as our minds, we can make safer choices.

3. Introverts and Extroverts

You mentioned that you're an introvert, and that plays a key part in how much time you spend interacting with people. Respect your desire for alone time and inward processing. Hashem has made you this way and as much as it is a gift to be an extrovert, it is also a gift to be an introvert. The world needs both.

4. Leaving a Friendship

Friendships are like icing on the cake of life. If they don't go on smoothly and if they don't taste delicious, then you're better off without the weight.

In your situation, having respect for yourself means you get to choose the amount of time you want to be spending listening to your friend. Maybe you've tried changing the subject by interrupting. Or maybe you've tried to express a desire to do something fun and light. Or maybe you were able to get honest and speak up about feeling drained by her venting and how that was affecting your health. If these actions work, great! And if not, then spending less time together may be exactly what your body and soul need. Saying "no" to something or to someone is saying "yes" to other very important things and people. It's your job as a wise woman to be discerning, and sometimes we can shift patterns in a friendship.

But the hard fact is that not all friendships last forever. Relationships change and you may move on from each other. Please have in mind that Hashem is always working behind the scenes and setting you up with whoever you are supposed to meet and when. While you are making discerning choices of connection, Hashem is orchestrating the show.

That being said, leaving a friendship can be awkward, uncomfortable, and painful. Sadness recognizes loss and is very real even when it was your choice to leave the relationship. Give yourself time to feel the feelings. Feel the sadness in your body. Is it in your chest as a heaviness? Is it an ache in your heart? Put your hands on it and lean forward. If tears are wanting to be released, allow for that.

You will move on. And at the same time, it is realistic to know that the sadness may come up again. You may feel sadness weeks after you have let the friendship go. And that is okay. Repeat the process above and just allow the feelings to flow. Emotions, as "energy in motion," pass through us when allowed, leaving us with the wisdom and insight to move forward.

***If there is a lot of energy coming up for you, please do the **ROAR! Process** from Chapter 2 to help you release pent-up emotion and energy. It's great to get larger with emotions than to hold them in and try to suppress them. If you're feeling anxious, scared, or mad, then **ROAR!** will help.

Homeplay Exercise

Grounding Exercise

You may feel awkward seeing the old friend after you've let the friendship go. Jewish communities are tight-knit and you will probably run into them. So, let's learn a grounding exercise to help with the awkwardness. Grounding is always good to use, but especially if there is an event where you know the past friend is going to be there. You're giving your nervous system the opportunity to feel safe in the present moment.

When you enter the event, take a moment to notice your senses (you can do this eyes closed or open):

What do you hear? Feel your feet on the floor and like a raccoon who is attuned to all sounds in 360 degrees, be the same. Throw your hearing sense outward.

What do you smell?

What do you see?

What sensations are happening in your body? If your mind is ruminating, then drop into body awareness. Is your stomach jumping? Your jaw clenching? Just notice, and if you can, place a hand on that area of your body. The energy will flow, your mind will calm.

With more of a calm space held within, choose where you want to sit at the event, who *do* you want to speak to, and how long you will stay, etc. Care for yourself by discerning what is right for you.

Homeplay Exercise

Laser Beam of Light

Once you leave a relationship, there is the risk of that past friend speaking negatively behind your back. Unfortunately, we can't control what others say about us. Even though lashon hora is a known no-no in our frum communities, there does seem to be a laxness at times. There is nothing you can do in these situations except stay grounded in your truth and know that Hashem sees everything.

Imagine a laser beam of light between you and Hashem. You are standing in the beam of that light. G-d is the only true judge and G-d knows why you left the relationship. Others don't have the full picture, but Hashem does. Stand strong in that confidence. You did the best you could not to hurt another person, and yet you felt it necessary to leave the relationship. Hashem knows it was not your intention to cause pain.

If you ever need to speak up directly, do so to bring clarity. Share what you need to, letting people know that the situation was complicated and you handled it the best way you could.

Here's a compassionate message you can give yourself: "*This is awkward, and I'm doing my best. Hashem understands why I left.*"

Since leaving a friendship can trigger childhood wounds, you may need the support of a healer. You don't need to go it alone.

May these exercises and suggestions help you navigate this friendship and may you welcome healthy patterns of connection!

Blessings!

Letter 2

People-Pleasing

Dear Miriam Racquel,

I'm a typical people-pleaser with my friends and my community. I say yes to setting up community events, yes to watching other people's children, yes to hosting sheva brachos. If I even think about saying no I feel like a bad person—like I'm selfish, or not giving enough, or not doing ahavas yisroel.

But the problem is that I often feel worn out and resentful. And then I complain non-stop to my husband. My husband feels this is an emergency situation and that it's affecting my health and our relationship. He also thinks that it's unhealthy for our kids to see such a burnt-out mom. Plus I'm more short-tempered and less patient with the kids because I'm so wiped.

Help! How do I say no and when do I say no without feeling like a wicked witch?

Dear Awesome Woman,

You can say no.

Not an easy thing for you? I do know that saying no can bring a whole wave of feelings such as guilt, shame, and internal self-criticism. I get that.

So, let's do something different. Let me replace your internal critical voice and be a voice of loving compassion that gives you permission to say no. This, I whisper to you: *"It's ok, honey. You can say no. You may feel some discomfort in your mind when you do, but your soul will thank you. There are times when your soul wants you to say no to preserve your energy, your strength, your health, your dignity, and your well-being."*

It's awesome to be a giving person, but drainage only leads to resentment and the opposite of good health. Finding balance is an important life practice.

Let's dig deeper, together.

Making G-d our G-d and Setting Boundaries

We really need to make our G-d our G-d. Meaning, if you're people-pleasing, then you are worshiping other gods. You are bowing to society, to your community, to your friends, co-workers, bosses, and you may even be bowing to family members.

You're listening to the people-pleasing yetzer hara. Chassidus says that the yetzer hara can dress up in all kinds of clothes. It can dress up in holier-than-thou clothes telling you to do something that may seem important, but which takes time away from other prioritized tasks.

In kabbalistic terms, there is the energetic flow of chesed, which is "giving" and gevurah, "constricting, limiting." The attribute of chesed is metaphorically on the right arm while the flow of gevurah is on the left. Somatic pain will sometimes present itself on corresponding sides of the body depending on the emotional/ metaphysical issue you are having.

At times, giving is appropriate for your mind, body, and soul; and at times, limiting your flow of giving energy is good for your mind, body, and soul.

How do you know which to choose? Check in with your body and soul to discern.

Homeplay Exercise

Replace "Shoulds" with "Coulds" Wisdom Flows

Where you are "shoulding" yourself? Turn the "shoulds" into "coulds" and notice your body sensations. Listen to the wisdom that flows. Journal it.

Example: *"I should host the sheva bracha."* Feel into your body what happens with this thought. Notice the physical sensations. Is there tightness or expansion? Does your jaw clench? Do your spirits feel uplifted? Only you know because it is your body.

Now change the sentence to, *"I could host the sheva brachos."* Notice the shift of physical sensations in your body and a new flow of thoughts. For example:

"I could host the sheva bracha, but then I would feel exhausted, overwhelmed, and resentful. It will take a lot of effort and my cleaning lady just quit, which means tons of pressure on me to clean up and cook. I will wind up snapping at my kids. The baby is still waking up at night and I'm tired. I'd rather have quiet time with my kids, slowly clean up when I can, and put my feet up and rest. This will make me a better mother and wife. It is loving and kind to me. I feel that I'd like to skip this time of hosting a sheva bracha."

continued

And breathe.

If your "could" in this example leads to a feeling of uplift in your body, but your mind warns of overwhelm, then determine how you can get more help or divvy up the tasks. What can you do to simplify?

Homeplay Exercise

How's Your Plate?

Check to see if your plate is too full, if your load is too heavy. Will giving to someone cause you resentment? How will your loved ones be affected if you do that thing that is being asked of you? Will you snap at your loved ones because you'll feel stressed and overburdened by saying yes to that extra task? Will you wind up in bed with aches and pains?

Homeplay Exercise

Hang These Words Up

Ask yourself, "Will I be able to complete my soul-driven tasks (wife-ing, mothering, working, creativity, writing, exercising, learning, etc.) if I say yes?

When chesed and gevurah are balanced—meaning both "giving" and "limiting" are being used wisely—you get the flow of tiferes, which is harmony. Your life and body run more smoothly.

Please hang these truthful and kind words up so you can see them:

It is human to disappoint people and let them down by saying no.

I choose to be kind to myself.

It's ok, honey. You can say no. You may feel some discomfort in your mind when you do, but your soul will thank you. There are times when your soul wants you to say no to preserve your energy, your strength, your health, your dignity, and your well being.

Your energy is a precious commodity. Your body has limits. Your soul has your divine tasks for you to do. Please treat all parts of you with care, kindness, and respect.

Blessings! 

Letter 3

Recognizing a Borderline Narcissist

Dear Miriam Racquel,

I just moved to a new community. Everyone is very friendly and I feel blessed. There is one woman though who was super friendly when I moved in and offered to do so much for me. She was really kind, generous, and fun. But now, it seems like she thinks I owe her something, like she is entitled to my time, attention, and energy. If I don't pick up the phone when she calls, she gets insulted or asks me if I'm purposely not answering her calls. How ridiculous! I've got young kids and a husband—I can't be at her beck and call!

What should I do? Do I owe her for all the help she gave me? My husband sees how torn up and confused I am about this person. He wants me to drop the friendship, but I think I'm afraid of her reaction if I do, and I do feel guilty—she really has done so much for me. Help! I'm so confused!

Dear Awesome Woman,

I'm so sorry that you're having this experience. It's definitely the last thing you need when you've got a family to take care of and need your head clear and focused and your body energized for that very important role. In fact, even if you didn't have a family to take care of, a relationship like this is just too draining and damaging for your body, mind, and soul. Your husband is very wise and is right about dropping a toxic relationship like this. It sounds like you've gotten caught in the web of a Borderline/Narcissist.

Borderline/Narcissists are delightful and fun people—until they're not. They're charmers, and extremely generous, at least at first in the courting and grooming phase where you're heavily dosed with it. However, once you're in their web, there may still be bits of charm and generosity; but then there's also manipulation and control, fear and entitlement—things you did not sign up for.

Your "friend," the Borderline/Narcissist, has trapped you in her web of FOG as Susan Forward calls it, or FEAR, OBLIGATION, and GUILT.

Homeplay Exercise

What is Your Body Telling You?

Your body has been trying to share messages with you. What are they? When the phone rings, does your chest constrict and your stomach drop? That is most likely the emotion of fear because, as you said, you're going to "get in trouble" if you don't answer right away.

When she says something funky, do you notice confusion in your mind, an incongruity in your body, a furrow between your brows? Does your jaw clench or your chest constrict when she talks about other people? That would be your anger. Borderline/Narcissists love to put others down (behind their backs) and that can be disguised as subtle snide and catty remarks.

continued

The truth of the matter is that you were duped. The Borderline/Narcissist drew you in with charm and generosity, but the relationship is not a loving, kind one; it is based on power-over and dominion. The Borderline/Narcissist must stay on top in order to feel good about themselves. Consider what their generosity and kindness will cost you: your spiritual, mental, and emotional health. That's a big price to pay.

Homeplay Exercise

Peel Off the Labels

It is part of a Borderline/Narcissist's power-over method to label people as selfish, ungrateful, and not as giving as she is. And even if it is not blatantly said out loud, you may still feel this energy from her.

This toxic "friend" has placed labels on you because she wants to manipulate you to do what she wants. This is called emotional blackmail. A real friend respects your time and space, your energy and health, your marriage and family. She respects your limitations. A toxic friend does not because she wants to own you and your energy.

Write these labels down, cut them out as labels, and tape them to a piece of paper. Then peel them off the paper, rip them up, and throw them away.

It's like you're peeling them right off of you.

Please give yourself lots of loving kindness. It is not your fault for getting involved in a toxic friendship such as this. Borderline/

Narcissists are master manipulators. They know how to play people so forgive yourself for getting stuck in their web.

If the labels continue to stick, look for professional help. I strongly suggest getting support. The slime of Borderline/ Narcissists is toxic and has a negative effect on the mind, body, and soul of their victims. Never be ashamed to get assistance in healing.

Homeplay Exercise

Getting Out of a Friendship with a Borderline/Narcissist

Here are 5 steps to get out of that toxic relationship:

Step 1: Keep your goal in mind and get your brave on.
One of the biggest fears of a Borderline/Narcissist is abandonment, so when you distance yourself from them, they'll not only smell it a mile away, but they'll get really mean and angry. They will sting. They will say things that are not true about you—not only to you, but to others as well. They will want to make you look bad.

You must get your courage up and keep your goal in mind, because leaving this kind of relationship can be scary. There are all kinds of slime. Know deeply that you are saving yourself and your soul. You are choosing to no longer live in confusion between the Borderline/ Narcissist's charm and their need for you to love them more than you love your-

continued

self. You are choosing to fear Hashem, rather than fear them. Hashem is your G-d, not the Borderline/Narcissist. No one has power over you or the right to frighten you into doing what they want. The only one you serve is G-d.

Visualize yourself being free from the Borderline/Narcissist's manipulations, their charm, their incongruity. Visualize yourself being aligned with your soul and with your spirit instead of with theirs.

Step 2: Do the ROAR! Process.

Your body has been in fight, flight, trauma, and freeze and needs to run and hit out. Your mind needs to empty out all those angry words that you needed and maybe wanted to say to this person when you felt something was funky, but you didn't because you were too afraid. And now you can say anything you want on paper. Saying the words you want to say to the Borderline/Narcissist probably will not help anything because they are master manipulators and will turn your words around on you. You will get more confused. It's not worth your effort.

Instead, do the **ROAR! Process (Chapter 2; Letter 3),** and you can send that difficult energy to Hashem to recycle into light.

Step 3: Line up support in the way of friends, therapists, and healers. You may need a village behind you on this one.

Because Borderline/Narcissists are liars and manipulators, you'll need sane, kind people to keep telling you the deep truth about you—that you are a caring, kind individual who is leaving a toxic relationship. I'm so glad that your husband sees the truth of the relationship. Not all people see the Borderline/Narcissist's true colors even when their colors are flying high. Count it as a blessing that your husband does see them.

The sanity of others will be your saving grace and lifeline so that you don't get stuck back in the controlling Borderline/Narcissist's web.

Though you can do the **ROAR! Process** by yourself, you may need more help to release your body from trauma. The work of somatic-based healing will help cleanse your being of the toxicity of the Borderline/Narcissist's poison.

You've been like a frozen rabbit, unable to access your body's natural fight or flight response. Your body has registered the lies, the manipulations, the incongruity of their outwardly nice, inwardly crooked nature. Your body wanted to run. But your thoughts, confusion, and fear held you in place.

When you finally leave a relationship with a Borderline/Narcissist, you'll need to process the emotional energies of anger and fear. Your body can finally release the adrenaline of your fight and flight response. All that energy can flow and your body and mind can heal.

Step 4: Just leave. Exit. No explanations, no rationalizations, and no excuses.
They will have a fit. No. Matter. What. The Borderline/Narcissist will be as angry as a hive of hornets. They will sting and slug all kinds of cruel, spiteful, and toxic language at you including labeling you as uncaring and selfish. They will feel rejected, which is natural, but what is different from a regular friendship is the severity of the insults they will throw at you. They will tell you that you hurt them without taking accountability for the pain they've caused you. And blaming you for their pain is just another manipulative tactic of FEAR, OBLIGATION, and GUILT.

continued

Remember: this is why you are leaving. Deep in your heart and spirit you know, no matter how kind and generous they have been at times, this person is capable of being cruel to you. Who wants to be friends with someone who wants to hurt you? (Hurting you is their way of having power over you.)

You may have seen this side of them before, perhaps in a hidden way or perhaps the way they have spoken about others. And it threw you out of alignment.

You didn't know what to make of it. Aren't they a kind person? At least they've expressed beautiful, warm and fuzzy traits, and with charm. And that's why you entered the relationship in the first place.

They were just so nice. And everybody said how nice they are (they can fool a lot of people). You believed everybody. But little did anyone know that this charming and dynamic individual was a Borderline/Narcissist. Sometimes, you've got to be somewhat deep in the relationship to discover this about them. By then it's too late; you are already in over your head and exiting will not be easy. They will attack and you will get bruised. And that's why you arm yourself with safe, truly kind, loving individuals, and professionals.

Because a hornet attack is dangerous. Dangerous to your mental, physical, and spiritual health. It is almost impossible to have clarity on your own at this point. That is the way with a Borderline/Narcissist. They are brutally confusing. There is no open communication or two-way communication. Those regular relationship rules don't apply here.

So, you must leave, and over time you'll find clarity. Your alignment will be strengthened, and you'll stop questioning yourself. Know that you will be grateful every day that you took that very brave first step to exit.

Step 5: Remain completely disengaged. No conversations. Receive no calls, emails, or texts from the Borderline/ Narcissist.

Block them from your cell phone and block them from your email. Block them on social media. Receive nothing of their attempts to lure you back with their twisted lies and deceptions—their cover ups, their deflections, their excuses.

Again, the name of the game they play, unbeknownst to you, is the power game. And each engagement with them—every phone call, text, talk, or email—will suck you right back into the game. This is not a game that you can win. They won't let you. Hence the lies, deceptions, and twisted arguments. Confusing for your mind, body, and soul.

I know these measures seem extreme. But notice the fear in your body. That is also extreme! No relationship should ever make you feel that way. They are the ones with bad behavior. They are the ones who don't have ahavas yisroel. They have hurt you, not the other way around as they claim. You are only hurting them by leaving, which cannot be helped, but you are being kind to yourself by doing so.

You must have ahavas yisroel for yourself, for your family, and for other friends you will love and care for. The Borderline/ Narcissist relationship is not a normal one, so you can't treat it normally. You're being tested to be courageous, to cling to Hashem, and to drop all people-pleasing behavior. Your body will thank you!

A Sum-up for getting out of this toxic relationship:

- align with your vision for freedom;
- fully accept and be clear that Hashem is your G-d, not the Borderline/Narcissist;
- line up your support;
- do the **ROAR! Process** again and again;
- exit and remain completely disengaged.

Meditate on this: Going vertical in strength, faith, and alignment with Hashem is the opposite of going horizontal with the fear of "what do others think of me?" Hashem sees everything and sees who you are and what is going on in your life—He is the one you account to. Please believe in yourself because G-d already does.

You can do this!

"My value as a person is independent of what any mortal thinks of me."

—Rabbi Zelig Pliskin

Homeplay Exercise

Ten Tips to Spot a Borderline/Narcissist

Once you've gotten out of this toxic friendship, it's important to know how you can avoid similar relationships in the future. Using the **BRAKES Method** (Chapter 4: Letter 1) is great for discerning how to move forward in any kind of relationship—whether it's dating, friendship, or even at work. The most important elements for a strong foundation of a relationship are emotional safety, vulnerability, and kindness. This foundation is not available with a Borderline/Narcissist because their game is power, not love.

Ten tips to spot a Borderline/Narcissist early so you don't get trapped in their controlling web again:

1. They're overly friendly, generous, and charming.
They have landed their line in you and are reeling you in. How do you know? Normal folks are kind and may offer help, but they don't need to charm and they're not excessively generous. If you feel yourself being charmed and doted on to the extreme, run the other way. A person with decent self-esteem doesn't need to charm and doesn't have the time to overly focus on you.

2. They "get" you. They've given you the impression that they understand you and where you're coming from. They emphasize that they "know how you feel." This is not empathy; this is part of the reeling in. They are superb manipulators and know what makes people tick. They know that they need to make you feel safe before they show their true selves and turn against you.

continued

3. They're multi-talented.

It's part of their charm. You're probably very impressed by them.

4. They move in quickly.

They know they want you, whether as a friend, a lover, or a close co-worker. You are their goal. They will court you.

5. They say odd things, but they are so nice that you ignore the funky feeling it sets off in your body.

You may even furrow your brows and feel a bit confused. Most likely you'll just smile awkwardly to be polite and not make waves. But something just doesn't make sense. It doesn't feel right in your body; something seems off, but you can't put your finger on it or are uncomfortable putting your finger on it.

6. They will talk badly about other people behind their backs.

They make fun of people, make snide comments, or put them down. I was once with a Borderline/Narcissist who looked another woman up and down! I had never seen such a thing before — I thought that was only in the movies! Borderline/Narcissists are deeply jealous of others and nasty digs (even visual ones) are their modus operandi.

If it is against your integrity to talk unkindly behind others' backs (and I hope it is!), do not walk—run away. And fast. Or speak up! Call them on it. Don't just try to defend the person who is not in the room with you. Say, "Hey, it's really rude to speak that way about another person. I'm not into that." If they put you down because you speak up or if they try to laugh it off, keep calling a spade a spade. Show that you aren't easily intimidated or afraid to speak your mind. And then walk away. They've shown their true colors.

Remember Maya Angelou's warning, "When someone shows you who they are, believe them the first time." Plus, you know that lashon hara is not okay — why are you allowing yourself to be exposed to it on a constant basis with this person? And know that if the Borderline/Narcissist is speaking this way about someone else, they are also speaking this way about you.

7. They won't like you if you don't show an interest in them.
So, don't. They want to have power over people. If they can't have power over you, they won't like you. One of the ways they do this is with their super charming personality and their many talents. Don't get that interested.

8. They seem really down-to-earth and deep.
But they're not. They're missing something inside. They want your energy and will suck you dry if you let them. You have something that they want. They are energy vampires. Maybe not at the beginning of the relationship—at the beginning they are generous, attentive, kind, thoughtful, etc. But don't be fooled. They will eventually become a vampire. Or Dr. Jekyll's Mr. Hyde. Not fun.

9. They're confusing.
They say something about you that makes you go "huh?" or feel defensive.

10. They try to get you to do something that you don't want to do.
They're persistent and you feel intimidated, not physically, but emotionally and socially. You feel uncomfortable saying no. You get a sense that they are judging you for not doing what they want you to do. And they may be. But in truth, their

continued

judgments are not the problem. Your judgments about you are the problem and the Borderline/Narcissist will use your weaknesses and vulnerabilities for their own devices—to get you to do what they want.

For example, there was a woman I was once friends with. Even though I had a young colicky infant, she would continually call me up and ask me to host her Shabbos guests for meals and for sleeping over. Meaning, she didn't want to host them but thought it would be nice if I did (though she did not use those words). I would agree to host though I was overwhelmed by my own life and lack of sleep. Why did I say yes? Because I was judging myself for being selfish if I said no.

When I went on my healing path, I recognized many of this woman's traits to be those of a Borderline/Narcissist. And also discovered that she had been speaking very nastily about me behind my back while we were "good" friends. I know firsthand the toxicity of a "friendship" with someone who has Borderline/Narcissist manipulative and unkind traits.

Another example: When I picked up my children from school, a neighbor's child always ran over to my car and asked for a ride. I often said yes. But then I caught on that I was being used. If the neighbor wanted a carpool, it would have been a give-and-take situation. But they only wanted to take and not give. My inner judgments were "How can I say no? It's not a big deal to take their child home. I should not be selfish." Again, I needed to wake up and accept the challenge of establishing healthy boundaries with someone who was being manipulative.

You too can stand up to a Borderline/Narcissist. You can set boundaries and say "I can't" without explanation. You can

distance yourself from that person. Do not engage in conversation or debate with them because they are masters in the art of domination.

The Borderline/Narcissist is a master manipulator, and you will become confused. Something is broken about them—a twisting of the mind—and they will defend themselves. Or maybe this time, they'll apologize. But at some point, they'll be expecting you to apologize and tell you that you hurt them. And then you will regret being involved with them, but too confused to figure out why.

Also, if they tell you something about yourself, keep in mind they may be lying. They want you to feel vulnerable and dependent on them. Pointing out your weaknesses or making them up is a power tool of theirs to get you in their web (and to stay there after you've lost your way). A Borderline/Narcissist will shame you about your personality. They want you to feel doubtful of your abilities. Please DO NOT give your power away to the Borderline/Narcissist. They'll only wind up hurting you.

So, you've spotted them. Now what?

As I said before, it's time to walk away. QUICK! Before they sink their line into you and become an energy vampire, draining you of your divine light, confusing you in a way that is so toxic, you won't know which way is up.

Step away now with clear boundaries—don't spend time with them, don't talk with them beyond brief, casual exchanges, don't respond to their advances, don't chat with them. No phone, no WhatsApp, no Facebook—in fact, unfriend them.

The kind but cold shoulder is best. And yes, this may feel extreme, but they are not a regular nice guy or gal. They are something different. They are a controlling Borderline/Narcissist.

continued

You don't need to become their victim. You don't need to be controlled by their manipulations. You can live free y and have kind, healthy relationships.

Homeplay Exercise

Be Your Own Best Friend

Remember this: You are more amazing than you know! Treat yourself kindly, with respect and care. Of course, be humble, but being humble just means recognizing that you're human, recognizing that you make mistakes, and that you can make changes. Hashem is your source and power and has given you divine gifts to share in the world. Do your mission knowing that Hashem is watching.

Peace to you as you get out of this toxic relationship and avoid others like this in the future. You will deeply appreciate the energy you gain back for your life.

Blessings!

Letter 4
Making New Friends

Dear Miriam Racquel,

I've just moved to a new town and want to make friends. Do you have any suggestions?

Dear Awesome Woman,

I do! A great way to enjoy new friends and create a small community for yourself is to arrange a gathering for a few women on the evening of Rosh Chodesh to do simple creativity. This can even be within a community that you've been a part of for a while and are feeling a bit lonely. If any factors make social distancing necessary, these gatherings can take place over a video call or in your backyard, with small tables placed apart.

There are numerous ways to be creative, and I have found collaging to be a great way to connect. All you need are glue sticks, scissors, and magazines for cutting. The women can do vision boards or just have fun collaging pictures of words and images that feel good to them. The joy factor is what is important, not the artistic factor. Magical things happen when you collage because you're drawing attention to what lights you up.

There are no "shoulds" to collaging. It's just choosing pictures and words that give an uplift to your spirit—where you feel "I like this,

this feels good," and there's no need to know why. Let it be a right-brain activity of imagination and not a left-brain activity of logic.

Women can also use watercolor pencils (they'll need watercolor paper for that), glitter, or any other creative ideas that they have. The key is that it's an evening for women to relax, connect, and enjoy—pressure-free.

Now, the most important factor to keep in mind is to start small and invite women who are non-judgmental and very kind. You want it to be a safe gathering for women to share and be vulnerable if they want to. If you're an introvert, you'll probably want to limit the group to 4-5 women.

I have had a group for a few years now, the same women meeting each month. There are other wonderful and kind women in the community whom I could invite, but because my intention is to keep it small and the women are already comfortable being vulnerable with each other, I continue to keep it a closed group. But I do encourage people to start their own groups!

Blessings!

5

Dating

Don't go for the bright, shiny object—
you know what I mean—the charmer.
The exciting one.
Instead, go for the kind-hearted,
the patient, the stable, the generous,
the responsible one.
Yes, you can have fun with this one too
and build your bayis ne'eman.
In an emotionally safe space,
the Shechinah can dwell.

—Miriam Racquel Feldman

Pre-Dating: Letter 1

Asking the Right Questions

Dear Miriam Racquel,

I'm a baalas teshuvah and I'm ready to start dating to establish my own bayis ne'eman. I went to a Shadchan and got a few resumes of potential shidduchim. The guys all look great on paper, but I know that their references need to be checked out. A very kind Shabbos hostess offered to help me by calling the references. She has not done this before (her children are not in the parsha yet) and asked me what questions she should ask. Do you have suggestions?

Dear Awesome Woman,

Welcome to the start of your very next journey on your baalas teshuva path! Your goal in getting married is a beautiful one—finding a loving partner to share your life with and creating a bayis ne'eman in which to serve Hashem. Deciding who will be the man you'll spend the rest of your life with, become vulnerable to, and G-d willing, raise children with is the most important decision you will ever make.

This is a time of great excitement and wonder. You are searching for your second half—the one whom Hashem has called out as yours.

Creating a home where there is emotional safety, kindness, peace, and love is the goal—this is where the Shechinah can dwell. This is a home where joy can be found.

To this end, it is wise to find a man who is caring in spirit and heart and a man who is yiras shomayim—meaning he will put halacha over his base taivos. Your husband can be an extrovert or introvert, a great businessman or not such a great businessman, a learner or not, but if he is kind and considerate of your needs, he is worth his weight in gold. Ideally, when considering who to establish a home with, you are looking for a man who matches your values, a man you can communicate with, and a man you enjoy being with.

Probe as much as possible about character.

A resume typically lists a person's qualities and their interests, but it will be up to you to look beyond the paper and discern whether this is the man to set up a bayis ne'eman with.

The references are people who wish to see this man get married and who have been asked to give a glowing report. Then there are the non-references to inquire of who are not on the paper. These non-references are the ones who have had interactions with the potential shidduch and can answer what they know about him that the references may not want to say or may not even know.

When speaking to a reference it's a good idea to jot down their answers.

Before we get to the questions, I'd like to make this point: in order to ask these questions, the researcher needs to put aside shyness and be direct instead. It may seem intrusive probing into someone's business when in Yiddishkeit, privacy is so protected. We're also told not to judge and not to speak lashon hora, so this process of deeply inquiring about a shidduch may feel very uncomfortable. But in the area of shidduchim, it's a mitzvah to probe, research, and discern.

Know the difference between judgment and discernment.

In trying to be a "good person," it may seem like a great idea to drop judgment. And this is true—judgment is unkind and...judgy—an ego creation. Besides, we know that the only true judge is Hashem. But Hashem has given us the ability to use wise discernment in determining which relationships will bring more kindness into our lives or more grief.

One of the best pieces of advice that I heard about marriage was from Rabbi Manis Friedman. He said that when choosing a person for marriage (though advice can go for all kinds of relationships—friends, business partners, co-workers), don't look at what you like in a person, because there is much to like in most people. **Look instead at what you don't like in someone and discern if you can live with that.** That is what you are doing in the shidduch process. You are not judging for the sake of judging, you are discerning for the sake of determining with whom you can best build a bayis ne'eman.

For example, if a man speaks petty and derogatory words about others, can you live with that? How does he behave when he doesn't get what he wants? Does he get nasty or does he stay calm? Is he manipulative, angry, or does he use emotional blackmail (pressure you emotionally) to get his way? Good to know and to decide if you want to live with that.

Keep in mind that using your gift of discernment will help you choose a marriage partner with whom you can, G-d willing, build a healthy and compassionate home with.

Celebrate yourself for having gone to a Shadchan and for taking this very brave step of inquiring about a future partner! **Put your arms up into the air in a V shape and say, "Yay me!"**

Your Shabbos hostess is very kind to do this probing for you. The following are possible questions to be asked of references and non-references.

Questions:

1. Can you tell me about him? Start off with this general question

2. Personality. Is he an introvert or extrovert? What is his sense of humor like? Does he have one or is he more on the serious side? Would you describe him as warm and connecting or more intellectual and shy? Is he laid-back or does he have more of an intense, get-things-done energy about him? Is he soft-spoken, demanding, generous, loud, bold—what is his personality type? How does he behave when things don't go his way? Does he have a temper?

Is he kind? How does this show? Do you have examples? Does he do a lot of chesed? Like what? How is he with his friends—teasing, talkative, quiet? Does he have lots of friends or just a few good ones? Who are they?

3. Frumkeit, Chassidishkeit, Religiosity. How does he dress—black and white, casual, colored shirts, shorts, etc.? Does he watch movies or TV? Does he want to learn full-time or work? Does he have a learning seder? Does he go to minyan? How often? Where does he go to minyan—which shul? Is he the type who sleeps in? Who is his Rebbe, Rabbi, Rav, mentor? How does he feel about his Rebbe? Rav? What hechshers does he hold of? Does he keep cholov yisroel? If he has a beard, does he trim it?

4. Parents, Family, and Relationships with Them. What kind of relationship does he have with his mother and father? Are they married or divorced? What kind of relationship do they have? What are their personalities like? You are not only marrying your husband, but a family as well—best to know up front what they are like. If the mother or father sounds like a Narcissist, has Borderline Personality Disorder or Bi-Polar Disorder (which can be controlled by meds) this is very important info to have—these personality disorders will not only have affected your spouse but will affect you as their daughter-in-law. What kind of relationship does he have with his siblings? Warm, close, distant, argumentative? Are there any personality disorders there?

5. Any health issues?

6. Activities. What does he like to do for recreation? Does he like adventure? Sports? Travel? Reading? Music, concerts, or TV? What are his hobbies and interests? Does he exercise?

7. Good with Kids? How is he with children?

8. Where does he want to live? Is he flexible about this?

9. What kind of career does he have? How would he support the family?

10. How is he with money? Saves money? Loves to buy and collect things? Generous? Tight? Concerned and worries a lot about it?

11. How much time, if any, does he spend on social media? Have you viewed anything he has posted? What kinds of things does he share online?

12. What is he looking for in a wife?

~

While collecting information to make your decision, keep in mind that **a woman's number one priority is to feel safe in a relationship.** From here trust and intimacy can flow.

An insightful shadchan and dating coach, Rivkah Leah Bernath (*Chicago Shidduch@gmail.com*), once told me that if a man and woman are on a date, and a person approaches with a dog on a leash, and the woman shies away because she is scared, does the man mock her or protect her? Does he act like a shield so she feels safe or does he tease and belittle her? Guess which one will be better for building a Bayis Ne'eman with?

Obvious red flags are tempers, addictions, control issues, treating people unkindly or curtly, and impatience.

A note about differing levels of observance:

If you choose to consider someone who is of a different hashkafa or is committed to less or more Torah observance than you are at the moment, you can consider a story concerning the Lubavitcher Rebbe's advice to a woman who was dating a man who had a different level of observance. The Rebbe focused on a fundamental principle of marriage—the couple understanding what each one wants most in their life. The man needs to know what the woman's vision is for her life and the woman needs to know what the man's vision is for his life. Even if they don't have the exact same vision, they must genuinely care that the other person reaches their goals.

Lots of hatzlacha on your journey!

Blessings!

Pre-Dating: Letter 2

How to Pick a Nice Guy

Dear Miriam Racquel,

I've been learning more about Judaism for the past two years now, and I feel ready to begin dating to find my marriage partner. But I'm afraid. My experience with men in college before I was religious was not great. Things would start out well and then go downhill. The guys turned out to be critical, and we fought a lot. I felt like I was looking for love in all the wrong places. Maybe it was because I don't have such a close relationship with my dad, who himself is critical and harsh. I want a kind, loving man with whom to build a home. How should I change myself so that I don't pick unkind men like I did in the past? How can I trust myself to pick someone kind?

Dear Awesome Woman,

I'm so glad that you reached out for help. Your goal is beautiful. Deciding who you will spend the rest of your life with, become vulnerable to, and G-d willing, raise children with is the most important decision you will ever make. You don't want to be in a marriage with a man who is critical, unkind, lacks generosity or is irresponsible, blaming or confusing. As you shared, you previously picked men who were critical and harsh—perhaps not realizing it at first. So, how can you change that? How can you change the inner programming that may have led to this?

One thing to keep in mind is who you are now is different from who you were in college. Your values have changed, and what you are looking for in a husband-to-be is different from the college guys you hung out with for fun. Have confidence in that inner change you've already made.

I see that you are concerned that you'll pick an unkind husband because of the unkind relationship that you had with your critical father. This is not necessarily true. Again, being older and wiser, with some Jewish tools under your belt, you are a different person. And as much as our childhood relationships have an effect on us, we are also quite free from limiting ourselves to those patterns.

One way to make sure that unhealthy patterns of the past are not locking us into future unkind treatment is to treat yourself more lovingly and respectfully (on the inside as well as the outside). Look at it from this angle: If you have a dad that criticizes you a lot, then you have most likely inhaled the habit of criticizing yourself. As children, we take those messages from our parents very seriously. But you are an adult now. You have a beautiful soul—a piece of G-d in you—and that critical abuser has to go. Starting today.

You have the opportunity to change the way you treat yourself. And with this gentle shift others will treat you differently, too. The beauty of this shift is that your internal kindness will have far-reaching effects—the more gentle and kind you are to yourself, the kinder you will be to others.

Move away from inner cruelty and move towards inner love and G-d's love. Rise from a woman who accepts negative treatment to a woman who only allows positive treatment. This opens up the pathway to having a husband who treats you with honor. Love is an inside job. Having warm regard for yourself is necessary for living a healthy, joyful and purposeful life. G-d believes in you, and *you* can believe in you.

Exercise 1: Change the Way You Treat Yourself

1. Ask yourself: What are the three most important characteristics or aspects that you want in a husband? Write those down.

2. Now with those three characteristics, turn them around towards you, putting each aspect in the blank.

> *"How can I be more ___________ with myself or others?"*

That's a surprising question, isn't it? But asking yourself this can tune you into certain characteristics that you expect to see in a partner and yet, you need to own them in yourself as well.

3. Come up with two or three ways to be that way with yourself and others now—not waiting for someone else to do it for you.

An example:

> Sara wants a husband who is trusting, honest and generous.
>
> She writes: "How can I be more trusting of myself, honest with myself, generous to myself?"

Continuing with the exercise:

Sara gets more honest and trusting with herself. She is pushing herself forward in a career that she dislikes strongly; she is putting too much pressure on herself in the dating realm, and so decides to trust in G-d and take it more slowly.

Sara finds two ways to be more generous to herself or others. She buys herself flowers for Shabbat; she says no to some social gatherings because she recognizes that she is an introvert and enjoys more time to herself. She decides to do a weekly gesture for a friend.

Exercise 2: Heal Wounds by Giving Yourself Compassion

I once took a 10-week course in self-compassion. At the beginning of the course, I asked myself how many classes (and these were two hours each!) can they give on this topic? Wouldn't one suffice? But the surprise was that self-compassion is amazing for our nervous systems. We don't realize that when we beat ourselves up psychologically, our bodies tense up—there's an inner fight, flight and/or freeze response created. All generated by us. We can be our own enemy making our nervous systems feel like we are being chased by a lion or attacked by a wild creature.

So instead, when you do find yourself hurting with inner criticism, take a moment to rest your hand on your heart and give yourself compassion. You can say these healing words: "I'm hurting now. May I give myself kindness."

And if a memory from the past pops into your mind, you can give compassion to the little girl inside you by saying: "I'm so sorry that happened to you."

Emotions like anger, sadness or grief may come up. Since emotions are "energy in motion" and present themselves as physical sensations, just take a moment to notice them in your body. The tendency many of us have is to leave our bodies and dissociate from the discomfort of emotional energy, but you can allow yourself to just gently sit with these sensations or even move with them. This brings flow and will provide healing for you on a deep subconscious level.

Practicing these two exercises will help you shift from the inside out, creating a vessel to receive more kindness in your life.

When you choose to begin dating for marriage, be mindful of choosing a kind partner. Kindness is such an integral quality that when Eliezer was searching for a wife for Isaac, he devised a test of character to see if the prospective life partner was kind. Make that your top priority. Beware of red flags, like overly charming or controlling men. Look for compassion, respect and accountability.

And remember that G-d is with you in your search, so have the courage to step into this exciting part of your life.

Blessings!

(Originally published at *TheJewishWoman.org*)

Pre-Dating: Letter 3

False Expectations of Love

Dear Miriam Racquel,

I've been on a few dates with some really nice guys, but I'm running into a problem. They all fall short of the romantic version of a husband that I have in my head. Maybe it's a skewed version of love since I grew up on Walt Disney stories, and romantic novels and movies. I've been learning more about Judaism, and I've come to understand that the Torah approach to love and marriage is different from the fantasies I was raised on. Do you have any ideas of how I can set my expectations more realistically and general tips to follow to nurture a fulfilling relationship?

Dear Awesome Woman,

Great questions! And I know that you are not alone with your false expectations of love.

As a woman who came to Jewish observance in my early 20s, I also grew up on the Hollywood and Disney model. I must have watched hundreds of romantic shows by the time I reached my teens. And on top of that, the amount of love-struck music that played on the radio everywhere was not helpful for realistic expectations of dating and marriage.

I see it now as an insidious form of brainwashing. As Swiss-born British philosopher and author Alain de Botton says so clearly:

> "... the classic Romantic model has sold us on a number of self-defeating beliefs about the most essential and nuanced experiences of human life: love, infatuation, marriage ...."

Many people are coming to recognize that these "fairy tale" expectations are not serving us well, and the high level of divorce certainly proves that the world does not educate properly on dating, relationships and marriage.

To juxtapose this, here is a beautiful story that sheds light on the real meaning of love and marriage:

A young woman named Chana Sharfstein once came to the Lubavitcher Rebbe for a private audience. He asked about her dating, and then upon hearing that she had rejected some good young men, said that she read too many novels. Then he shared some very timely advice that we can all take to heart. Thank you, Chana, for revealing this personal information so that the world can learn from the Rebbe's wisdom.

In her words:

> "Love, he explained to me, is not that which is portrayed in romantic novels. It isn't that overwhelming, blinding emotion that is portrayed in a romance. These books do not portray real life, he said. It is a fantasy world, a make-believe world with made-up emotions. Fiction is just that—fiction—but real life is different.

> And then, as a father to a daughter, he began to explain to me the meaning of real love.
>
> Love, he told me, is an emotion that increases in strength throughout life. It is sharing and caring and respecting one another. It is building a life together, a unit of family and home. The love that you feel as a young bride, he continued, is only the beginning of real love. It is through the small, everyday acts of living together that love flourishes and grows.
>
> And so, he continued, the love you feel after five years or 10 years is a gradual strengthening of bonds. As two lives unite to form one, with time, one reaches a point where each partner feels a part of the other, where each partner no longer can visualize life without his mate by his side.
>
> Smilingly he told me to put aside the romantic notions developed by my literary involvement, and view love and marriage in a meaningful way."

From the Rebbe's very powerful words, we can see that where there is kindness, generosity, respect and partnership, love can grow, and a marriage can be nurtured.

It's such a brave act to partner up with someone, and false ideas of how relationships "should be" could lead us away from our soulmate instead of closer together. My suggestion to you is to choose someone compassionate and respectful, and to be this way as well.

And please be careful not to swing the completely opposite way either—meaning, don't think that there should only be the rational objective of a paper perfect spouse. The Rebbe was very clear that one should have an attraction of the heart (hamshochas halev).

Your feelings count!

I'd also like to share with you two tips for when you are dating and even more so when you are married, G-d willing, in the near future. These are not taught in the Disney shows:

1. Know your desires and state them respectfully: Say "I'd like" or "I'd love" without the word "you." Avoid phrases like, "Let's … " or "Don't you want to … ?" Instead, when you have a request or preference, state it: "I'd love to go out for sushi." "I'd like to take a walk by the boardwalk."

Surveys show that husbands want to make their wives happy and want to fulfill their desires, but reject and feel belittled by subtle words of control. The word, "Let's" means "Let us." For women who are relationship-oriented, it may feel very connecting. But for a man, it could feel like he is being controlled or "led." And "Don't you" can be taken as a bit forceful because what if he "doesn't want to … " but would be willing to do something because it would make you happy?

2. Another word about respect: Male culture is such that it can be a bit harsh and critical. Growing up in this culture, husbands are sensitive to "trying to be made better" by their wives—they are allergic to shame and have an adverse reaction to negative judgment. Like all of us—women included.

And yet, since women are divinely gifted with an abundance of the ability to discern (binah) and the desire to improve and better the world, we can typically turn that ability on our spouses and make them a "home improvement project." It doesn't work and can lead to much conflict.

Many women don't realize that they are being disrespectful even if they are doing it with the best intentions and care. Again, if you see something that you'd like improved, use "I'd like" or "I'd love" without the word you. Sprinkle in plenty of gratitude and appreciation for all the things that your (future) husband is getting right by you.

With a caring heart, kindness and some marriage skills, you will G-d willing, have a marriage that the Rebbe is referring to—one in which the bonds of love strengthen over the years.

Wishing you well on your journey and good for you that you're taking responsibility to change your perspective on love and marriage. You and your future spouse surely will benefit greatly, and nurture a home of peace and kindness!

Blessings!

(Originally published at *TheJewishWoman.org.*)

While Dating: Letter 4

Nerves

Dear Miriam Racquel,

I have a date in an hour and my palms are sweating, my heart is pounding and I feel so much anxiety. It's always like this for me. I'm a nervous wreck. How am I supposed to calm myself down enough to have a decent conversation and appear somewhat normal?

Dear Awesome Woman,

First of all, normal is overrated. Hashem has created each one of us from a unique mold and as similar as we all are, we are also blessed with different personalities, different genes, different looks and different soul-qualities. Hashem has a perfect partner for you *who will appreciate you for you,* including the fact that dating makes you nervous.

Second of all, I'll share with you three great somatic techniques to help calm your nervous system.

Homeplay Exercise

Stay in Your Body

We all tend to want to escape our bodies when we feel the discomfort of nervousness, but the safest and most healing place to be is "in your body." By this, I mean to put your awareness on the physical sensations coming up.

*Place your hand on your heart and notice the pounding.

*Take some soft, calming belly breaths as your hand rests on your heart.

This small action will have the effect of dialing down your anxiety to a more manageable place. You can also bring your awareness to the rest of your body. Where does the anxiety sit? Is it jumping around in your chest, in your stomach? Just feel safe in noticing those sensations. This allows for a flow of energy that calms your system.

With this calmer energy, listen for intuition or choose an empower-ing thought: "Even though I'm a bit nervous, I'm moving in the direction of my desires." And then throw your arms up and celebrate yourself.

Homeplay Exercise

Do ROAR! to Release the Nervous Tension

ROAR! it out. Please see The **ROAR! Process** in Letter 3 of Chapter 2: Self-Care. And do it! You can scribble your nervous thoughts on paper, rip it up, and then do the O and A actions. This "getting big" energy will help you release some of your very normal fears and nerves. You will feel more comfortable in your body and more present for your date.

Homeplay Exercise

On the Date, Tune In to Your Senses

On the date itself, tune into your surroundings. Your date won't even realize that you are doing this and it only takes seconds.

- Feel your feet on the ground as you're walking or sitting on the chair.
- Notice the sounds around you—throw out your hearing as far as it can go. What do you hear?
- Take a breath in—what do you smell?
- What do you see with your eyes?

Being in touch with your senses will make your nervous system settle in real time making it feel safe and aware, grounded and present. You'll be in your body and more in touch with your intuition.

Please take a moment to celebrate yourself for taking the brave journey of dating. It's an act of courage and Hashem loves you for it. Put your hands up in the air in a V for victory and say—"Yay, me!" This somatically brings blood flow and oxygen to the brain, boosting your body with good-feeling endorphins and dopamine. Giving yourself loving messages is an act of compassion. Do that for yourself as you would for a friend as you embark on this precious life journey.

I love to breathe into the energy of this quote by Tony Robbins: *"Stop being afraid of what could go wrong, and start being excited of what could go right."*

Blessings! 

While Dating: Letter 5

Dating with Discernment: BRAKES and Somatic Wisdom

Dear Miriam Racquel,

I loved using your discerning questions about a possible shidduch. Now I'm ready to actually date. What advice do you have on the dating process itself?

Dear Awesome Woman,

Your discerning process has moved from paper and fantasy to real life. Now that you are ready for your first big date, it is important to set proper expectations for the next period in your shidduch journey. Ideally, you will feel emotionally safe, excited, and happy around the man you will be dating.

That being said, it would be unrealistic to insist on someone who is perfect and who doesn't have qualities that will annoy you or frustrate you at times. The Jewish belief in soulmates contains room for conflict, growth, and the acceptance of imperfections. However, what is important is that your potential husband has the middot, yiras shomayim, and ability to work *together with you* in creating a home of kindness, peace, joy, and wellbeing.

What I'd like to teach you is the **BRAKES Method** as well as somatic wisdom to continue to discern as you move forward. Both will help you identify potential obstacles, as well as joyful possibilities, in creating such a home. Here we will discuss not only what to watch-out for, but also how to pace yourself during this phase. My goal is to encourage women to vet their shidduch wisely, to have smart boundaries as they slowly get to know the man they are dating, to pay attention to the wisdom of their bodies, and to recognize red flags that may show up as G-d's chesed to them.

When you date, try not to talk too much out of people-pleasing habits and nerves. People-pleasing behaviors in the dating stage can be hazardous to your future. You must keep checking in with your body to know if this is someone with whom you can set up a safe home with—both emotionally and physically.

Be less concerned about making conversation and wondering how he feels about you, and instead, take time to pause, breathe, and put awareness on your body (a somatic approach) so you are in touch with how you feel with him. Stay open and receptive to your own reflections about the person you are with.

Also, if you're overly concerned about what he is thinking about you (as if you can see into his brain!) then you'll be even more frazzled and nervous. This will make it harder for you to be a good listener and listening is such an important relationship skill.

Finally, enjoy yourself as much as possible. The energy of the masculine has a somewhat playful quality to it so being with that energy can bring lightness and laughter.

Now, let's dive into the **BRAKES Method** for shidduchim. You may have read the **BRAKES Method** in the earlier Chapter 4: Friendship and Community. I'm reiterating it here with detailed specifics regarding the dating parsha.

Homeplay Exercise

The BRAKES Method for Dating

The six principles of the **BRAKES Method** will help you be wise and choose honest, trustworthy relationships thoughtfully, whether these relationships are with co-workers, friends, and/or shidduchim.

BRAKES simply refers to putting the brakes on our vulnerability and intimacy with a person, remembering to take our time and ask ourselves a few questions as well as feel into our body, before becoming too close.

Sometimes we're so eager for a relationship to meet our needs that we ignore important things. As I mentioned in Chapter 4, backing out of a relationship after moving too quickly is much messier than going slow to begin with. People get hurt, offended, and attached—it's much easier to go slow from the beginning.

Also, sometimes a person may pressure us to get closer faster than we feel comfortable doing. Using **BRAKES** will caution us against that as the principles help us set boundaries for ourselves while we discern moving forward with a relationship. In addition, please be sure to study the **RED FLAGS** section in this dating chapter.

Read through these questions and keep them in mind when you date.

1. BOUNDARIES. Does he respect and honor your boundaries? Your personal boundaries define what your values and limits are. It's very important to marry a man who respects and honors yours (and you, his). While dating, notice if your date respects and honors your boundaries, values, and sensitivities. What

continued

happens when you say "no" to him? Are you afraid to say "no" because when you have said "no," he gets mean and nasty, overly hurt, threatening, manipulative, or has a temper tantrum claiming that you don't like him?

2. RESPONSIBILITY. How responsible and reliable is he? With your shidduch, does he follow through and do what he says he will do? Or is he busy juggling and over-committing himself to a lot of stuff that he can't possibly do and then backs out at the last minute?

3. ACCOUNTABILITY. How does he show up when it comes to taking accountability? With your shidduch, have you experienced him owning up to his mistakes? Does he apologize and then make changes? Some people are great at apologizing, but then do not follow through with making changes. If this is a pattern, then take note and make changes yourself. Don't be a victim and continue to blame the other person (that will get you nowhere). It is important to open our eyes to what people are showing us about who they are and make the changes necessary to honor ourselves.

4. KEEPERS. Does he keep what you share with him private? While dating, your shidduch will be sharing things about you with mentors and family, just like you will be sharing things about him. This is part of the discerning process of deciding to move forward with a shidduch. This is normal and to be expected. However, can you get a sense of how he is with people's private information? Does he share a lot with you about others, perhaps things that another person wouldn't want him to share? It's an important part of feeling emotionally safe in a relationship to know that what you do share is kept confidential and that your vulnerability is honored. Can you imagine him being the type of person to honor that if you do marry?

Also, once a couple is married, they are better off not sharing private information with family members unless there is abuse going on and they need help. Otherwise, it is highly advised that married couples go to mentors, rabbis, rebbetzins and coaches, either together or individually, for shalom bayis issues. Family is not objective and it can lead to challenging problems, G-d forbid, for the married couple if they get involved.

5. ENERGY EXCHANGE. What is the energy exchange between the two of you? Are you a high or low priority for him? A wife needs to be a priority for her husband, above community, above his friends and above his family members. And a husband needs to be a priority for his wife, above community, above her friends and above her family members. This is the most important relationship you will have—it is the center of your life and home. If a marriage is tense or difficult, G-d forbid, the ramifications radiate into all areas of a person's life. On the other hand (and what you are aiming for!), a solid, kind marriage will be a source of stability and centeredness as life's joys are shared and life's challenges are tackled.

6. SYNC. Is he in sync with your values and his own values? Does he have integrity? Do you respect him? Does he make choices in line with your values? Does he even make choices that are in sync with his own values or does he just talk about them? If asked, would he be able to identify your values and whether they line up with his? Does he understand how your choices are in sync with your values? Actions speak louder than words. In every relationship, but especially in dating, pick people who are in sync with your values and with their own values.

Homeplay Exercise

Somatic Wellness

Pay Attention to Your Body's Wisdom

Emotions are "energy in motion" and show up as physical sensations in the body, starting out very quiet and subtle, almost vibrational. The key here is to notice these physical sensations which is our body trying to communicate with us. When we focus our awareness on the sensation, the energy flows and the body registers that its message to you has been heard. This process requires awareness and honesty (with ourselves).

As you date, continue to make a practice of listening inward—pause, breathe, sit back, and feel into your body. Pay attention to the information you find:

- **Excitement**—An uplifting of the chest that energizes you positively.
- **Nerves**—A mixture of excitement, vulnerability, and fear of the unknown.
- **Fear (dread)**—A message from your body asking you to pay attention to something that doesn't feel safe. May be felt as a sinking in your stomach.
- **Anger**—A surge of energy trying to set a boundary. Asks for action to be taken—words to be said or physical distancing—a protection of sorts. May be felt as a constriction in the chest, a tightening of the jaw, a furrowing of the brows or a tingling in the extremities.

With a potential spouse, one of the things you're discerning is whether you can trust him or not. Trust is built over time and people are human, not perfect angels. Since you're an adult,

I'm sure you've had many interactions with people, and even the most trustworthy can disappoint. This will be true with your husband as well. But for the most part, you are looking for a dependable, kind, and responsible man to set up a Jewish home with. One where the Shechinah dwells, one who you'll ride the waves of life with.

So, how do you know whether you can trust him or not? How do you learn to trust yourself to even figure it out? The best way I know how is by using your body like a compass.

Your body picks up so much information in your interactions with others. Your mind, on the other hand, sometimes wants to shut that information down because it may threaten the status quo of the relationship.

The challenge for you is to "ignore" your mind and tune into your body. Your mind may want to keep things hidden from you by giving you "shoulds" like — "I should ignore that weird thing that he just said." Or the mind wants you to rationalize, "He was really late again, but I should give the guy a break." It's best to pay attention, be honest, drop the "shoulds," and notice how you feel.

Example #1: You're looking out the window waiting for him to arrive for your third date. Just like the second date, he is more than fifteen minutes late. Notice how your body responds. Do you feel your chest constrict or your jaw tense? Put your hand on that area of your body. Let that wise energy flow. These sensations can indicate anger—a boundary violation—you stopped what you were doing to get ready on time for the date and you feel that your time is not being honored. On the date itself (not the first thing) you can tell him, "I'd love when we decide on a time that we stick to it. Otherwise, I stop doing the important things I'm doing in order to get ready and then find myself sit-

continued

ting around waiting." You're not judging him for his lateness, but you are respecting your own need for greater punctuality. You didn't let your mind hijack you by ignoring your body's reaction (tight chest, tense jaw—sensations of annoyance). Anger requires taking action so you spoke up.

Now, notice how he reacts to your respectful way of communicating. Does he apologize? Does he get defensive? Does he take accountability? Does he admit that punctuality isn't his strength and that when you guys decide on a time, you should add fifteen minutes onto that? Your speaking-up can lead to honest communication in getting to know one another. This is a blessing.

And if he is a person who is chronically fifteen minutes late, can you live with that? If you love his other qualities, then you may decide this is something that isn't a big deal to you.

Example #2: Your shidduch tells you that he is a very patient person, yet you feel this wave of rage coming from him when he's driving behind a slow car. Your body registers that incongruence—his mouth is saying one thing and yet his body is saying something else.

Your body is a highly sensitive processing machine and is picking up "that something else" signal. Our logical, conscious mind processes about fifty bits of information per second, while our body and unconscious mind can process as many as eleven million bits of information per second.

Turn inward and notice the physical sensations that are happening in your body. What does your stomach feel like? That is usually where fear sits. When someone is not being congruent, our body's natural reaction will be fear. Put your hand on the physical sensation that is being present with you. Let that energy flow and give you honesty and wisdom.

Let me explain further: A horse is a highly sensitive being. Its body registers heart rate, blood pressure, and other autonomic body responses in another being. If a person walks into a horse pen and is afraid, but is pretending to be happy, the horse will feel the tension in the person's body. Sensing the incongruence, the horse won't trust that person and will shy away from them. But the moment the person admits to themself that they are afraid—gets congruent with their emotions—the body's autonomic functions change, and the inner tension drops. The horse feels safer which is indicated by it walking over to the person because it feels safe to do so.

We want congruence in a person. We want what's being said to match up with what's really going on in their insides. You can feel when someone says how happy they are for you, yet you register jealousy. Their incongruence, their dishonesty can be felt viscerally by you. Your body has a "horse sense" too. If your date says he is a patient person and you feel an underlying impatience or rage from him—pay attention to your body's sense, not your mind's attempt to convince you differently.

Example #3: You're on a fourth date with a guy that you've enjoyed spending time with. You're beginning to feel that he's the one. And then in conversation he says something nasty about the waiter and you grimace. He laughs at you, annoyed by that look on your face. "Can't you take a joke?" he says.

Your mind may be confused. *Hey, I've really liked this guy—he's been really nice. And others say such great things about him. Maybe he didn't mean what he said.* But if you tune into your body—the grimace when he insulted the waiter and the flinch when he was sarcastic to you—you'll realize a few things:

continued

1. You didn't like how he behaved.
2. You didn't like how he reacted to your reaction (his energy was one of intimidation). With honesty, you can say to yourself, "I don't like that he made fun of the waiter. And I don't like how he responded to my reaction to the remark he made."

Your mind may want to rationalize the event or come to his defense. Your mind may want to dismiss the sinking in your stomach or the tightening in your chest. But don't let it. Don't let your mind ignore your body. Listen to the wisdom. If your body feels anger, it is setting a boundary.

Registering your body's response doesn't necessarily mean dumping the guy right then and there. But it does mean taking note of that interaction with him if you decide to continue to date.

I know that you are in a very exciting part of your life and are ready to set up a Jewish home. Now, you get to find the partner that you can do this with fully. Awesome!

But we don't want that excitement and hope to waylay the wisdom that your body and soul want to share in discerning whether this is the one—even if they sounded so great on paper. The mind has the potential to dismiss red flags, funky feelings, confusion, and doubt in order to fulfill your desire to be married.

In the dating process, you really have to draw on your faith and connection to Hashem. When you see something that you don't like in a potential partner, the fear that "I'll be alone for the rest of my life" may kick in. That is your yetzer hara. Hashem is in charge of your shidduch and you're using your G-d-given discernment skills to make a wise choice. Better to not be married for a little while more than pick a partner where you've ignored the red flags.

Like Rabbi Friedman said, "What is the 'bad' that you can't live with?" Only you can discern that, but my suggestion is that if a guy has a more relaxed taste in clothing while you're into fancy or if he is more on the quiet side while you're on the louder side—these are the kinds of "bad" that you can live with. Being mocked, put down, or controlled are the sort of bad things that you cannot live with because they will stifle your spirit, mind, and heart.

Again, we're not being nitpicky here. We're being honest with ourselves. No partner will be perfect, not even your bashert. Him not knowing how to respond sometimes, or being awkward, a bit shy, a bit nervous—all of these reactions are ok.

It's the mean, angry, sarcastic, controlling, or dismissing vibes, big and small, that we're paying attention to.

A mentor or a relationship coach can also be helpful to you during this time, particularly one who is aware of the somatic.

People act in the best way possible (even Borderline/Narcissists) while dating. That is why you are doing **BRAKES** and tuning into your body's discerning wisdom which will, G-d willing, prevent you from rationalizing away any red flags.

As you continue on your dating journey, may you find a kind, caring partner to set up your bayis ne'eman with.

Blessings!

While Dating: Letter 6

Red Flag

Under Pressure. The Guy Who is Right About Everything—But What Does Your Body Say?

Dear Miriam Racquel,

I'm dating a guy who I like very much on so many levels. He looked great on paper, the shadchan really speaks highly of him, he has a good job, I'm attracted to him and he makes me laugh. Problem is that he thinks he is right about everything—like that his opinions are fact. He even insists on it. I'm listening to what you share about tuning into my body's reactions and every time that we disagree about something and he pushes his point of view, my stomach sinks. I think that it's a feeling of dread. And intimidation. What should I do? I'm even afraid to break it off with him. We're already texting each other and setting up the dates between us instead of through the shadchan.

Dear Awesome Woman,

I'm so glad that you reached out when you did—before it was too late. Good for you for listening to your body's messages! That feeling of dread and intimidation is true fear. It's asking you to check your environment for what feels unsafe and to take action accordingly. This guy who appears so great on paper and has a good relationship with the shadchan is showing his other true colors with you—and they ain't pretty. Your body may be telling you to run for the hills. If you're afraid of him now, what would be in the future? Who wants to be intimidated by their spouse? Is that the kind of foundation for building a bayis ne'eman? Can the Shechinah dwell in a home where the husband's ego is so big that he insists on being right all the time? Please ask yourself those questions.

In order to end dating in this kind of relationship, you will need to be very firm. You will have to hold your ground against the pressure of the shadchan and the guy himself. If your goal is to leave the relationship, then it's best not to share too many reasons why. The shadchan and the guy may insist that you're interpreting things wrong, that he's a great catch, that you won't find anyone else, and that you are misunderstanding him.

Don't fall for it.

You know what you know and as Rachel Bluth, a columnist of the Jewish Press, advised in a lecture about red flags,

> "Listen to your gut and that if something doesn't feel right, it probably isn't."

The letter writer, a mom who had attended the PTA lecture given by Mrs. Bluth, was expressing her deep gratitude. Her daughter had been redt a shidduch to a great yeshiva bochur, described as top of his class from a very well-respected family. Even after the first date, the daughter expressed that "he was not for her." The parents were shocked and the daughter couldn't describe anything specific. The shadchan called the following day with the news that the boy wanted to see their daughter again. The parents implored the girl to give it another shot and go out again. The daughter returned from that date with the statement, "He's not for me." She was adamant that she would not date him again.

The letter writer informed Rachel Bluth of the shocking news that six weeks later this bochur married another woman. After a few weeks of marriage, the kallah was back home with her parents. There were supposedly issues with violent behavior, mental issues, and physical abuse. The mother remembered that her daughter had said after the second date, "He seems a bit loud, and there's this odd thing he keeps doing with his hand, thumping on the table with his fist every few minutes. It made me nervous."

Maybe your date isn't as obvious with his behavior, but clearly there is something deeply bothering you and it's smart of you to pay attention to it. In the letter writer's case, when she told the shadchan that her daughter did not want more dates, the shadchan said they "were giving up the cream of the crop, the best of the best," and that their daughter would never find someone like that again. Wow! Now that's intimidation as well! Feel that in your body!

Breaking Off a Difficult Shidduch

Step 1: Get strong in yourself. If you have someone that you trust to open up to, then do that. If they don't believe you or encourage you to continue dating or to try to "fix" this middah of his, find another friend or mentor to confide in and get support. Your body is telling you something and it's important to listen. And even more importantly, your body is expressing fear in breaking off with this person, and this is even more of a telltale sign of potential problems in the future. It's normal to feel bad when you break off with a shidduch—that can be discomfort, guilt, or anxiety around the fact that you'll be hurting another person's feelings. But you express in your letter that you are "afraid" to break it off with him. Again, there's the intimidation factor.

Step 2: Use "I" language to share what isn't working for you with the shadchan if they ask. If the shadchan argues with you, that may be a sign that this is not a shadchan to work with in the future. Your points need to be heard and validated. You are not making excuses. You have true legitimate fears and those need to be taken seriously. Plus, you know that you don't want to continue. That middah he is showing would be "dangerous" in a marriage considering that you are feeling intimidated. If the shadchan is a good shadchan, then they can share your points with the bochur as a means to encourage him to see a trait in himself that he may want to get help for. But that is between the shadchan, the bochur, and Hashem.

Step 3: Fortify your trust in Hashem. Know Hashem is with you on this journey and ask for help and courage. Hashem is in charge of shidduchim and since you are ending this shidduch for very good reasons, Hashem can give you strength to do so. Fearing Hashem is a mitzvah; fearing a human is not.

I know that this may sound like a difficult road, but it's better to break off dating someone than find yourself trapped in a fearful marriage.

Blessings! 

While Dating: Letter 7

Red Flag
Love Bombing & Borderline/Narcissists

Dear Miriam Racquel,

I'm dating a guy who really likes me (we've gone out three times). I know that sounds weird to say, but he is the one saying it. He says that he felt a click right away when he first saw me. He tells me how wonderful and special I am, how warm and generous my spirit is, how smart I am, how I'd make such a great wife. It's very flattering and hearing that does wow me a bit. He also treats me like gold, and he's polite and very kind.

On the other hand, sometimes he says things that make me feel guilty, things like, "C'mon, don't you trust me already?" Or, "I say so many nice things to you, why don't you say the same things about me?" In following your advice, I've been listening to what my body is sharing with me and there's definitely an incongruence between what my mind is saying ("He is so generous and caring!") and the twisty-turny sensation that I have in my torso when he says things like that—I feel like an amoeba cringing away from an irritating stimulus.

He loves spending time with me, wants to date often, and is pushing for feedback on my feelings for him. I'm not sure what to do. Help, please! I don't want to give up someone who seems like my bashert and like a really good guy, but I'm also feeling confused and overwhelmed.

Dear Awesome Woman,

I'm going to get right to the point—it sounds like you are being love bombed and emotionally blackmailed. These are both things that Borderline/Narcissists do to get you feeling dependent on them. No wonder your body is reacting as an amoeba wanting to move away from a stimulus—these tactics feel just like what they are—manipulative and intimidating.

Borderline/Narcissists love bomb to reel you into relationships with them. The love bombings are dressed up as floods of compliments, flattery, gifts, favors, and promises for the future. But these are traps—like a spider that weaves a web around its victims. Please see Chapter 4, Friendship and Community: Letter 3, to see the list of traits of a Borderline/Narcissist in order to identify them and avoid them.

Besides being love bombed, it sounds like you are also being emotionally blackmailed. Emotional blackmail is a term used by author Susan Forward in her book *Emotional Blackmail—When the People in Your Life Use Fear, Obligation, and Guilt to Manipulate You.* Here is how she describes emotional blackmail:

> "Emotional blackmail is a powerful form of manipulation in which people close to us threaten, either directly or indirectly, to punish us if we don't do what they want.... Emotional blackmailers know how much we value our relationship with them. They know our vulnerabilities. Often they know our deepest secrets.

> And no matter how much they care about us, when they fear they won't get their way, they use this intimate knowledge to shape the threats that give them the payoff they want: our compliance.
>
> —*Forward, 1997, p. x*

Unfortunately, this form of manipulation may be found in any kind of relationship. Mothers, fathers, husbands, siblings, wives, friends, bosses, co-workers, and children may use this harmful form of disrespecting boundaries. An emotional blackmailer's goal of getting their way is of utmost importance to them. They want something from another person and will pressure, demean, and hurt to get it. Their tools are blame, sarcasm, criticism, cruelty, manipulation, and threats.

Some typical emotional blackmail phrases used are:

"If you really cared about me …"
"I've done so much for you …"
"I'm so generous to you …"
"You're so selfish …"

Even if other phrases are said that are more subtle than this, the goal is the same—to get you to do what they want you to do.

Some of us may have even used these bad habits to get our way. If so—we need to stop now. There are ways to express our needs in a respectful way, even using assertion if we have to.

Hashem is ultimately the true source of fulfilling our needs—not a human. If someone is emotionally manipulating you or if this is your habit to use in getting your way in relationships, reach out to a professional coach, healer or therapist for help—it's that important for your health to make changes.

Emotional blackmail is extremely toxic to your mind, body, and soul. When someone uses emotional blackmail with you, as this man seems to be doing, your body reacts accordingly. Emotions are physical sensations that carry messages. The energy of fear which may sit in your stomach as a jittery feeling or in your limbs as a prickly feeling is a warning signal. It is telling you to be alert to the present moment because there is a threat to your wellbeing. With emotional blackmail, the threat is emotional, as abandonment or an uncomfortable change to the relationship. Of course, if there is a physical threat, leaving or calling 911 is the answer.

You may feel a tightening in your chest signaling anger in which your body is sending up a protective boundary, like a plate of armor.

Emotional blackmail is a toxic form of communication in any relationship, in particular in marriage. Pressuring and entitlement are huge red flags. I have many clients who are victim to Borderline/Narcissistic spouses or are exes to this type of person—it is both traumatic and frightening.

Questions to Determine Emotional Blackmail

If you are still unsure whether you're being emotionally blackmailed or not, ask yourself these questions:

1. Is he being uncomfortably persistent?
2. Do you feel intimidated?
3. Do you feel uncomfortable saying, "No, I'm not ready to give you feedback?"

4. Do you feel judged for not telling him what he wants you to tell him or for not doing what he wants you to do?
5. Does he criticize you or belittle you for not telling him what he wants to hear or doing what he wants you to do?

Answering yes to any of these questions signals it's time to break off the shidduch.

So, how to break things off?

If your parents are the go-between, then great! Let them tell the shadchan that you no longer want to continue. If you're a baalas teshuvah, then the shadchan can do it for you. This is the emotionally safe way to take care of this situation. And no, you are not being a coward by refusing to speak to him directly.

If he has Borderline/Narcissist tendencies and you attempt to speak to him directly, then he may try to bully, intimidate, or pressure you into continuing. Or he may want explanations as to why you don't want to continue.

You cannot engage in arguments with people who have these tendencies. They will never hear you and you will never win against them.

The game of Borderline/Narcissists is about powering over, not about love and connection.

When you break things off, they will tell you that you hurt them, and this is true. People do get hurt when they feel rejected or when a shidduch is broken off.

However, the difference here is how a person with Borderline/ Narcissist tendencies will manipulate this hurt. They will lay on guilt heavily and really focus on how much you have hurt them, while refusing to take accountability for how they've hurt you. They make great actors in being victims and they try to break people by hurling insults and criticisms. All that love bombing and complimenting goes right out the window when a Borderline/Narcissist feels rejected. It gets replaced with blaming and shaming, confusing their victims to the core. Borderline/Narcissists are adept at running circles around people.

Some Borderline/Narcissists will even apologize. These apologies are only another way to manipulate and confuse. At some point, he will expect you to apologize to him, leading with how much you've hurt him.

Your safest bet is to break off the shidduch through the shadchan. G-d willing, she has learned about red flags and is understanding and supportive. If she invalidates your experience, it brings into question her capability as a sage and safe person to work with.

Take time to celebrate yourself after this experience is over. You just dodged a toxic bullet by listening to your body. Yay, you! You are moving forward on your path to find a truly kind and caring bashert!

Blessings!

While Dating: Letter 8

Red Flag
Defensiveness, Sharpness

Dear Miriam Racquel,

I've been on four dates with a guy and I basically like him. But one of the things that I don't like is that when we're driving and I point out a parking spot that's close to the place we're going, he gets annoyed, defensive, and speaks sharply to me. How serious an issue is this?

Dear Awesome Woman,

This could be a serious issue. Though many men do not take kindly to driving or parking advice, let's consider how they handle these suggestions. How defensive do they get? What are their middos when that happens?

The guy that you are with may feel controlled by your suggestion. Relationship author Laura Doyle points out that what may be considered helpful in the world of women can be considered controlling in the world of men.

A woman may appreciate a friend pointing out a parking spot or hear it as her friend telling her where she would like the car parked. A man on the other hand may hear the suggestion and feel that the woman is "telling him where to park." It feels disrespectful and degrading to his ears. I know, I know, to us women, that may sound absurd! But there *are* differences between the female culture and male culture. If there were another man in the car, he would probably never suggest where the guy should park. It just wouldn't be done. It would be like stepping on the driver's toes—it's his business where he parks the car.

There are great ways to share suggestions with a man—and that is through the expression of "desire." Meaning that if you'd like the guy to park somewhere close to the restaurant, you could tune into that desire and say, "I'd love to park as close as possible since these heels make it hard to walk far." You're using the phrase "I'd love" without the word "you."

Or you can ask yourself, do you really care where your shidduch parks the car? Maybe it doesn't really matter.

All that being said, the question still needs to be answered: how serious of an issue is it that when you do point out a parking spot, he gets defensive and responds sharply? How does your body react? Do you feel like you just got punched? Or do you wince at the sharpness? Does your throat close or your chest tighten? Those sensations can tell you a lot. Even if he doesn't like you suggesting a parking spot, he can respond respectfully. He could have said, "Would you like me to park there?" Or, "I see another one up ahead, but thank you for the suggestion." The sharpness is exactly that—sharp. And sharp hurts.

Bottom line, many times during a lifelong marriage a wife will offer suggestions, share her ideas, and worries. If the husband is defensive about her sharing her ideas about a parking spot, how much more defensive will he get about more significant and potentially stressful things? So, to answer your question, his sharpness could be indicative of a serious issue that will affect your ability to feel emotionally safe in your marriage.

Blessings!

While Dating: Letter 9

Parent's Relationship

Dear Miriam Racquel,

I like the guy I'm dating very much. I mentioned his name to a married friend of mine and she told me that she has been to his parent's house many times for Shabbos and noticed that the father speaks very condescendingly to the wife. She and her husband had even stopped going because it was so uncomfortable. She was concerned about this and wondered if the guy I'm dating would be the same way to me because this is what was role modeled in his home?

Dear Awesome Woman,

Great question. This is something that can certainly be addressed and brought into the open in a wise way while dating. If your shidduch has been treating you respectfully and kindly and you haven't had any funky indications of the opposite, then you can broach the subject by asking him these questions: how is the relationship between your parents? What do you like about it and what don't you? In no way indicate what your friend shared. That is important information that Hashem has given you through your friend, but it does not need to be divulged to him.

These are fair questions to ask, and he should feel comfortable asking you the same. Be open. Remember, dating is for information gathering—body and mind information—and it's important to gain insight into how he was raised. What affected him growing up as a child in his home? How does he feel about it now as an adult about to embark on his own mature journey of establishing a home?

Notice if he mentions that he's unhappy with some aspects of his parents' relationship and expresses that he'd like to do things differently. If he is a gentle and honest soul, you may see that he's been hurt by what's been modeled in his childhood home and will be willing to create something different for his future family.

Blessings!

While Dating: Letter 10

Eating Junk Food

Dear Miriam Racquel,

I'm in the dating parsha and when my mind starts ruminating about my last date or my talk with a shadchan, I grab sugar instead of something nutritious. I feel terrible afterwards. Any advice?

Dear Awesome Woman,

Reaching for sweets is a very common choice when we're experiencing stress. The best thing we can do when we catch ourselves ruminating is to release those thoughts on paper.

Homeplay Exercise

Let It Out

Scribble down those swirling thoughts without filtering them. This is not journal writing, but a way to release tension from rumination. Rip up the pages using big arm movements when you're done. Then take a deep breath and stretch your arms up above your head. Do the **ROAR! Process** for extra release (Chapter 2: Self-Care, Letter #3).

With some of that tension released, your mind will have fewer cravings for unhealthy food choices. And remember—a little chocolate is good for a woman's soul.

Blessings!

While Dating: Letter 11

Friend Engaged

Dear Miriam Racquel,

My best friend just got engaged. I'm really excited for her, but feel sad that our relationship won't be the same. Am I a selfish friend for having these feelings?

Dear Awesome Woman,

First of all, "Mazel tov!" for your friend's simcha. Second of all, you're human and Hashem created you with the ability to have contradicting emotions at the same time. Joy, sadness, excitement, fear—emotions as "energy in motion" ebb and flow like the ocean waters.

Homeplay Exercise

Accept and Allow the Flow

When you feel the sadness surfacing, notice it in your body —is there a heaviness in your chest or a tightening in your stomach? That's ok. Just sit and allow that sadness energy to flow. It will cycle and pass. Give yourself compassion for the change and loss that's taking place. You'll go through a range of emotions as your relationship shifts. By allowing the sadness rather than suppressing it, you'll be able to feel the excitement and joy when that emerges as well.

Blessings!

Saying Yes!: Letter 12

Is He the One?

Dear Miriam Racquel,

How do I know that he's the one?

Dear Awesome Woman,

Okay, you've dated. Now ask yourself these questions:

- **What do you like about him?**
- **Why do you enjoy being with him?** He's got a great smile. He makes me laugh. I love talking with him, etc.
- **What, if any, red flags came up for you?** Check in with your body!
- **In what way does he make you feel protected?** When you share either in words or actions that you're afraid, how does he respond? With respect, teasing, or denigration?
- **Do you notice anything out of the ordinary regarding his family relationships?** How was his mother treated in his home? How was his father treated? What is their relationship like?
- **Do you respect the person he is and how he treats others? Does he speak kindly about others?** There is such a thing as "male culture" and men often tease and joke with each other in ways that may surprise a woman. I know—I have sons, B"H,

and I see the way they interact at times is just like lion cubs playing with each other—a little rough, but they're having fun. I've learned to respect the male culture and not think that men have to be like women—nurturing, comforting, vulnerable—to be okay. **This behavior is not what I'm talking about with this question.** In spite of the goofiness men may have around each other and the roughhousing in words and playful actions, ask yourself: is he someone who is petty, puts others down, or is highly critical and judgmental? Or does he refuse to speak badly about others, which shows him to be of a higher character?

- **What behaviors and choices of his do you respect?**

- **What are his qualities?** Is he courageous, gentle, warm, intellectual, outgoing, quiet, cheerful, optimistic, pessimistic, serious, generous, stingy, more on the gevurah side or chesed side, meticulous, neat, relaxed, willing, communicative, kind, prompt, spiritual, easygoing, straightforward, ambitious, cautious, empathic? Does he have healthy boundaries and know when to say no? Does he feel comfortable saying no? Does he overcommit to people and activities and then run into accountability issues? Just ask yourself what you're noticing and jot a few points down. Again, be attuned to your body's reaction to him as well as noting these qualities.

- **How does he treat time?** What I've noticed over the years is that people regard time in interesting ways. People who are perpetually late will generally just be that way for a lifetime. They get caught up in what they are doing, they think that it only takes five minutes to get somewhere when it really takes ten, and so on. Then there are those who need to be early or get anxious around time. Getting somewhere promptly is very important to them. I won't make a judgment about either quality, but what I will advise is that since marriage takes team effort, consider how you partner up with your shidduch's sense of timing. If he's someone who loves getting places on time and finds that respectful, and you're someone who is fine being late, then how will that play out in a marriage? Sometimes it's great if both people are always fashionably late and then neither gets mad at the other because it's the way they both treat time. And if promptness is important to a couple, then that's great too. With this question, just notice how your shidduch treats time and see how that makes you feel. Is it something that you respect? Is it something that bothers you? If it is like one of those things that Rabbi Friedman said about really not liking, can you live with it?

- **Can you be vulnerable with him?** How does he react when you share your emotions? Is he empathetic? Again, kindness is key. Even if emotions aren't something he is in the habit of expressing himself, can he deal compassionately with yours? My boys have rarely seen me cry as their mom. If I ever cry, it's in private or with my husband, friends, or healers. But I remember one instance where I was so emotionally pained by something, that I did break down in front of one of my sons. He comforted me and was extremely kind and understanding. He couldn't fix the issue and didn't try to offer solutions, he just sat with me and listened. This is what you're looking for. A compassionate reaction.

- **If something happens that's uncomfortable between you, how does it get resolved—do you open up and talk about it or just ignore it?** If there's a misunderstanding, do you feel okay sharing your perspective on the situation? Also, check your shidduch's heart message. Sometimes he may act in a way that you feel confused by, but check what is the seeming intention behind it. Did he mean to be caring, but it came out all wrong? This is not the same as manipulation. A heart message is when there is care and kindness. If your body senses incongruence, then the intention may not be from the heart, but from the head as a manipulative act.

- **Do you find him attractive or cute?** Does he have warmth in his eyes, a kind smile, a fun way of being?

- **Realistically, will you be able to depend on him to financially support you or at least be a partner in that?** Marriage in many Orthodox circles happens in the younger years, and he may not have figured out what he wants to do. That being said, has he been working up till now? Does he seem responsible in the area of finances?

- **Does he have addictions?** Taiva addictions are a big deal; don't make light of them.

- **What are the things that you don't like about him or don't enjoy about him, and can you live with those?** Everyone has stuff—we're not perfect beings. When you marry you are basically asking your partner to live with the stuff about you that he may not always appreciate or find easy. And vice versa, there will be stuff that your partner does that you don't like all the time or that may annoy you. While you're in the dating parsha and in the mode of choosing a life partner, get honest and real about what you see in your shidduch that is negative for you (what is negative for one person, may be a quality enjoyed by another) and decide if you can live with that.

Finally, review the BRAKES list and get a realistic assessment (Chapter 5: Letter 5). Again, it's very important to see a person for who they are, not who you wish them to be. Of course, marriage changes and matures people (or maybe not!), but have your eyes open to who you are dating. Being honest with yourself (as well as with your mentors) will help you make this very important decision in your life.

Is he the one?

So, you've asked yourself a lot of important questions. Now for the finale:

What does your body say? Is there a feeling of comfort when you see him? Is there a feeling of uplift or expansion, a feeling of excitement or giddiness when you see him? A feeling of security, safety, care, attractiveness, appeal and joy? A sense of knowing that this is someone you want to spend your life with?

Can you authentically share your thoughts, ideas, and worries with him? You will be sharing your everyday life with him—are you on the same team about many of the things that occupy your mind? My husband and I do things very differently; yet, we've always loved spending time together and sharing our ideas and thoughts. On Shabbos mornings, we love to sit together before he goes to shul and just talk. When the weather is warm, it's especially nice to be in our garden, enjoying the sunshine, flowers, and bird chatter, discussing life as we see it.

My hope for you with listening to your body's wisdom and asking yourself these questions is that you'll choose an incredible bashert to set up your bayis ne'eman with.

> "As two lives unite to form one, over time, there is a point where each partner feels they are a part of the other, where each partner can no longer visualize life without the other."
>
> *—Rabbi Menachem M. Schneerson, The Lubavitcher Rebbe*

Blessings!

6

Marriage

The potential of male and female relationships is like atomic energy. When used in a positive and holy way, there is nothing more powerful and precious. However, when used recklessly, without sacred context, it can be the most destructive force in existence.

—Rabbi Menachem M. Schneerson,
The Lubavitcher Rebbe

Letter 1

An Introduction to Marriage: Male Culture vs. Women's Culture

> *Dear Miriam Racquel,*
>
> *My husband seems to come from a totally different culture than me—the male culture. I just can't figure it out. Can you explain?*

Dear Awesome Woman,

Sure! There really is a male culture and female culture—this is spiritually based, society based, and biologically based. Understanding this and knowing that there is incredible power in the relationships between male and female, how can we help create love and peace in our marriages rather than disconnection and war? Though it is not only up to us as women to create an atmosphere of respect, kindness, and connection in our homes—our husbands have obligations as well—we do have tremendous power to direct and navigate our relationships.

The Lubavitcher Rebbe teaches that, "Judaism is, essentially, a 'feminine' religion," and then goes on to expand this concept by explaining that it's women's nature to nurture, as opposed to what it says in the Talmud about a man's nature being to conquer. Through support, affection, and nurturing, women can bring out the highest potential of things.

We can refer to the wisdom of the Rebbe's words to approach our marriages, for our marriages are the microcosms of the world. How can we nurture our relationships with our husbands all while nurturing ourselves? Just to be clear and prevent any misunderstandings, nurturing our relation-ships does not mean becoming a schmatta for others or having no boundaries. The strength of being a nurturing woman includes boundaries, limits, and wise discernments. The somatic wellness way of the feminine involves respecting our emotions and processing them to extract wisdom. At the same time, it is also important to know that as the feminine, we have tremendous potential to elevate our marriages.

Getting a peek into the masculine culture will give us a wise understanding of our partner. Men in general are raised in a societal environment rampant with humiliation and shaming. The Torah says that a man's nature is to conquer by force. We can see this in competitions, in teasing that often seems quite cruel to women, and in the sometimes harsh expectations of society for men to "toughen up, be brave, stop whining, just deal with it like a man."

Compassion is not usually expressed to them in educational settings, in sports settings, or among male friends. And sometimes not even in the home. Being teased and being told to "toughen up" leads boys to reject the vulnerability of not knowing how to do things, the vulnerability of getting things wrong, the vulnerability of making mistakes. That vulnerability can make them feel stupid, less than, and ashamed.

Unfortunately, this male culture primes a man's nervous system to be in a highly alert state—they will detect any whiff of negative judgment or disrespect. As wives, we may unknowingly activate this highly alert state in our husbands with our tone, our complaining, our directives, our advice, our criticism, our judgment, and our expressions of disappointment or feeling let down by them—all indications that they have failed us somehow.

I like the term "highly allergic" that I once heard Shterna Ginsberg use. The societal expectations that men have been raised with causes many husbands to be "highly allergic" to anything that smacks of disrespect, criticism, or judgment of them.

Any time that you, as a wife, express yourself in language that is indicative that your husband did something wrong or has failed you will trigger that shame and humiliation. Any time your husband feels negatively judged, it will trigger the fight/flight response of their nervous system, hence snapping at you (a fight response) or shutting down (a flight response).

Even if you're not directly saying it, the *energy* behind your words can reveal disdain or condescension. A highly allergic husband will smell it, and it will trigger that shame attack. If your husband is feeling shamed, he may lash out at you. Imagine a trapped and wounded stray dog that lashes out with its teeth and nails. **That's the fight response.**

Or imagine a little boy who got a poor grade on a test and his father shakes his head in disappointment and scolds him for not doing well enough, not trying hard enough, or not being smart enough. The little boy wants to slink away in shame. He finds a corner to curl up and brood in and builds up armor so that he'll never be hurt again. **That's the flight response.** We can see this same reaction in a husband shutting down. He may leave the scene physically or emotionally or both, closing his heart to you.

As a woman, perhaps you have also experienced being criticized and shamed. These feelings are not exclusive to the male experience.

The difference is that women tend to be relationship-oriented beings, so they'll go to their friends and share their feelings when hurt. They'll cry and get empathy, compassion, and nurturing.

But in the male culture, it is admired to be stoic and brave. Most boys will keep their feelings in, not sharing with anyone that they are sad and hurt. They want to just keep up the tough exterior that they're ok and that nothing (and no one) can touch them. Vulnerability is a big no-no for boys and men. Hopefully we can change that as we raise our sons, and also change the education system, but many of our husbands have been raised being shamed for their vulnerability, rather than encouraged and supported in dealing with their pain.

I believe that the key to healthy marriages in which intimacy and joy can grow is to nurture emotional safety in the relationship. How emotionally safe do you feel with your husband? How emotionally safe does your husband feel with you? Are we accepting, kind, and understanding of each other's quirks, idiosyncrasies, likes, and dislikes? Do we have space to breathe in the relationship, to do our own thing and yet come together for fun, discussion, and laughter? If not, can we make this happen? Yes!

We must understand that we are all walking nervous systems. When we feel safe, loved, and protected, our minds and bodies are relaxed and respond accordingly. When we feel under attack (judged, criticized), our minds and bodies prepare to protect and attack or take flight. When there's a feeling of hopelessness or freeze (can never get anything right or it's never good enough), our instinctual reaction is to withdraw and shutdown.

Let's look at this from a biological nervous system perspective. Dr. Porges of the Traumatic Stress Research Consortium identifies three nervous system reaction states: ventral vagal, sympathetic, and dorsal vagal. In the ventral vagal state, we feel safe, loved, and protected, allowing our minds and bodies to relax and communicate easily. When threatened or feeling unsafe, the sympathetic state is triggered and responds accordingly by increasing the heart rate and blood pressure. The nervous system prepares the muscles to protect and attack or to take flight. In situations where escape seems hopeless or we feel incapable of an adequate response, the body enters a dorsal vagal state. We instinctively withdraw, shutdown, and freeze.

In which state do you think joy, love, connection, partnership, and intimacy will grow for both of you?

You may be trying to be helpful to your husband by using constructive criticism, or telling him how to do things better, offering suggestions, advice. Laura Doyle shares that what feels helpful to women, can feel controlling to men. Unwittingly, you may be triggering your husband's nervous system to go into attack, flight, overwhelm, hopelessness, or withdrawal which then triggers your nervous system to do the same and bam!—the emotional safety of the home went out the window.

Especially if your husband is highly allergic to feeling ashamed and judged, then he will go into protective mode very quickly by fighting back, shutting down, or walking away. Now, you may have just asked him to do the dishes. What could be the problem with that? Nothing—except for the fact that he may be primed for defensiveness (from childhood/societal wounding) in his most intimate, vulnerable relationship. Not all husbands are primed the same way. Let's find out more about yours with a quiz to see just how "allergic" to shame your husband is.

This quiz will gauge the "defensiveness" in your husband, which will key you into how much you'll need to use and practice the marriage tips I share in the following letters to achieve emotional safety in your home. And as I said earlier, this nurturing of emotional safety will help promote more relaxed nervous systems for both you and your husband (and your children, if there are any), providing space for increased love and joy in your microcosm of marriage.

Homeplay Exercise

Quiz: How Allergic to Shame Is Your Husband?

Use the table below and reflect on how your husband usually reacts to the given situations. Write down a point value in Column A and B based on how often he displays each kind of response.

Often: 2 points, **Sometimes:** 1 point, **Never or Not Relevant:** 0 points

How does your husband respond when ...	**Column A** He smiles, does what you're requesting and/or acts with kindness, concern, care, sensitivity.	**Column B** He gets defensive or dismissive. He tells you not to tell him what to do or calls you controlling. Doesn't do what you ask or does it with annoyance.
You ask him to take out the garbage: "Honey, the garbage is full. Can you take it out?"		
You say, "Gosh, look at this disgusting garbage. Can you please take it out? Isn't it your job?"		

continued

How does your husband respond when ...	**Column A** He smiles, does what you're requesting and/or acts with kindness, concern, care, sensitivity.	**Column B** He gets defensive or dismissive. He tells you not to tell him what to do or calls you controlling. Doesn't do what you ask or does it with annoyance.
You make a request: "Can you change the baby? I'm so tired."		
You ask him if you can talk to him for a minute about something.		
You make a request: "The sink is full and the cleaning lady won't be coming tomorrow. Can you do the dishes?"		
You talk to him about carpool: "There are too many carpool obligations for me to handle. Can you do any or can we hire someone?"		
You say, "I'm worried about our finances."		
You're having issues with a friend and you vent, complain, cry.		
You complain that he is going out with his friends or dealing with community stuff again.		
You complain to him that he comes home from work too late and you need his help with the kids.		

How does your husband respond when ...	**Column A** He smiles, does what you're requesting and/or acts with kindness, concern, care, sensitivity.	**Column B** He gets defensive or dismissive. He tells you not to tell him what to do or calls you controlling. Doesn't do what you ask or does it with annoyance.
You're traveling on an airplane and are dealing with the kids all by yourself. You ask for his help.		
Total		

Often: 2 points, **Sometimes:** 1 point, **Never or Not Relevant:** 0 points

Add up the scores in each column. It's pretty simple: **the higher the score in column B, the more important it is for you to use the tips.**

Please note, no matter how high the score is in column B, if you're married today and in it for the long run, you can use the tips I'm sharing **even if** you're considering divorce. I coach women individually and together with my husband (Building Great Marriages) and many marriages have been turned around with amazing results! There is tremendous hope. That being said, I'd like to mention that if a spouse has extreme Borderline/ Narcissistic traits, a more serious discussion is needed and even the best tips may not help the marriage. You will need outside help for discernment and problem-solving solutions.

So what can we do?

For a husband who is highly allergic to shame, realize that a little humiliated boy sits inside that mature man's body, and in an intimate relationship they will lash out or shut down if they so much as sense the energy of criticism and negative judgment.

As wives, we don't want to trigger that shame. It certainly does not lead to an emotionally safe atmosphere for our husbands or ourselves. But if you're like me, you may not have known that you were triggering any of this in your husband. Growing up in a secular culture meant saying anything on my mind. Being completely honest. "Say what you think!" was the philosophy encouraged when I was growing up. But guess what? That is a terrible philosophy for marriage (and just about any relationship).

It's not that we should shut down our own voices, but we can choose to use our voices wisely. It is possible to get our needs met in a more respectful manner. There are words and energies we can use to encourage and support rather than put down—these lead to goodwill. These shifts we choose can create an atmosphere of emotional safety for both ourselves and our husbands.

Homeplay Exercise

Quiz: How Critical a Wife Are You?

This one's for you! You didn't think that I would leave you out, did you? Women come from the middah of gevurah and some of us have a lot of it. We can use our awesome discerning powers (read more about the difference between discerning and judgment in Chapter 5 on dating) for good—knowing who to hire or, become friends with, noticing and guiding who our children become friends with, and so on—or for the negative—only seeing the negative in our spouses or being nitpicky and controlling.

Besides coming from gevurah, many women judge and control from a place of fear. In fact, when an issue comes up and my response feels controlling to my husband and we start to butt heads, we both have come to the realization that I've most likely moved into fear mode. If I catch it first, I'll say to him, "What's the question I'd like to be asked?" That prompts him to ask, "What are you afraid of?" And then I launch into all my fears around a situation. I tend to be super practical and like order; my husband tends to be risk-taking and more spontaneous. This opposite dynamic can cause combustion! After over 30 years of marriage, we finally figured out how to bypass a lot of conflict this way!

So, let's get honest and see how you may unconsciously be showing up as controlling, shaming, blaming, dismissive, bossy, or negative-judging to your husband.

How often do you ...

1. **Ask him to take out the garbage with a criticism: "Why don't you ever remember to take out the garbage?"**
2. **Get mad at him for leaving his clothes around the room.**
3. **Tell him that you don't like his friends.**
4. **Tell him how to dress or make negative remarks about his looks.**
5. **Tell him how to eat.**
6. **Tell him his ideas are bad ideas.**
7. **Direct him how to take care of the kids.**
8. **Tell him when and how to ask for a raise.**
9. **Go on your phone when he is around.**

continued

10. Put him down for not bringing in enough money.

11. Appreciate and compliment him.

12. Avoid sexual intimacy with him. He may have given up asking, but that doesn't mean he doesn't desire it.

There's no scoring for this one—just a reality check for you. If you're often criticizing him or telling him how and what to do, you're probably strangling the bejeebers out of him. Let go of the reins and free him to be his own man, do things his way (even if they don't work sometimes—he's human and can make mistakes) and make his own choices. And don't worry —the tips I'll be sharing will help you get your concerns and needs met, too. A kind partnership in marriage is a real thing. Let's help get you there.

If you've taken the time to do both these quizzes, good for you! Getting honest with yourself and your marriage is the first step to creating change that will produce positive results. Please take a moment to celebrate yourself and say "Yay, me!" for taking the first leap into increasing the emotional safety and intimacy in your marriage! This is the most important and foundational relationship in your life.

Blessings!

Letter 2

Emotional Safety: The Foundation of Marriage

Dear Miriam Racquel,

What are your favorite tips to having a good marriage?

Dear Awesome Woman,

Great question! Here are eight tips that can make a good marriage even better and turn a difficult marriage around quickly. For a good marriage, the tips increase the emotional safety *you already have* in your relationship. Since we all have our childhood wounding, our cultural wounding, and our very interesting and varying personalities, nurturing emotional safety in our homes creates an atmosphere of respect, kindness, and love.

If you have a difficult marriage and are lacking emotional safety in your relationship then it's more of an emergency to start these tips right away!

Feeling lonely and confused? Resenting his shut down or defensiveness when you offer the best advice? Having trouble finding the good in him? Wondering why you ever married him?

If you answer yes to any of these questions, then negative energy is radiating out of you.

As I mentioned in the introduction, we are all walking nervous systems and your husband will feel like he's being attacked even if you're not saying anything. The atmosphere in the home will be bitter and unpleasant to say the least. You may *both* feel like the marriage is doomed. Perhaps despair has set in, a sense of hopelessness that positive change can never happen especially if you've gotten help from therapists or read marriage books but nothing has made a significant difference.

Read ahead for help. Positive change can happen and happen quickly! The tips are gold for your marriage. Each time you do even one once, it's like putting a gold coin into your marriage bank account. Those gold coins add up and switch the home atmosphere from doom, gloom, and walking on eggshells, to hope, lightness, and peace. Your investment in your marriage is the most important thing you can do as the akeres habayis. You have a lot of power.

We'll dive into each one of these tips in detail, but for right now, I'm going to give you a quick summary of each one:

TIP 1: The ROAR! Process

This somatic technique was discussed in Chapter 2 Self-Care, but I'm including it here to highlight how it can be used specifically in the context of marriage. It is a fantastic help to your shalom bayis. You are releasing steam in a very safe way like a pressure cooker does—no one gets hurt because the **ROAR!** is done in **private.** You are *not imploding* with your emotions and you are *not exploding* all over your spouse (or kids). You are taking the time to somatically process your feelings.

When you feel your needs aren't being met, it is natural for the emotions of disappointment, sadness, shame, guilt, fear, and anger to arise. With **ROAR!**, these "energies in motion" won't get suppressed. Instead, you're getting honest, allowing energy to flow. You may even change your perspective on the situation because you released what was triggering to you—you're not perfect, after all. None of us are.

The resulting release and clarity also paves the way to hearing your intuition. And your insight will give you a good sense of what action to take—whether to speak up (read ahead for using wise "husband language") or not. Yes, *not* speaking up is an action—sometimes a very wise one.

TIP 2: Self-Care

In addition to reading the self-care tips that are specific to marriage, please review Chapter 2: Self-Care. The act of self-care is about taking accountability for your happiness—not putting that burden on anyone else, especially your husband. Bored? What can you do to add some spice to your life? Overwhelmed? What can you do to dial down the stress? Overburdened? Can you tap into your feminine energy of receiving? Sad? Can you sprinkle in daily moments of joy? When you practice self-care, you become more creative, more energized, more loving and kind to yourself (and others), and more comfortable with setting limits.

TIP 3: Don't Jump the Net

Bring to mind a tennis court, with a net in the center. Respectful communication is founded on staying on your own side of the court—a tennis analogy for not jumping over the net onto another person's side of the court. In this case we're talking about your relationship with your husband, but this analogy can be imagined for any relationship.

a recipe for marriage, this would be the secret sauce and one of the most important ingredients. I don't call it "Miriam's Somatic Temper Tantrum Release" for nothing. You live with your husband day in and day out. Marriage is an incredibly intimate relationship on all levels—mental, emotional, physical, sexual, and spiritual. You're dancing the dance of this intimate relationship at the same time that you are trying to manage so many life's challenges and wonders. How could you not feel triggered at times?

The **ROAR! Process** has many benefits in general, as we saw in Chapter 2, but how can it specifically benefit your marriage?

The Benefits of ROAR! to Marriages

Allowing negative energies to sit and build up in your body and mind isn't healthy, especially when it's related to someone you live with and are so intimate with. When you can discharge that energy, you'll see tensions release and your physical health improve.

If you're angry at your husband because he was late in taking your child to school, then your jaw might be clenched. If he criticizes you for the pile of dirty dishes in the sink, then your stomach might sink, your chest may tighten. When you pay attention to these physical and emotional signals, you can give your body the release it needs to be healthy.

With this process, you will be able to have this release of emotions while also preserving your marriage as a safe space for you and your husband. Rather than letting tension build in yourself and ending with you lashing out, the **ROAR! Process** can help direct your emotions in a positive, productive direction.

Homeplay Exercise

The ROAR! Process (Miriam's Somatic Temper Tantrum Release!)

Now that you know about the benefits, let's try out the process itself. Do this in a private space—your bedroom, your office, your car, even a bathroom is great.

1. Rip. Start by writing, scribbling, or drawing your anger, frustration, annoyance, or disappointment towards your husband onto paper. It may feel uncomfortable to write words of anger and frustration about someone you love so much, but remember that he will never read them, and it's important to get those feelings and thoughts out. This is not the time to edit. Just let it out! Pour out anything that is steaming in your mind that is causing you to feel frustrated, sad, hurt, or emotionally unsafe in the relationship. I believe that words suppressed can lead to thyroid or throat issues, G-d forbid. The emotional energy of pain is stuck in the throat with unspoken words. Better to privately and safely release rather than ignore or suppress. Doing this will help remove the tension and prevent resentment from building.

After writing or drawing, rip the paper up. The act of destruction leads the way for new space and creation.

2. Open (combine with step 3). Open your mouth in a silent scream or scream for real into a pillow! Or do a dragon breath. While doing this, you can imagine yelling at your husband which you may feel like doing when you're at your boiling point. Doing this step along with the others will prevent you from doing this in reality.

continued

3. Action. In this part, you're giving your body action. Run with your legs (either in a sitting down position or actually run around the room) and punch out or hit the air with your fists. If this feels too uncomfortable, then just stretch out in different directions. Even just walking around is fine—the goal is to give your body movement. You're angry, mad, sad, or feeling humiliated. You're getting bigger with your energy rather than suppressing it. The situation with your husband may have caused you to feel like running away; or you may have clenched up or froze. You're activating your body's flight response by walking or running and the fight response by hitting out. And no one is getting hurt.

4. Released. Congratulations! You've just released pent up energy in a healthy way. You've let out words, and the resentment, anger, sadness, or hurt while maintaining emotional safety for you and your husband. As part of this release, push your palms upward and send all that released energy to Hashem to recycle into love and light, away from you, your home, and your family.

Take a moment to allow your heart to settle by resting your hands over it. Then consciously breathe, listen to the sounds in your surroundings, and give yourself some love.

Notice if any intuition pops up in your mind. An intuition should feel somewhat neutral and brief, and give you a sense of relief.

You may get a new perspective on the situation or insights of actionable steps to take (using husband language—read on!).

Homeplay Exercise

Celebrate you for getting honest with yourself!

Arms up in the air in a V for celebration—get that oxygen rich blood flowing into your brain. Getting honest with yourself by doing **ROAR!** is not always easy or comfortable, but is beneficial for your health and for the health of your marriage.

TIP 2: Self-Care

In Chapter 2, I dive deep into different ways you can treat yourself with more self-care in all aspects of your life, and these can be applied to your marriage, too. You're taking responsibility for your day-to-day mood.

Also, one of the most important aspects of self-care in a marriage is your ability to receive from your husband. This means accepting assistance, compliments, and gifts. Women today are very focused on being independent (and doing things their own way) that they don't realize when they are rejecting their husband's care and offerings.

*****A special note:** Yes, we are going to request help and other resources from our husband. And G-d willing, he is the kind of man who is a partner by your side and does a lot. At the same time, it is important to keep in mind that husbands carry a heavy load on their shoulders between work, family, community, and religious obligations. Perhaps your husband can't help as much as you'd like. Since it's important to be respectful of his time and energy, hiring help when you can is amazing self-care. **Even if you feel money**

is tight or your husband has expressed that money is tight, keep in mind to look to Hashem for money and resources. Prayer and intentions are powerful. Hashem is the true source of money so turn to Hashem and ask for the money to get the help needed to make life easier. Set this intention: "*We always have plenty of money for our needs and more.*" And be grateful for every dollar that comes in.

Homeplay Exercise

Let Your Husband Handle Difficult Situations

Receive help from your husband by letting him deal with things that can be especially emotionally triggering or difficult. That conversation with a teacher because Berel is acting up in class? Let your husband handle it.

Wherever you see that your husband's leadership, diplomacy, and guidance can step in, allow that. The more trust and success created in this area, the better. He may not take care of it the way you would, but if you could let go of control, you may experience a sense of protection and relaxation as his male energy is allowed to take charge. I've done this more and more over the years and wow! What a difference it makes to let go of the wheel and just be a passenger at times. Doing this along with the other tips I'll share in this chapter, your husband will feel more confident in the marriage. His leadership abilities, those of a true mashpia, will rise. And remember, Hashem is behind the scenes. Trusting Hashem and your husband to take care of things can take a heavy load off your shoulders.

TIP 3: Don't Jump the Net

When we play a tennis game, it would be rude to jump over the net onto your team player's side. Imagine doing this and telling them how to hold their racket, how to serve the ball, and how to dress to be in the latest tennis fashion. When we tell our husband's how they should think, dress, act, speak, and do, we have jumped onto their side of the court.

As women, according to scholar Rabbi Moshe Y. Wisnefsky, we have a "heightened presence" of binah—understanding—in our psychological make up.

We take this heightened sense of understanding and apply G-d consciousness to the world. This means that as women, each of us has great ideas for elevating this world to a higher place—that was Chava's gift.

But our ways are not the only ways to do things. **Cultivating respect for our husband's ways and choices of action will save us a lot of hardship in our marriages.**

In Chapter 2: Self-Care, hopefully you got a better understanding of yourself, so you're more attuned to what lights *you* up, what *you* enjoy, what drains *you*, and *your* best way to action in the world. Be on *your* side of the tennis court—own it. Take up space—on *your* side.

But don't trespass onto your husband's side. Practice sacred silence by not telling him what to do. His way will be different from yours. And different doesn't mean wrong. Marriage gives us a wonderful opportunity to learn humility.

For example:
My husband and I have known each other for over thirty years, since we were teens in college. Back then, I actually thought we were quite similar. But now, what continues to amaze me is that I keep discovering how radically different we are. And these differences can be challenging to navigate at times.

I love to get to the airport a good two hours before the flight. He can only tolerate sitting at the gate for about ten minutes. This means we've both needed to compromise greatly on what time to leave for the airport.

I'm an introvert and am careful to schedule quiet time into every day. My husband is an extrovert. Having a lot to do and interacting with an abundance of people energizes him.

We are both active on social media. I enjoy Facebook, where I share somatic wellness tips, spiritually uplifting messages, and garden and family pics. I have developed a circle of kindness on that platform and love peace, courtesy, and gentleness. I engage once or twice a day consciously, remaining aware of my energy.

My husband, on the other hand, loves Twitter (X) and tweets about fifteen times a day. As a marriage and family therapist, he dispenses relationship and marriage advice as well as kabbalistic wisdom. He engages constantly and doesn't mind being involved in controversy that Twitter is famous for. If he is "attacked" for what he has shared, he has fun responding in creative, non-confrontational ways which he has developed over the years. He doesn't get riled up or insulted from the criticism, and even tries to befriend those who disagree with him. It's become an art form for him.

My revelations? We are so opposite. And I notice, for a lot of my friends, this is how their marriages are as well—they are matched up with someone who is mostly their opposite.

G-d has a great sense of humor because as much as we may have sought out these differences when we were in pursuit of our soul-mate, we never expected the challenges that could result.

If I were to tell my husband to just relax at the airport during a two hour wait, look at him weird for loving a very active social life, and advise him to get off of Twitter because of the nastiness found there, I would be jumping over the net into his side of the court. It's not my place.

Homeplay Exercise

Refrain!

Not jumping the net means refraining from telling him what to do and how to do it.

- **Stay on your side of the court and refrain** from advising him the "best" way he should go about asking for a raise, getting a job, bathing the kids, choosing friends, and dressing himself.
- **Don't share your amazing ideas.** Be quiet and send up a prayer. We will have other tips to make your desires known without criticizing him or bossing him around.
- **Take a second to imagine** how you feel when someone tells you what to do, what to wear, how to drive, how to run your business better, when to do something, or how

to change or dress your child. You may not appreciate all that advice—most people don't—and your husband is no different.

- **Contemplate this fact:** Our mind often tells us lies. We have a yetzer hara, and as the Lubavitcher Rebbe says, "It can dress up in a Tzaddik's clothes." Or any kind of clothes, for that matter. It can be self-righteous or it can be super religious. It can cause us to believe that we are being humble when in fact we are treating others unkindly. It can be wrong and lead us astray.

- **Whisper to yourself twice a day:** "My husband is capable of doing great things."

Now I'm also going to say loud and clear—staying on your side of the net does not mean stuffing your feelings down, or if there is a safety issue, not speaking up. This also doesn't mean if you have a suggestion to make, not making it. You do not stay quiet if you are concerned or frightened by something. It is your divine privilege to speak up, and there are ways to do this in a respectful way. When an atmosphere of kindness, appreciation, safety, and love exists in the home, your voice is appreciated and welcomed.

But more often than not, give your husband the space to be him. Remain on your side of the court and do the scary thing of trusting Hashem to lead and guide your husband. Not jumping over the net means seeing your husband as an intelligent and wise being—not perfect, but if you chose to marry him, then you saw good in him. Sometimes after the chuppah we lose sight of that goodness, and marriage gives us a holy opportunity to find it again.

TIP 4: Speak "Husband Language"

Numerous studies show that the most important thing to a husband is his wife's happiness. I know, I know, it can seem like the opposite of that sometimes, but when surveys are handed out and interviews are completed, this is what the husbands are saying. They want their wives to be happy (I'm not talking about husbands who are Borderline/Narcissists where their twisted thinking distorts this G-d-placed desire in them).

With the first three tips, hopefully, you've begun to be happier, which is an energy that your husband feels. You have the **ROAR! Process** to release anger, disappointment, stress, and make helpful changes. You're practicing more self-care and not burning yourself out, hopefully feeling more at ease with yourself, and certainly being kinder to yourself, which is a healthy place to be. You're staying on your side of the net which relieves you of the pressure of controlling everything on your husband's side. With all these tweaks, you are becoming more of a receptive vessel for joy.

This increased state of happiness will bring your spouse a sense of emotional safety. Why? Because the nervous system of a person who is grumpy, burned out, and overwhelmed radiates irritation and anger. Being around that energy puts someone in a state of high alert and defense. A person who has a nervous system that is more relaxed and centered radiates calm. Being around that energy allows for breath and space. So, in other words, your husband can feel your happiness and satisfaction and this gives him a sense of safety in your presence.

"Husband language," our fourth tip, will bring more peace and love for your relationship.

Remember what I shared earlier about men being allergic to anything that makes them feel shame? Speaking husband language helps avoid that shame trap. It is non-critical, non-judgy, and leaves expectation-energy behind. This requires a change in paradigm if you've been using a different habit of communication until now. Speaking husband language is like using a new muscle, which needs to be exercised regularly—not perfectly, but regularly. And trust me, you'll get the hang of it. If I can, you can! Just ask my husband!

And once you get the hang of it, you'll feel the difference in your relationship. The way I express myself now to my husband feels so much better for him and the peace in our home is tangible. He also has done a lot of work on his own, but the tools that I share here helped make that happen. The "shame attack" approach and head-on, direct approach just wasn't getting us to a good place in our marriage. Once I began doing my inner work, he had the safety to look at how he was showing up and to make changes.

Even if your husband doesn't consciously do "his work," the increased emotional safety in the marriage will naturally have him responding in the way of his higher self. For sure, cortisol (the stress hormone) levels decrease when there is more respectful communication.

So, let's start building these husband language skills.

How can he make you happy? A husband wants to know.

As I mentioned earlier—I know, I know—you may be shaking your head and laughing (or crying) right now. You may be saying to yourself with a shocked expression, *"My husband wants to know how to make me happy? I've told him a thousand times and he never listens!"* Or *"When I do tell him what makes me happy, he gets mad and defensive. I can never win.*" And what I often hear from clients is, "*When I'm frazzled and complain, he either shuts down or snaps at me.*"

I get this. I used to be perplexed by this very notion myself. But after making my own inner changes and making a paradigm shift about marriage and the language I use, I see the truth of this. Most husbands truly do want to make their wives happy.

Even from a kabbalistic perspective, this makes sense, as men are the mashpia and women are the mekabel. In this male/female dynamic of creation, men give and women receive. This does not mean that women aren't mashpi'im in their own right, since as teachers, mentors, friends, moms, and wives, we all have the capacity at times of giving over and sharing. But in the context of marriage, kabbalistically, husbands are the mashpi'im.

Homeplay Exercise

I'd Like or I'd Love Without the Word You

How can you express your wants and needs respectfully, in a way that feels safe for him—without being demanding, bossy, critical, negative, or full-of-expectation?

Here's how—the two-step process:

1. Know what you desire.

You are the only one who knows what you desire. If you're doing your self-care, then you're more in touch with this. What desires can be shared with your husband to help make them a reality?

continued

Do not expect him to guess—that just isn't fair. Even if something is so obvious to you, it may not be obvious to him. He has a ton of things on his mind and shoulders. Are these obvious to you? Probably not because we are not privy to each other's thoughts. Your husband is not G-d; he is not all-seeing and all-knowing. It's on your side of the court to know what lights you up, what help you're needing, what wishes you have, and then to make requests, keeping in mind the importance of maintaining emotional safety in the marriage.

2. Express these desires using the words of desire: "I'd like" or "I'd love."

Relationship author Laura Doyle shares that "I'd like" and "I'd love" are effective and respectful communication phrases to use with your husband. And it's best to speak these phrases without using "you" as in "I'd like you to ...." and without the energy of expectation. If you're "shoulding" him in your head as "he should do this," he will pick up on that demanding energy. Respect means also giving space for someone to *not* fulfill what you're requesting.

What's the difference between saying "I want" and "I'd like"? Feel in your body what it feels like when you imagine saying to your husband, "I want," as in "I want the garbage taken out," or "I want more help." What I notice in my own body is a tight, determined sensation. This can come off as demanding.

Now feel into your body when you use the language of "I'd love" or "I'd like." For me, there is softness and even a feminine flow of energy.

Your husband may not be able to fulfill your desires as expressed, but at least he'll have heard you because you've done your part in creating the space for your wishes to land respectfully and kindly.

Example: Laura Doyle told a story of wanting to take a couples dance class again with her husband. She looked at her husband and said, "Let's sign up for dance classes again." He gave her a look. She then countered, "Don't you want to?" He gave her a look again. (Remember, she's the author of a book on how to express desires to your husband, so it seems that her husband is making her walk the walk.) She then got an aha moment and rephrased her desire. "I'd love to sign up and take dance classes again." His response: "Sure."

What can we learn from Laura's example in terms of communication with her husband?

"Let's sign up for dance classes again!" may have been felt as another thing on her husband's to-do list or an obligation. The question "Don't you want to?" is very pointed, and the truth could be that he didn't want to. Maybe he'd preferred to lounge around and watch TV instead.

But when she clearly expressed her desire to take the dance class with "I'd love to ...," she made him aware of how he could make her happy. Whether he loved the dance class as much as she did, was not the point. He was just being given the opportunity to fulfill his wife's desire.

Example: Once, my husband took over my carpool because I had been down and out with a cold. It was amazing to me how our differences showed up even in this small area of life. He's Mr. Fun so he turned carpooling our neighbor's kids and my daughter into Entertainment City. He had the rambunctious children dancing and singing in their seats and my daughter joining in from her seat.

How did I know this? While stopped at a stop sign, he took a video of the scene and forwarded it to me. It was super cute.

continued

But I noticed that the neighbor's children didn't have their seat belts on, which is the first thing that I have them do when they get in the car. I laughed about the video, but also called him and said, "I'd love the seatbelts on, please!" That was my desire which he was happy to fulfill.

Let's walk through two examples to help illustrate the two-step process:

Example 1: Your birthday is coming up.

Step 1: Know what you desire.

Do you desire jewelry? New clothing? A night out to your favorite restaurant? A trip to a spa? Remember—the first step is knowing what you desire and what is meaningfu to you.

Step 2: Express in a way which is respectful to him and does not have entitlement or judgment energy. Use "I'd like" or I'd love."

> *"I'd love a date to my favorite restaurant for my birthday."*
>
> *"I'd like flowers and a gift card to this store for my birthday."*
>
> *"I'd love a gift certificate to the spa and babysitting help so I can go."*

Example 2: You're feeling overwhelmed and need more help, or just feeling a need for more quality time spent together.

Step 1: Know what you're feeling and desiring.

Don't limit yourself—Hashem is the true source of your needs. You may not get, but you can know and ask. I am confident that when I express my desires to my husband, Hashem is listening as well. If my husband can't fulfill them, then maybe Hashem will.

Step 2: Express those desires respectfully—use "I'd like" and "I'd love" without the word you. Let this land and give him time.

> *"I'd love more help with the kids at night. I can't do baths, bedtime, and nurse the baby at the same time. I'm exhausted and drained and find myself holding back tears.*
>
> *"I'd like date night during the week to do something fun—even a nature walk would be great. I'd also love a vacation together."*

Depending on the kind of person your husband is or on how he has been showing up until now, you may need to be very specific with how you would like his support. Be open to his suggestions as well. For example:

> *"I'd like to make supper tonight and would like help with the dishes."*
>
> *"I'd love to feel our toddler is safe and occupied while I help the kids with homework."*
>
> *"I'd love to go on a vacation somewhere warm where we can find relaxation time together. I'd love help in figuring out the details."*

Maybe your husband will offer his help. Maybe he'll offer to get more cleaning or babysitting help. Maybe he'll suggest starting with more low-key outings and think about planning a vacation later. Each husband is different and while one wife's husband needs specifications about the support she needs, another wife's husband may feel those specifications are too controlling for him. Try to get a feel for what works best for your husband.

continued

Beware of this pitfall—expectation energy: I believe that expectations are "false visions of the future" and they can get us into a lot of trouble in our relationships with others (and with ourselves). As often as we can catch ourselves "shoulding" or holding tightly to expectations, this is how often we need to release them. Make sure to do your **ROAR! Process,** and the Own Your Shadow Homeplay Exercise later in this chapter. Having our desires and requests met every time, no matter how carefully we express them, is an unrealistic expectation. But knowing our desires and respectfully sharing them gives the opportunity for our husbands to fulfill them.

Desire journal: Make a daily practice of writing down your desires. What would you like or love? Send those intentions to Hashem. Some may be able to be fulfilled by your husband (expressed using husband language) and some not. But Hashem is listening and is very creative.

Homeplay Exercise

Tell Him What You're Afraid Of

Instead of going head to head in an argument, allow yourself to be vulnerable. Many times, when we dig our heels in and dive into a conflict, there is the underlying presence of fear. When you notice that you're triggered by something your husband said, when your chest feels tight, and you start to argue, pause and express your fears by saying, "I'm afraid..."

With my husband, we've made a bit of a game of it. I'll notice when I start to argue, revved up by fear, and say to him, "Okay —ask me the question." He knows this code. Then it's his turn to pause and ask, "What are you afraid of?" I'll then launch into my underlying fears on the topic that we're discussing. Sometimes I'll even throw my arms up and pretend to stomp around (the temper tantrum release part of the **ROAR! Process**) as I share my fears. This makes us both laugh and the tension between us falls away. We know that we're on the same team though we have differing opinions and ways to get there. A peaceful discussion follows where we both share our concerns; then, we can get to solutionizing without war.

Homeplay Exercise

Let Him Lead

Sometimes, husbands *want us* to go bounding onto their side of the court. They ask us what to do or whether they should do something or not. When this happens, keep your mouth shut as much as possible so he can take charge of the situation. You may even have an opinion, but if it's not something that important, let him come to a conclusion and lead. Obviously, if it involves you and you have a preference, then use the phrase of desire that we discussed above. But with other things that are on his side of the court, let your brilliant ideas fall to the wayside, tell him you trust him because he makes good decisions, and just say, "I don't know."

Of course, sometimes it is important to share your suggestions. My husband and I work together with marriage coaching and my input is needed.

If at times, your husband needs you to be a listening board, then by all means be that. You can also help him reiterate the issues in order to get clarity by saying: "I'm not sure. What do you think?" This will help him find his power.

Homeplay Exercise

The "Ouch" Factor

Sometimes your husband may criticize you or say something sarcastic that is hurtful. Laura Doyle has the perfect tip for not entering the war zone after a hurtful comment has been launched at you. She says to just say, "Ouch."

It's an amazing concept because most of us are taught to retaliate, speak up for ourselves, be honest, and not let others get away with things. With one simple word, "ouch," you're letting the ball he just launched at you to hit the net and drop down on his side of the court. When you say "ouch," your husband knows he hurt you. He's left to deal with his feelings of having pained someone he loves.

After saying "ouch," you can take your hurt feelings, leave the room, and do the **ROAR! Process.** Notice if insight arises during the process of releasing your pain and anger in that sacred **ROAR!** space. People make mistakes and blurt out what they're thinking. I'm sure you've done the same to him and others. That's called being human. He may even apologize for the hurtful criticism. But you can feel proud and dignified that you've avoided a battle that most often goes nowhere.

> "We are all walking nervous systems."
>
> *—Miriam Racquel Feldman*

Homeplay Exercise

Communication Checklist

- Am I staying on my side of the net?
- Am I telling him my desires in the way of "I'd like... or I'd love" without the word "you"?
- Am I letting him lead?
- Am I telling him what I'm afraid of instead of arguing?
- Am I doing "sacred silence" and not offering my opinion and advice, letting go of my need to control?
- Am I saying "ouch" when hurt?

TIP 5: Gratitude & Appreciation: Never Take Anything For Granted

Your husband needs to know what he's getting right in his marriage. And he needs to feel successful with the most important person in his life—you. When people feel successful, they want to increase that success.

Homeplay Exercise

Let Your Husband Know What He's Getting Right By You

As women, we can be very discerning creatures and we can all too easily list and point out all the ways that our husbands are getting things wrong or failing in life or marriage. This is an unkindness to both you and him.

continued

Where your attention goes, your power goes. As life coach and sociologist Martha Beck once shared from her conversation with a white-water rafter, "If you pay attention to where the water flows between the rocks, that's where you'll go. If you pay attention to the rocks, then, bam!—that's where you'll go." Instead of always paying attention to the rocks—the things your husband messes up—give power and attention to what he does right.

What qualities of his do you appreciate?

Can you appreciate the lightheartedness he brings to the home? Okay, he may tickle your youngest and keep him up later than you like, but kids do need fun, laughter, and play and the male species is usually quite adept at that. Tell him that you appreciate the fun he brings to the home, that you love that quality in him.

Some men are the opposite and bring more seriousness to the home. Remember that opposites often marry. You may be the lighthearted, playful one. So, can you appreciate the steady, stable presence he brings? Tell him that you respect that about him.

If he has a job, can you tell him that you respect the fact that he cares for you?

Are there ways to bring to light that you feel protected by him? Supported? Loved?

Do you respect his determination, his tactfulness, his diplomacy, his mentorship, his tenacity, his commitment, his dependability, his easygoingness? Even if your husband doesn't get it completely right, notice what he did get right and compliment, appreciate, and qualify your experience.

Just think of the times when you get complimented. Maybe it feels like an uplift in your body, a lifting of your spirit. He'll feel that too! He'll know that he added to your satisfaction and happiness in some way.

And again, this doesn't mean to suppress your feelings, your emotions, your fears, your complaints, your dissatisfactions, your disappointments. I've shared the **ROAR! Process** for processing all those honesties that I want you to have for yourself. Venting, complaining, and noticing what isn't working for you is important to release—in private. And you have "husband language" for turning those complaints into desires to get your needs met using respectful energy.

But to add **GOLD** into your relationship? That's through expressed appreciation.

Every day, share words of gratitude with your husband. At least twice a day if not more. Each one is a gold coin in your marriage bank account. These can be done face to face, in a text message, or in a kind note left on the fridge. Any way of expression works.

I've become aware of the fact that some people have difficulties expressing appreciation so I'll share a few examples.

> *"Thank you for taking out the garbage. The house smells much better and it's off my to-do list!" (Even if you two have agreed on the fact that taking out the garbage is his task in the home, you can still express gratitude to him for doing it).*

> *"I appreciate you giving Shmeryl a bath. He loves spending time with you! I saw his face light up when I told him that Tatty was giving him the bath tonight."*

"Thank you for .... It's such a relief for me and I know I can lean on you."

"Thank you for going shopping. I love that I don't have to go with the kids. You make my life easier."

If he forgot the milk but got basically everything else on the shopping list, you can say: *"I'd love milk—it's such an easy breakfast for the kids to have cereal in the morning."* If he says that he'll make them pancakes with almond milk for breakfast, that could work too. Be open to his way of doing things.

By bringing words of success to his attempts at adding to your happiness, he will naturally choose to do more. Wins inspire the desire for more wins.

Of relevance: *There are exceptions to everything and there are unfortunately some marriages that may not work no matter how much gratitude you share, no matter how much effort you put in to trying to create emotional safety with your husband. If he is a Borderline/Narcissist, expressions of gratitude won't work because of entitlement and power/control issues. I'll cover this topic later in this chapter.*

Homeplay Exercise

Never take anything for granted

Having trouble finding things to appreciate? Try this!

Get a whiteboard and dry erase markers. Every morning jot down this phrase: *Never take anything for granted.*

List three things about your husband and four that are general. What things that if you didn't have them today, G-d forbid, you'd feel the loss big time?

The three about your husband, you can express to him as appreciations. The others are a private exercise for you.

I won't leave my bedroom in the morning until I've grabbed my whiteboard and done this exercise. It's that important.

I also initiated family appreciation practices at mealtimes once a month—at the Shabbos or Yom Tov table or even during a regular weekday dinner. Each member of the family will share what they appreciate about each other. What a gift. The positive vibration in our home and family is palpable.

TIP 6: Apologize

Yup, you're human and make mistakes. If you've come at your husband with aggressive energy, apologizing goes a long way in restoring emotional safety in the marriage. Being humble and getting vulnerable by owning your mistake brings closeness. Do this when you've been bossy, judgmental, unkind, or critical. And if there's been a conflict, it's most likely not all your fault. But you can own your part—apologize for that piece.

TIP 7: Bring A Tzaddik Into Your Imagination

We all use our imagination. When you imagine the worst-case scenarios regarding anything, G-d forbid, your body reacts with fear as if that event is happening at the moment. Cortisol increases, and your body tenses up with the freeze, fight, or flight response. If you can use your imagination in the negative, you have the power to also use your imagination for the positive.

Homeplay Exercise

Tzaddik or Compassionate Angel to the Rescue!

When you have something important to say to your husband or if there is a conflict going on, try to bring a Tzaddik or an angel (cherub) into your imagination. By holding in your mind's eye a spiritual figure that is higher than this physical world, your energy will sync with that higher vibration making you feel safer.

Your nervous system will be in a calmer, safer state and this will help bring wise words for you to speak. Your spouse will thereby also feel safer because energy is tangible. The whole situation will be uplifted to an increased spiritual vibration.

This is the opposite of coming with angry energy in which dialogue will be confrontational. Bringing a Tzaddik or an angel into your imagination is a powerful tool for creating a peaceful resolution.

TIP 8: Sexual Intimacy

Sexual intimacy can be a great source of pleasure. It can even be part of your self-care! As Avraham Peretz Friedman writes in his book *Marital Intimacy, "The Torah's view of sexuality is a perfect illustration of the general Torah attitude towards the physical world and its pleasures:* The Seer of Lublin *(Rabbi Yaakov Yitzchak Horowitz, 1745–1815) emphasized that a person must feel and express gratitude to the Almighty when experiencing sexual pleasure. Sexual pleasure, like all physical pleasure, the Seer explained, is an opportunity to feel gratitude to G-d."*

And,

> *... the sexual relationship between husband and wife is the vehicle for achieving a very great spiritual goal: the pleasure that results propels the marital relationship to higher levels of solidity and vitality—beyond what intellectual interaction alone could accomplish.*

Jews are fortunate to have taharas hamishpacha, sacred family purity laws, to enhance marriage and physical intimacy. With all niddah's details and seeming "restrictions," its actual result is an expansive keli for bettering marriage. As Friedman explains in his book, Rabbi Meir asks and answers the question about niddah, "Torah's desire to increase the love of husband for wife, and wife for husband .... The laws of Niddah, calling as they do for periodic separation and abstention, protect a couple from overindulgence, and overfamiliarity that quickly lead to jading, dissatisfaction, disgust and restlessness."

Non-Jews do not have these halachot—they can have sexual intimacy as much as they desire—no restrictions; yet, with all this "freedom," many couples aren't having! Over time, their desire has waned, gone cold. In our marriage program, Recreating Intimacy, my husband and I counsel couples who haven't been sexual for years! There's a lot to be said for Hashem's wisdom.

Physical intimacy is ideally supposed to nurture love and trust in your relationship. As Jennie Rosenfeld and David Ribner, authors of *The Newlywed's Guide to Physical Intimacy,* write so well, "*Your enjoyment as sexual partners is more than just physical; it can bring you to a place of closeness with another person that no other experience can provide. Your sharing of physical intimacy creates an emotional bond that should include feelings of trust, acceptance, caring, and mutuality. Your intimate relationship, which includes your sexual and emotional attachments, is the glue that binds your marriage together."*

All this being said, sexual intimacy can also be a huge point of contention in marriages. What if you're not enjoying sexual connection with your husband? There may be leftover resentment from disagreements, hard feelings from fights, and just plain exhaustion from busy days.

I hope that practicing the first seven marriage tips will better your health, lessen conflict and, G-d willing, create a more peaceful, loving relationship —one filled with more emotional connection and safety. All this can nurture your desire for your husband.

At the same time, often husbands are more desirous of sexual intimacy than wives. There are biological, chemical, hormonal, and energetic explanations for this. As energy practitioner Donna Eden explains, "Energetically, arousal for a man quickly ignites the genitals, and the energy moves up toward the heart and warms it. For a woman, arousal starts in the mind or heart and then travels to the genitals."

This illustrates even more so why a woman needs to feel safe with her husband and emotionally cared for by him in order to even want to have sexual relations—for her it begins in her mind and heart. It also helps us understand why self-care is so important; a woman must have the space in her being to choose to be together with her husband.

That being said, there may be times when a woman does not "feel" like being together with her husband. Try out these perspectives and suggestions:

1. **Look at sexual intimacy as an opportunity to receive.** When I trained in Laura Doyle's relationship coaching program, "receiving" was a term emphasized. You can enjoy the pleasure of being touched and desired by your husband as an act of receiving. Express the desire for back rubs as part of intimacy times and delight in having the tension of the day melt away.

2. **Make intimacy date nights.** Spontaneity may not work in many marriages. Plan ahead of time with your husband to have certain nights that you'll be together. This will also be a plus for emotional safety for your husband—he won't have to risk rejection. Also know that biologically, a woman's sexual desire is usually ignited once physical contact begins as opposed to a man's, whose desire may start beforehand. Mark Gungor has a funny Youtube video about this.

   Also, make sure that you're doing your self-care and garnering help from your husband, especially if you have little kids, in order to be able to show up on those nights. And I know that life can be very complicated with lots of worries on your mind, but you'll need to put those away for a time when you've committed to being with your husband. Being a worry machine all the time isn't good for you, nor for any relationship that you're in. Just like at work, you focus and prioritize. At home with your husband, you can do that as well.

3. **Know that you are fortifying the glue of your marriage and shalom bayis.** This is another gold coin in your marriage bank account. Your willingness and receptivity will be appreciated. Since marriage is a holy institution, you are serving Hashem in this act.

4. **Keep in mind that it's disrespectful and unkind to constantly turn a husband down.** As I mentioned, my husband and I coach couples. Many come to us when there hasn't been sexual intimacy in a year or even years, and that's not a marriage, really. A marriage does involve sexual intimacy; that's the difference between being roommates and being husband and wife. Hard feelings require being worked through, unless you desire a divorce. If you have resentments that have festered and prevented you from emotionally wanting to be with your husband, then do the tips I've suggested as well as reach out for assistance. I've helped many women somatically heal and reignite love and positivity in their marriages.

5. **Realize that hormonally, your husband feels *emotionally* connected to you through the sexual act.** This is because of the oxytocin being released. You may feel emotionally connected to your husband through words, gifts, kindness, and help with chores. But, for a man, his heart is warmed by sexual intimacy. Donna Eden explains that, *"Oxytocin, the "tend and befriend" hormone, is associated with women bonding with one another and nurturing their families. And indeed, it is often ten times as concentrated in women's bodies as in men's. Except at one particular time—during orgasm. That's when men get to have a deep bonding moment. Their oxytocin jumps to five times normal levels."*

This means that men feel loved and more loving through the sexual act—their oxytocin dictates that feeling. All that stuff that he does for you as your partner—going to work, helping around the house and with the kids, listening to you when you share your worries and issues—are ways that he shows his love and care for you and the family. Your words of appreciation are important, but when you make time to be together with him, bonding sexually, he feels your love and care for him. And during the sexual act itself, his love for you strengthened because of that huge input of oxytocin he received. We are human after all — souls in physical, hormonal bodies.

6. **Use natural products for lubrication and dryness.** Organic apricot oil is one such product; and another, called Neu Eve, was especially formulated by gynecologists to help with dryness, which can especially be an issue after menopause. Neu Eve is made of natural ingredients and can help heal tissues. These products are easy to purchase online.

I'm hoping that as you start practicing these eight tips and the many Homeplay exercises, you'll feel rejuvenated and empowered in your marriage.

Blessings!

Letter 3

Tension With My Spouse Regarding Important Decisions

Dear Miriam Racquel,

My husband and I keep butting heads on important decisions. We both have such differing opinions about how to run a home, how to discipline the kids, our work schedules and even the food we eat. What can I do to have my opinions and decisions respected and avoid feeling like we're battling all the time?

Dear Awesome Woman,

I'm so sorry to hear of the tension going on with your husband. That's definitely a difficult place to be in a marriage.

When I have times like this with my husband—that time of butting heads about important things—I try to remember this: We're on the same team! And according to Torah, we're not just on the same team, but actually one: A husband's and wife's soul are two halves of a whole. There's no tug of war and no winning side; we both need to win as one entity working together towards peaceful wholeness and unity.

Our desires are the same—we both want what's best for each other, our family and our home. Once I click into this very important truth in the midst of a clash, my energy shifts. My guard drops, my nervous system calms down, and my ego releases its very selfish grip. As two Jews coming together, our G-dly soul can overpower the evil inclination's goal of division. This is an empowering thought and brings such spiritual strength to the situation.

Another technique I'll use to help elevate the situation to a higher spiritual vibration so that peace can prevail is to bring into my mind a mentor or righteous individual. I'll imagine that in the room with us is someone of great Torah standing, and this will also help shift my energy to a calmer state. Peace within ourselves helps to bring peace outside of ourselves.

Then, if I can give affection, I do—I'll take my husband's hand and say, "Hey, we're on the same team! We both want what's best. So how can we work together to make this happen?"

With this calmer energy, I also share with my husband what I'm afraid of. Oftentimes, when tensions rise, we're both fearing something—a loss of time, connection, health, money. Especially when it comes to the kids, there are many fears. When we're locked in a "debate" of sorts, I'll prod my husband to ask what I refer to now as the magic question—"What are you afraid of, honey?" When he asks me this question, my guard immediately drops, and I'll share with him what really is concerning me about the subject that we're in conflict about. That question is so helpful in bringing us together rather than apart.

I'll give an example because storytelling is an easier way to remember things.

Once I found out that my children who left the house with my husband on their way to synagogue on Shabbat were told to continue on their own when my husband had to stop off first at a neighbor's house. Meaning, instead of my husband having the children wait for him, he told them to go ahead and walk on their own.

I'm more protective of my kids in terms of walking around the neighborhood than my husband, and our synagogue is a good 20 minutes away with some busy streets to cross. When my daughter mentioned it to me that afternoon, I felt my nervous system rev way up. The heat rose to my face; I was not a happy camper. My mama-bear energy had arisen!

The question was: How was I going to speak to my husband about this in a respectful way without locking horns? How was I going to not come off in an attacking manner that would rev up his nervous system, get him defensive and result in me not being heard? And that's when I used the techniques that I share above.

Resting in my recliner that Shabbat, I came to see that we're on the same team, wanting safety for the kids. I realized that we obviously have different ideas of what that looked like. He obviously felt comfortable with them walking to our synagogue alone; I did not. Later that day, I had a chance to speak to him (after his nap!), imagining someone I highly respect sitting there in the room with us. I took my husband's hand and said, "I know that we both want what is safe and best for our children. I'm concerned ...."

I believe that because my nervous system was in a calm state and I had started the conversation with connecting energy, my husband heard my fears and acknowledged them. He agreed that in the future, if he needed to stop along the way, he could just have the kids wait for him because that's what made me feel better and safer. The conversation concluded with closeness and agreement rather than distance and dispute.

I invite you to try these suggestions—spiritually raise the atmosphere, expose your feelings, get vulnerable and find agreement. Connection is the key to resolving the tension. And remember, you're on the same team!

Blessings! 

(Originally published at *TheJewishWoman.org*)

Letter 4

Introverted Wife, Extroverted Husband: How to Have Shabbat Guests

Dear Miriam Racquel,

My husband is an extrovert, and I'm an introvert. He wants a lot of guests on Shabbat, and I don't. I'm tired from managing the home all week and as a result of other responsibilities, including work and the kids. Plus, I'm not so into entertaining. But my husband works hard all week and loves to be with other people on Shabbat, so he'd like us to have guests. What should I do?

Dear Awesome Woman,

First, celebrate yourself for who you are and how much you're handling in your life, especially as an introvert who requires more down time than an extrovert. Good for you! Put your hands up in the air and say, "Yay, me!" You need to be your own cheerleader. I know that may seem silly, but recognizing how well you're managing helps maintain your empowerment, giving you strength and positivity to continue your role as a Jewish woman, wife and mother.

Also, have compassion for yourself. Of course you're tired! The fast pace of life in this day and age is even more of a challenge than it used to be for introverts. Self-care is a must for maintaining grace and good mental health—for remaining grateful instead of resentful, accomplished rather than defeated, and healthy instead of drained.

When I use a flowing pattern throughout the day of inward energy, outward energy, inward energy and outward energy, I can be my best self and show up for my loved ones and the world in a positive way. Downtime is the essential ingredient for staying centered and being kind to myself and others, and I intersperse that inward energy with chunks of outward action in order to "get things done."

Inward energy involves things like meditation, prayer, contemplation, inner processing, conscious breathing, walking or sitting in nature, breath exercises, journaling, resting and reading. Outward energy activities include work, socializing, talking, playing on social media, decluttering, exercising, doing errands and going over my "To Do" lists. These can all be mixed around, but with the continued pattern of inward energy, outward energy, inward energy and outward energy.

Now, back to your question—entertaining guests for Shabbat. I think it's important to clarify that while it's a wonderful thing that your husband wants to have guests, the real mitzvah of *hachnasat orchim* is inviting those who are in need of a place to stay or eat (examples could be guests who are traveling, or who live alone or who have a hard time making ends meet, or those who are just beginning to keep Shabbat and need support on their spiritual journey, etc.). Just having friends over, while a very positive thing, is not necessarily a fulfillment of the mitzvah of *hachnasat orchim*.

That being said, how can inviting guests be manageable for you, as well as enjoyable, practical and comfortable? Your mental, emotional and physical health is a priority along with a calm rapport with your children. Since you're an introvert, being respectful of your energy is key. So, what things can you and your husband put in place to make this mitzvah possible?

1. Establish Boundaries

Do you feel comfortable having a few guests twice a month? Once a month? Discern what would be OK for you, feel that in your body (expansion, stress, tension, relief or neutral), and then consider where you can come together with your husband about this.

You can share with your husband how you'd like to have guests in the way you feel you can handle because he's expressed that it's important to him. Remember, you are on the same team of raising your family and honoring each other as husband and wife.

"I'd like to have guests twice a month, about three people at a time, because I know that's what you would enjoy. I'd also like to end the meal at a certain time—one that we decide beforehand—so it doesn't go on too long and I can get some downtime afterwards. I can only entertain for so long before my energy feels drained. I'd also love more cleaning help and help with food shopping."

2. Be Selective in Who You Invite

Being careful with who you invite is very important as well. Choose people who are respectful of your time and your needs. As you know so well, too much conversation may drain an introvert, so being aware of your own boundaries and need for quiet time is very important. This is why you can be selective about the type of guests that you have.

Is it too much for you to have guests with young children? Does that feel chaotic and overwhelming, or is that actually wonderful for your children? Maybe they'll be more entertained that way.

If there are guests who talk too much or require a lot of attention, those may be best saved for when your kids are grown. Though our hearts go out to everyone, if engaging with certain types of people causes you stress that you cannot handle (a constriction in your body, a tightness in the chest and jaw, a drop in the stomach), then they may be best left for others to have.

3. Minimize Your Work

Make it easier for yourself by choosing simple recipes. When you have young children, too much time in the kitchen with fancy recipes can lead to neglect of what's really important. Your children need time and attention, and guests usually feel very grateful and content with a warm atmosphere, simple food and Torah conversation.

Keep the food light, healthy and easy to prepare so you won't fall into the resentment trap. Fresh salads, cut-up vegetables and store-bought dips are filling. Crockpots and air fryers for either fish or meat can cut preparation time in half without standing over a stove. Also, if your guests offer to help serve and clear, let them! Receiving help is not only good for you, but for the one offering, it makes them feel useful. Trust that if they didn't want to, they wouldn't offer. But hopefully, you'll be inviting guests who do offer.

This way of compromising and working together with your husband is a beautiful thing for your marriage. Respecting your husband's desire for guests, as well as attending to your introverted nature, is definitely possible. These tips will help you do that mitzvah of welcoming guests in a way that is kind to you and to others.

Blessings!

(Originally published at *TheJewishWoman.org*)

Letter 5

Dr. Jekyll/Mr. Hyde Behavior or is My Husband a Borderline/Narcissist?

Dear Miriam Racquel,

I think that my husband may be a Borderline/Narcissist. Things he says just seem so twisted. At times he can be loving and generous and at other times, he seems so mean, gives me long lectures about how everything is my fault and blames me. He never seems satisfied with me—nothing I do ever seems to please him enough and he calls me selfish. I tried using some of the tools you shared in the 8 Tips to Nurture Emotional Safety and sometimes they work and other times not. Even if I give him sincere appreciation, he acts entitled and things don't get better. I feel like I'm living with Dr. Jekyll and Mr. Hyde. All this behavior of his started after we got married—while we were dating he seemed so normal and even loving and attentive. I don't know where things got off to the wrong foot, but I feel really crazy at times and I'm sinking into a depression.

Dear Awesome Woman,

I'm so sorry to hear this. From what you share, it does seem that your husband may have toxic Borderline/Narcissist tendencies. In

Chapter 4, I discuss Borderline/Narcissism with respect to friendships. Much of the same advice applies to spousal relationships. The big difference is we're going to do everything possible to help a marriage thrive (especially if there are children), whereas toxic friendships have to be ended. Your feeling of craziness and depression is a result of living under a cloud of FOG—fear, obligation, and guilt. This is emotional blackmail that your husband is using to keep you walking on eggshells. Susan Forward's and Donna Frazier's insightful book *Emotional Blackmail: When the People in Your Life Use Fear, Obligation and Guilt to Manipulate You* describes how people who are close to us, and are the ones who have shown us love and caring get mean, nasty, threatening, and manipulative when you don't give them what they want.

Like a two-year-old in an adult's body, they seemingly have a temper tantrum and claim that you don't love them enough if you say no to something or try to set limits or boundaries to your time, space, being. They throw labels at you—calling you selfish, greedy, cold, rigid, and other nasty things. They try to break you down so that you'll give in to their wants, needs, or fantasies.

Since your husband is doing this, please do not believe him. He is just trying to use manipulative lies and put downs to get what he wants from you. This is a power-over relationship, not a loving, kind Jewish marriage. In your body, these interactions will be felt as pressure, discomfort, shame, and fear. Your nervous system will be in disarray, wanting to take flight or fight back, but instead gets locked into a freeze state.

Because Hashem is unlimited and does create miracles, there is the possibility of change for your marriage. Please use the **ROAR! Process to get out of the freeze state,** and do self-care even if your husband calls you selfish. It's ok to be selfish, otherwise there is no self for you to be. As Hillel says in Pirkei Avot 1:14, *"If I am not for myself, who will be for me?"*

Hashem sees all. Hashem knows exactly what is going on. The Baal Shem Tov was told by his father before he passed, "Fear no one, but G-d alone." Your husband is not your power, Hashem is. And it is your G-d who you need to fear, not your husband.

It is hateful to Hashem that your husband is mean to you—this is certainly not a G-dly trait. Do not allow it to continue because that is abuse to yourself. Things need to shift now. You cannot keep falling for the manipulation and lies, the emotional blackmail, and blame/shame attacks that your husband is throwing at you. Your being and your body cannot continue to be abused by emotional blackmail. It's extremely toxic.

You need outside help—this is not something that you can navigate by yourself. Your self-esteem has been whittled away and you'll need a life vest from a sane professional. Friends can't be expected to carry this burden, nor are they trained to. It's very important that the kind of help you get is with a Rav, Rebbetzin, somatic-based coach, healer, or therapist who understands Borderline/Narcissist behavior. They must be attuned to this type of behavior. Borderline/ Narcissists are expertly manipulative—they can even manipulate professionals unless the professionals have awareness, education, and experience with this personality disorder.

One of my expertise is working with victims of Borderline/ Narcissists. We address the trauma that is in the body. Living in FOG with someone who is supposed to be a loving spouse is terribly traumatic to the nervous system and gets lodged in the cells as terror. Somatic healing helps with this as well as shifts neural pathways in the mind so self-esteem and healthy boundaries are established and upheld.

Do not share with your husband your suspicions that he is a Borderline/Narcissist, thinking that he will have an "aha" moment and make changes. He won't believe you. In fact, he most likely will call you the Narcissist.

There is no guarantee that your marriage will survive the changes you will make to regain your health and sanity. Your husband may change or he may not—he has free will, so we can't prophesize. But you do not have to walk the journey alone.

Blessings!

Letter 6

Nitpicking — Own Your Shadow

Dear Miriam Racquel,

I find myself nitpicking every little thing that my husband does. He is too lazy, slobby, irresponsible, impractical, foolish—my mind just jumps around and grabs anything negative that it can. Obviously, this is not great for shalom bayis. But I can't seem to help myself. There is evidence of all his negative traits everywhere! Help!

Dear Awesome Woman,

Thank you for reaching out and sharing something that is so human and common. And as you mentioned, terrible for shalom bayis!

When you're extra nit-picking your husband, check in with your self-care. Are you feeling extra tired or overwhelmed? Are you not taking enough time-outs for yourself to fill your tank? Are you refusing help? Are you making life harder than necessary—taking on too many community obligations, saying "yes" when a simple "I can't" is needed? Please review Chapter 2: Self-Care and take my words seriously. Honoring yourself by recognizing your limits, your boundaries, your care, and your creativity is so important!

And remember, part of your self-care is **ROAR!**ing. Are you **ROAR!**ing enough? I take my **ROAR!**ing very seriously. If I'm emotionally triggered by something small or big—whether it's a technical glitch on my computer or a global situation in the world—and don't take a few moments to sit down and write, rip, temper tantrum, and tap into my intuition, I will feel stuck, heavy, get a migraine, or shoulder pain.

We especially need to take time to **ROAR!** about our husbands if we find ourselves nitpicking him in thoughts or words. Being angry with our husbands will leak out into finding fault with him *all the time*. This sounds like it's happening with you. Doing the **ROAR! Process** allows a productive release for your mind and heart to vent all that negativity and complaining and will pinpoint what's really going on with you—hopefully bringing some relief, clarity, and guidance. If not, hire professional help to get greater insight and heal what's going on for you as well as what's going on within your marriage. Don't allow your marriage to slide downhill. It's just not smart to put your most important relationships (the one with yourself and the one with your husband) on the back burner.

Also, make sure that you're speaking up about your desires, preferably using "husband language."

All this being said, you're noticing traits about him that bother you. Truth is, we are not going to like our husbands all of the time. It's not possible—we're separate bodies, with personality quirks, separate egos, and opinions. But criticism and negative judgment can destroy relationships so we want to clear this energy up as fast as we can.

First, I'd like to clarify the difference between judgment and wise discernment because we're often taught the Torah edict of judging people favorably. Now this is great, but what is omitted from that teaching is our G-d given ability to discern. And we cannot ignore that. If we only judge people positively and ignore our wise discernment, then we're at risk for being treated unkindly in our relatioships; we're at risk for ignoring our emotions and rationalizing people's bad behavior; we're at risk for being abused by Borderline/Narcissists at work and in the community. Many of us have had painful situations where we've ignored our wisdom, our discernment, and trusted people we should not have.

Let's make a clear distinction between discernment and judgment.

Discernment is when there is a neutrality around what we are seeing in someone else. It's a noticing, an awareness of someone's personality traits. An acceptance. We are free to like or dislike what we are noticing, especially when it has a negative consequence for us.

For example:

- when a co-worker is continuously late.
- when a friend doesn't follow through on commitments.
- when a child leaves messes around.
- a spouse is critical.

In these cases, we allow ourselves to use wise discernment to take action. It's our job to keep ourselves safe, healthy, and whole.

Judgment on the other hand comes with a lot of ego-charge—a strong emotional trigger with the thought—"I would *never* do that!" In judging others, we act on the belief that we are more perfect. We feel so self-righteous!

Homeplay Exercise

Owning Your Shadow

We're not to ignore our ability for wise discernment like stated above. It's certainly reasonable to know what is okay for us and what is not okay. But the negative judgment energy of thinking, "I'm more perfect than him" or "I would never do that!" has got to go.

When there is strong judgment towards another, it's an indication that our shadow needs to be owned. **The shadow is the rejected part of ourselves—*our* shortcomings and defects.**

The Baal Shem Tov taught that the world is a mirror, and that the defects we see in other people are only a reflection of our own defects. We are likely to be oblivious to our own defects, but can easily detect shortcomings in other people. The Baal Shem Tov instructs us to take such observations as indications that we have these shortcomings ourselves.

—Rabbi Abraham J. Twerski, 1996

Those traits in your husband that are driving you crazy? Maybe you've got those too!

Our souls want us to drop ego and get rid of blind spots therefore becoming more whole. Owning our shadow parts gives us an opportunity to do this and thrive as a soul in a body.

My motto is: What the ego resists, the soul persists in showing us again and again.

So what better time than now to own these shortcomings, change what we can, dissolve our egos, and get more divinely aligned? Our marriage is the petri dish for this.

Also, walking around with negative judgments of others creates a lot of inner tension. This leads to physical pain symptoms in the body and can have us running to doctors looking for a purely physical cause instead of an emotional cause. Plantar fasciitis? It's the shoes. Migraine? It's the weather. Sciatica? It's a herniated disc. Of course we can get support from better shoes, nicer weather, and exercising, but it is also beneficial to examine what's going on inside of us.

I invite you to try this **Owning Your Shadow** exercise:

1. How are you "shoulding" your husband?

Write these thoughts down:
My husband should ________________.

2. Now translate those "shoulds" into judgments.
When you are emotionally triggered by your husband or anyone for that matter, your mind fills with judgment and your body fills with tension.

"How could they have done that! They're so ___________." And you fill in the blank. As your mind grabs onto that judgment, notice how your body reacts. Is it communicating tension through tight shoulders, a constricted chest, or a clenching of the jaw (possibly leading to a headache later on)?

Take a look at your list of judgments. Maybe you are thinking that:

- He is irresponsible.
- He is lazy.
- He is so selfish.
- He is so impractical. How could he think that could work?
- He is inept at his job.
- He makes bad decisions.

3. Now I'd like you to do the ROAR! Process. Do a quick one—scribble, rip, and temper tantrum with a silent scream. Move your arms and legs or stretch out in all directions. It's safe to be honest with yourself and recognize that these traits you're seeing in your husband annoy and frustrate you. You can be very judgy on that paper you'll be ripping up—that's what it's for. We don't want to keep that tension energy inside. **The ROAR! Process** will give a release for your body. Let that energy flow.

4. After that temper tantrum, put both palms out in front of you, facing the ceiling. Imagine pink watery bouncy balls in each palm.

5. Feel your feet on the floor and take a belly breath into your stomach and release out.

6. Gently wiggle the (imagined) pink watery bouncy ball in your right palm and say: "Sometimes he is so_________." Fill in the blank with the judgment word that you have towards your husband.

7. Then gently wiggle the (imagined) pink watery bouncy ball in your left palm and say: "Sometimes he is not__________." Fill in the blank with the judgment word that you have towards your husband and let your mind come up with a few examples of times when he has not behaved in the way you are judging. I'm sure there are moments.

8. Return back to the right palm and gently wiggle the (imagined) pink watery bouncy ball and say: "Sometimes I am __________." Fill in the blank with the same judgment word you had against your husband finding examples of where in your life you are not perfect and do (even on a subtle level) exactly what you're complaining about.

9. Then go to the left palm, gently wiggle the (imagined) pink watery bouncy ball and say: "Sometimes I am not ________." Fillin the blank with that judgment word.

continued

10. Feel your feet on the floor and take a belly breath into your stomach and release out.

11. Wiggling both palms at once, say: "We are all this."

12. Notice if the tension inside you has relaxed a bit. Perhaps there is more expansion in your chest, an ease of breath, a relaxed face, and settled shoulders. By owning and processing how we are judging others, we get to claim our shadows and be free. We let go of the inner tension caused by trying to hide from these rejected parts—our shadow parts—and free up the energy spent on holding something at bay.

This little exercise may sting a bit and that is the ego letting go of its self-identity. It's dissolving and that can feel uncomfortable at first. But when you get into the habit of owning all your parts, it's extremely freeing, releases tension in your body, and improves your marriage. You can also use it for other relationships when you find yourself being judgy.

You are still going to make wise, discerning decisions about what you like and don't like, who you friend, who you hire, and who you work with, but by owning your shadow parts you'll be coming from a more expansive, soul-wise place. You won't be left with a migraine, digestive issues, or pinched nerves.

Becoming whole and healthy means owning all our parts—the traits that we don't believe we have. It's all too easy to point the finger at social media strangers, at family members, at our children and at our spouses, and to judge them for being lazy, selfish, stupid, foolish, arrogant, cheap, irresponsible, inept, messy etc. Who wants to believe that we also carry those traits? These judgments we have are so normal and human.

But they are also projections that Hashem is showing us in order to integrate what is inside of us. These judgments are our shadow parts and instead of rejecting them, we can accept them and love ourselves more fully—the good, the bad, and the ugly. By becoming whole, we will find more love and compassion for our husbands and others, creating a more peaceful home and world. Our health will also improve as a result of less tension—more inner peace leads to more outer peace.

Blessings!

Letter 7
Wrong for a Married Woman to Be Friendly With Men?

Dear Miriam Racquel,

I've been happily married for a few years, and my husband and I are very committed to each other. But recently, my husband has asked me to distance myself from men I'm friendly with. There's a male co-worker I chat with during lunch at work; there's an ex-boyfriend from high school I keep in touch with through social media; and there's a male neighbor I run into when I'm walking the dog, and we tend to shmooze. I don't see the problem with these relationships and even share the conversations with my husband. But he tells me that my friendliness with these men makes him uncomfortable. I feel that he should trust me. What do you think?

Dear Awesome Woman,

I hear your disturbance. You'd love for your husband to accept you as you are and feel safe that you wouldn't do anything improper outside the bounds of your marriage. On a philosophical level, this makes sense; however, your husband actually has a good point.

Besides the fact that he is feeling uncomfortable and, as spouses, we try to accommodate each other's feelings, your husband isn't lacking trust in you; he is actually understanding a Torah concept and wanting to keep a fence around the sanctity of his marriage.

The Torah's perspective regarding men and women is that there is a natural, G-d-given attraction between them. Adding to this, there is something called ruach shtut, which means "a spirit of foolishness." This is not just plain foolishness we are all capable of but one that can override our better judgment. It's as if an irrational force grabs us, and we get lost in it. This combination creates a dangerous situation when it comes to men and women hanging out together.

Maybe you've heard stories about normally wise men and women from good marriages breaking trust with their spouse to indulge in a dream/fantasy that falls apart immediately when exposed. Often, they do not understand what they were thinking to have engaged in this sort of behavior; they broke all integrity and are not that sort of person. They will admit that they may not even understand what change came over them. Torah, the blueprint of life, warns us about this and has laws regarding friendliness between men and women to protect us. An example is the laws of Yichud in which an unmarried man and woman cannot be secluded together in a private setting.

So even though you are a trustworthy woman and your love for your husband is strong, it's worth lessening your friendliness with these other men. You don't need to be unkind, but a formal distance would be wise. Drop the unnecessary chatting. This may feel odd and even uncomfortable at first, but recognize that you are putting a fence around the sanctity of your marriage. And if the men that you have been friendly with comment about your new distant behavior, you can let them know that your marriage is very important to you and that you prefer to lessen your casual interactions with other men. If they don't understand, then just let it be. You're being a great role model by upholding a new standard for yourself and your loved one.

Just two more things that I'd like to add:

1. Desire and romance are not the glue that keep marriage together; these feelings come and go. Commitment is the glue. Gratitude for what you have and never taking anything for granted is an incredible bond.

Philosopher Alain de Botton says, "… the classic romantic model has sold us on a number of self-defeating beliefs about the most essential and nuanced experiences of human life: love, infatuation, marriage …." As opposed to this, the Torah's philosophy is long-lasting and never goes out of style.

2. Beware of "compare and despair." Social media is a loaded gun. Thankfully, you are happy in your marriage. But some people are not. And seeing pictures of happy couples on social media in addition to the constant broadcast of glossy marriages can be deceiving to the reality of life.

Never compare your insides (challenges, dissatisfactions, self-judgments) with others' outsides. As happy as a couple looks—and G-d willing, they actually are that happy—never underestimate the effort that it takes in real life to keep a marriage going. Acts of kindness, appreciation, compromise, humility, holding your tongue, overcoming your emotions—all of this creates a healthy partnership and a joyful home.

May you continue to enjoy your marriage and recognize the blessing in having a husband who cares for protecting the sanctity of your home.

Blessings!

(Originally published at *TheJewishWoman.org*)

Letter 8

The Case for the Unemotional Man

Dear Miriam Racquel,

My husband is quite the stoic guy. I know that he is deeply feeling on the inside but not so much on the outside. How can I appreciate this about him?

Dear Awesome Woman,

My husband, Dovid Feldman, LPC., once wrote a very moving newsletter about my father. My dad, Melvin Cook (may his memory be a blessing), was a deeply feeling man who from childhood wounds, life experiences, and survival reactions, chose to cover up the vulnerability inside of him (a protective measure for sure). Your husband may not be coming from the same place— his more stoic style may just be his personality "quirk"—but perhaps you can gain some appreciation from the touching words my husband shares.

The Case for the Unemotional Man

"I was never married to my father-in-law, Melvin Cook, may his memory be blessed. But I did marry into his family.

I've never seen him cry. Legend has it, he did. Times, dates, and places are well recorded in the memories of his three daughters and his beloved wife.

Over the 30 years I shared with him, we had perhaps two conversations where he opened up to me about his feelings, both of which were about his family. Surprisingly, they were meaningful and connecting, something I wasn't used to feeling around him.

But even though opening his heart in conversation wasn't his norm, it certainly was in his behavior. Mel Cook was a man who could always be depended on. He was always on time, always thoughtful, and always more concerned about you than you were about yourself.

At family gatherings, he refused to take a seat until everybody else had a place around the table. He never took the first piece or the last. Even in his eighties, he lugged the extra folding chairs from downstairs. He made sure you were comfortable, and created spaces and experiences for life and joy to happen.

His jokes were sometimes funny, many times off, but he would laugh at them nonetheless. He shied away from attention, preferring to pass that baton to his accomplished son-in-laws or his daughters. If he had any problems, you didn't know about them—his difficulties were held close to his chest, so as to never burden others with his issues. He was the quintessential 1970s family man.

He wasn't nice. He wasn't "emotionally available."

He was stoic, powerful, principled, disciplined, and quiet. Always there, always available, he was the loyal rock of his home for 60 years, providing safety, shelter, and life for his family.

And he was in love with them. With each one of the souls he took responsibility for. When his son-in-laws came, his care and concern expanded to include us. And when the grandchildren came, they folded into his protective bubble like they were his own.

He passed with the same enduring qualities as he lived. Fanfare, celebrity, and fuss were absent and replaced with legacy, consideration, and foresight. His dearest wife, my mother-in-law, opened the packet he arranged, containing everything she would need to continue living in safety, security, and dignity. Their relationship continues and deepens after his death, as she finds herself speaking to him and sharing with him now more than ever.

In many ways, I'm his opposite. Perhaps that's why his daughter fell in love with me. Perhaps that's why I'm shedding tears as I write, something he would never do.

Mel was the salt-of-the-earth man that built this world. He sacrificed everything for those he loved, his only goal to leave this world a better place than how he entered it — for others, not for himself. While he wasn't "emotionally available," he was perhaps one of the most available men I've ever known. I miss him, and men like him. And so should you."

Blessings!

Letter 9

Money, Love & Joy

Dear Miriam Racquel,

I've been a widow for many years and recently have been dating a man whom I'd like to marry. The thing is, I have a lot more money than him and am used to a more extravagant lifestyle. I'm not sure how to deal with this.

Dear Awesome Woman,

When my father-in-law was widowed, he was in a situation similar to yours but from the opposite side. My husband, Dovid Feldman, L.P.C., wrote a beautiful newsletter about the decision his father, Gene Feldman (may his memory be a blessing), and his fiance made before they married. It truly opened my eyes to possibilities, paradigm shifts, and old-fashioned values. Thank G-d, they went on to experience a very generous and loving marriage. May we learn much from wise elders (family or not) and may we create marriages that not only work but make us better human beings.

Happy to Trade Money for Love

"My father was widowed at age 65 upon my mother's untimely death. He entered the dating market after grieving the loss of his darling wife and was greeted with many options.

Being a modest man, he was retired, living on a small budget of about $3k/month. He owned his home, had a modest car, ate dinner out 1 x a month, and took a vacation 1 x year.

He loved reading, painting, gardening, hosting friends, learning, taking classes, and going to the theater. He was a sophisticated yet simple man.

As it happened, an extremely wealthy woman named Barbara, with many homes and much money, fell for him hard. They dated and soon decided they wanted to marry. My father was happy but concerned about the financial discrepancy.

So he offered her a choice. They could both either live his frugal life together or her extravagant life together. But he wasn't willing to have two economies in one marriage. The choice was hers, but whatever she chose, money would be shared evenly.

She took some time to respond but eventually came back to my father and sealed the deal in his heart. She said to him: "Gene, the choice isn't mine, as I've already made my choice—I've been poor, and I've been rich. I'm not interested in money, but I do want to share my life with you no matter what. So tell me, which type of life do you want?"

My dad was shocked. Who was this woman who loved him so deeply she'd trade in her riches for his modest life?

Having only been lower middle class, my father decided to adopt her lifestyle for some of the best years of his life. In between enjoying his modest garden and taking classes at a local college, they traveled the world together. They went on safaris in Africa, explored the Far East, and entertained friends and family at their multiple homes. I'll never forget the beautiful estate they created together in St. Thomas, a place we were invited to often, escaping the Chicago winters for just a bit.

Sadly after 11 short years together, Barbara fell ill with a rare brain tumor. No stranger to tragedy, my father nursed her and sat by her side every day, as he did for my mother, till she passed on several months later.

Barbara and Gene were more than a power couple. They were an inspiration, a testament to rebirth and sacrifice for life and love. Our blended families melded together instantly, as we were all so thrilled they found each other.

So many people put superficial constraints on who is deserving of their love and who they will allow to love them. I bless every man and woman who understands the depth and power of this real-life fairytale: may we all merit to have such a person in our own life whose love goes beyond the physical and well into the spiritual.

And, most importantly, may we all have the strength, wisdom, and good fortune to be that person to someone else."

Blessings!

A Final Note for the Marriage Chapter:

I hope that the suggestions and exercises in this Marriage chapter have provided insight and guidance for bettering your marriage. It's good to remember that our husbands are the second halves of our souls. We start as one soul in the heavenly sphere and then separate in this physical world to then find one another again and become whole—one soul creating heaven on Earth through love, connection, and acceptance of both ourselves and another. By fostering emotional safety, communicating with kindness, doing self-care, and giving priority to the most important relationship that we have, we can nurture this heavenly bond and create a beautiful home.

Blessings! 

7

Parenting

By creating an emotionally safe space
for your children, Torah can bloom.
In fact, everything can bloom.

—Miriam Racquel Feldman

This parenting chapter could be a million pages long. And I'm not exaggerating. Parenting issues, complications, and joys are infinite and truly there are no right answers set in stone for each situation that pops up. Parenting is a very brave journey and for those who have this blessing in life, it is a mighty journey indeed. What I offer here is a compilation of what I've learned along my parenting path as well as information that I've gathered throughout the years. Celebrate yourself for being on this road which has twists and turns, potholes, and uplifts. It all starts with us and the more we come with self-kindness, compassion, humility, and deep connection to Hashem and Torah (and I'm not talking about how "religious" you are here), the easier the path will be to walk. And the more resilient you will be to keep picking yourself up (and your kids up) when there are challenges.

Parenting is a blessing and children are a blessing. Each and every one of them. And they are here to teach us so much, as well as help us complete our gilgulim. Parenting children is probably the hardest job in the world, and the most important, because you are essentially building human beings and nurturing souls. A big task and a grand responsibility indeed. We are not alone in this task—Hashem is with us every step of the way, though at times we may not necessarily feel that. I hope that my words in this chapter will be one way that Hashem is revealed to you and helps you on your journey with your children.

Okay, all that being said—now let's dive in.

One of the most significant lessons that I've learned over time and the one which I wished I had known earlier on is that parenting is all about: *relationship, relationship, relationship.*

Let me repeat: relationship, relationship, relationship.

Not religion.

Torah cannot be taught and practiced in a vacuum. Or even worse—in a negative, critical, pressured environment. Religion must never get in the way of a compassionate and kind relationship with your child.

No matter how excited you are as a baalas teshuvah or as an FFB to pass on the Torah torch to your clan of children, to educate and parent them in the ways of the holy book as you may not have been parented and educated, your path has been and will be different than your children's.

Specifically, if you are a baalas teshuvah, you chose Torah and did the very hard work of transforming yourself to live according to the Torah paradigm. You dropped the societal expectations that you grew up in to become a Torah Yid. Your path required incredible mesiras nefesh and a tremendous commitment and willpower from within your being. This is not the path of your children. They are being raised as FFBs, but with a bit of a twist. You are not passing on the Torah tradition from your childhood home because you weren't raised in a Torah home. Most likely there are no bubbies and zaydes, savtas, and sabas who are keeping the faith with all the intricacies as you are trying to do.

Unlike FFBs, your children come face to face with the secular influence of very loving and kind extended family members all the time. The pictures of your parents on the walls don't show sheitels and yarmulkes. Your children's bubby may drive on Shabbos and wear pants. I remember when my son was about four years old and he asked me why grandma drives on Shabbos. "Isn't she Jewish?" he asked me with his sweet face turned up to mine. I saw how his little mind tried to make sense of the answer I gave about grandma being Jewish, but not really understanding Shabbos. That confused him even more since his comeback was simple: "Just tell her so she'll understand."

I sighed as I tried to explain vaguely (since I was speaking to a child's mind) that it wasn't that simple. I wanted my son to respect his grandparents as elders though they did things differently than us.

Certainly, I didn't want him to think that it was okay not to keep Shabbos; after all, my husband and I were raising him in accordance with all the halachas that Shabbos involves. "Don't do this, and do this" is kind of difficult to implement when he sees people he loves and who love him not following those rules. Kashrus was the same, when we brought over our own kosher food to relatives' homes. Even though we tried to bring really delicious things, it was still odd for the children to "take this dessert, but not that dessert" because one was kosher and one was not.

This is just one of those "twists" of raising FFB kids as a baalas teshuvah. These are not problems, but do require different maneuverings along the path of parenting. Secular society is not far removed from your children. Secular issues that directly conflict with Torah values such as modesty, kashrus, and Shabbos are in close proximity to your children. Although your children's grandmas, grandpas, bubbies, zaydes, aunts, uncles, and cousins may be great role models for your children because of how loving, connecting, fun, generous, and kind they are, you'll also need to find additional role models—those who live and practice Torah values.

As an adult, you are always forging your own path, but now you have little ones for whom you are responsible—they are expected to forge a path along with you. There's no way to possibly cover the gamut of questions, concerns, and confusions that parents go through in raising children, but I'm hoping that the tools and advice I share here will at least ease the journey as you continue to forge new paths as a parent.

When I got married as a baalas teshuvah, I was uber excited to have children and build my bayis ne'eman with them. Little did I know what I didn't know—parenting would be the most amazing and challenging ride of my life. And still is.

I had very little skills as a parent considering that I was rarely around younger children growing up. I was the youngest of three girls and my siblings were much older than me—one eight years older and one ten years older. I did not have young cousins and my closest friends did not have young siblings in their homes.

What I did have was a lot of pets—cats, dogs, bunnies, turtles, and ducks. I even grew up wanting to be a wildlife veterinarian. Well, that sort of came true when I kept having boy after boy after boy after boy after boy. Whew! I got my wildlife for sure. And then I did get a girl, B"H.

When I did become a baalas teshuvah, I swapped my wildlife vet desire for a mommy desire—the desire to raise Torah frum kids to the best of my abilities. I certainly knew how to nurture since that is what I had been doing most of my life with animals, but all my other parenting skills came with lots of trial and error and research, doing the best I could with what I knew at the time.

Now I'm here to share with you what helped me and what perhaps could help you, what I wish I knew along my parenting journey, and what I use today, since I do know better. And I'm here to tell you to forgive yourself for what you have judged yourself for getting wrong. Change does not come through self-criticism. Change comes through self-kindness and self-compassion. From this healing space we can make different choices in our thoughts, speech, and actions.

When I was feeling sadness about past parenting mistakes in a particular painful situation, healer Moshe Weinbaum said something beautiful to me, "Yes, you could have done better. And yet what happened was meant to happen."

If you beat yourself up for your mistakes, you will not be a better parent. In fact, you'll feel such tension and pressure inside, that you'll want to lash out more—you'll want to hurt what is outside you because you are hurting so much inside you.

So, let go of your inner critic, lock the door and throw away the key. It won't help you. If you are critical, judgmental, and pressuring yourself on the inside, you will be that way to others too. These habits can be hard to break, but it is possible. A Jewish neshama is limitless when it comes to being able to make changes.

And with certain tools and knowledge, you can at least know that you're doing what you can to show up for your children in the best way you can.

I believe that the most difficult points in parenting can be boiled down to the following:

- **Your child or children not doing what you expect them to do.**
- **You're worn out—your battery is drained.**
- **You're putting yourself down, beating yourself up.**
- **Children have different personalities and challenges**—I like to say that some kids you can have 10 of and some kids even half

of one is so trying. And they sometimes take turns. An easy baby may in the future become a teenager who goes against your grain. Parenting a challenging child does not make you a terrible mother—it makes you a woman trying to do her best in a difficult situation.

- **Unhelpful expectations.** My definition of expectations is "false visions of the future." Keep checking your expectations for each of your children and let go of unhelpful "shoulds." This practice will release tension in the body, which helps you to be healthier as well as to create more emotional safety in your home where your children can bloom. Children (even more so than adults) are intensely aware of "expectation energy"—that inner tension that radiates outward—and will rebel or feel shamed as a result of it. I love this quote from Ruchi Koval and have it hanging by my desk:

> *I thought that setting limits and teaching values was the main objective of parenting, but I now know that it's this: making your home the most safe, fun and loving place to be. I wish I could reach a long arm back through time and hug those kids and also myself. I would say, "Oh honey. Just breathe. It's good enough. You're good enough. Love. Just love."* —Koval, 2019

A safe, fun, and loving environment is what your children need. Not judgmental, harsh, domineering, critical, and dogmatic.

This does not mean that boundaries and limits are not set. Honoring one's parents and respect for others are very important values to teach children. One of the main goals of parenting is to raise these little human beings to be responsible, accountable, and respectful adults.

- **Fighting amongst kids.**
- **Lack of shalom bayis, which means tension, lack of support and unity.** Please refer to Chapter 5: Marriage for clarity and help. Shalom bayis is the most important foundation for raising children. Not only are you and your children's father role models for your children, but when there is constant conflict between adults in the home, the children do not feel safe. And as in marriage, emotional safety is key to keeping your children's nervous systems in a state of calm, leading to greater joy, health, and laughter. Torah will feel good in that environment. And if you are a single mom, then you can do your best to have peace (or no contact, depending on the situation) with your ex-spouse and maintain emotional safety in your home.
- **Being afraid to say no or set limits.** Your job as a parent is to teach your children empathy, compassion, and menschlichkeit to the best of your ability. In your parenting role, there is no place for unhelpful patterns of people-pleasing behavior. You cannot be afraid to say "no" to your child. Raising a child is not a free-for-all. Your relationship with your child is of utmost importance, but that includes being an authority figure, a person they can trust and lean into. Children crave being given limits (though they push against them) so a healthy sense of gevurah needs to be used.

My suggestion for this chapter is to read all the parts. It is best to do something that NLP (Neuro-Linguistic Programming) refers to as "Preframing." Preframing means establishing concepts that prevent issues down the road.

As an Orthodox Jew you have halacha as a preframe to tell you what is true and what is not true. The same goes for parenting. You can have principles to live by and to keep directing yourself to as you navigate your parenting. Fixing your mind to truthful concepts can relieve tension and produce more effective results. We do not know what Hashem will throw our way (I like to say that Hashem is very creative), so preframing and having some knowledge beforehand goes a long way.

Blessings! 

Letter 1

Parenting Each Child Uniquely

Dear Miriam Racquel,

I'm having a really difficult time parenting my children—each one is so different—what works for one, doesn't work for the other. Any suggestions?

Dear Awesome Woman,

Thank you for your question. There's no complete guidebook or recipe that works for all kids and all families, but there are certain flexible techniques that can be used to help dial down the chaos and confusion, resulting in more peace and emotional safety in the home.

Homeplay Exercise

What is Your Child's Energy Profile?

I believe that understanding who your child is, as well as who you are, is super helpful for parenting them. I am what is called a Fact-Finder, and I love gathering info to understand myself and others better. I have found that understanding my type and my child's type has been life changing in terms of how I parent; it helps me to better know what I need and what my child needs.

Carol Tuttle, author of *It's Just My Nature* and *The Child Whisperer,* believes that each one of us is born with a dominant energy as well as a secondary energy. We have all four within us, but our dominant and secondary energy (or nature) shows up in our facial features, our personality and how we tick. Please see Letter #2 of Chapter 2: Self-Care for a full description of these energy types, and then read on to learn about how it applies to parenting.

Type 1: Air. These children will have an extroverted personality, with a kind of bounce and playfulness to their step. They will laugh easily. Their energy may feel more random, and they may have difficulties with being on time since they lean towards being unstructured.

Type 2: Water. These children have a very gentle, subtler energy. They will be more introverted and want to be comfortable in inter-actions with others and wear comfortable, soft clothing. They have a steadiness about them, though they may have challenges in making a decision because of suffering from self-doubt. They are full of questions.

Type 3: Fire. These children are very action-oriented and have a swift, dynamic energy about them. They are extroverted, confident, and may be considered pushy at times.

Type 4: Earth. These children have an introverted and bold energy to them. They are structured, precise, organized, and exact, wanting to be their own authority even from a young age. They may be considered stubborn or blunt at times.

In parenting, understanding the primary and secondary nature of both you and your child can make things a bit easier.

For example, if you're a primary Type 2—steady—and your daughter is a primary Type 1—random—what is the most

continued

realistic way to approach her in terms of bedtime, eating, play? If your child is a primary Type 4, which means claiming their own authority is fundamental to them, how do you get them to eat their veggies, share their toys, socialize? Tuttle has suggestions that may enlighten your interactions.

Here is a personal example: I have a child who has the profile of 3 and 4 and a child who has the profile of 2 and 1. The 3/4 child is very self-disciplined, keeps their personal things organized, and needs little encouragement to get things done that they know are important. The 2/1 child has somewhat of a random flair about them and is different with time. This child has discovered ways that work, like wearing a watch with a timer and setting an alarm. With the 2 energy, their room is a bit messier, and so keeping it organized and clean is more of a challenge. Having an allowance chart that includes tidying the room before Shabbos is one way we work together in fulfilling my expectations of a clean room and this child's nature to pile stuff up. They definitely need more incentive to keep order than the 3/4 child who thrives off of seder. As you see, it's not that I don't expect the 2/1 child to clean their room, it's just going to be done differently and I don't expect neatness to be a primary concern for them. Fun, though, is super important to this child, who has a bounce like nature and lights up all the rooms of the house with their vibrant energy.

If your child has a Type 1 nature, then they'll be more extroverted. If they're a 4, then they'll be more introverted, but extremely loyal, steadfast, and true. Moms that I have coached have worried that their child doesn't have enough friends, but if that child is a 4, then most likely they won't, and that's okay. It's just their nature. And knowing that, a parent can take comfort in the fact that even though that child is different than their bubbly, Type 1 sibling, they don't need to push or prod that introverted child into being someone they are not. Even without energy profiling, those actions don't help, but I love hearing the sigh of relief from a parent who realizes it's just their child's G-d-given nature and that they're fine as they are. Tuttle explains that children who are Type 4 are also more often picky eaters and to just let them be. This understanding can take a weight off of a caring parent's shoulders.

It's fascinating to see children's natures shine through in their personalities and it's great having that awareness so that we can stop expecting them to do things the same way as others with different energy types. With this information, your preframes will be more aligned with what natures your children have, and you can work from those contexts. Unhelpful expectations and negative labels will be put to the side and emotional safety will reign.

Homeplay Exercise

What is Your Child's Conative Learning Style?

Kathy Kolbe's father developed cognitive assessment tests, yet she herself struggled with them. She had a different learning style and went on to become a pioneer in the business and educational field in defining something called conative styles. Conative styles are instinctual—meaning a person is born with these patterns and the four different approaches refer to their "typical action pattern."

Each person has all four types of styles within them—Quick Start, Fact Finder, Implementer, and Follow Through—and yet their more dominant ones drive the way that they take action in the world. Knowing your child's (and your own) conative style will help you understand them better, therefore giving you insight into parenting them and educating them. I'm going to give you a breakdown of each style which can give you wisdom in recognizing yourself and your loved ones.

Quick-Start. With this style, change is welcome. It is almost unbearable for things to remain the same. As a Quick-Start, your child may have many ideas looping in their head and start these as projects. They may then become bored with the follow-up and leave things unfinished. Research is not as important as getting started with the project. Basically, if the Quick-Start mode is dominant for your child, they prefer diving right in. Many Quick-Starts may be mistakenly diagnosed with ADHD, when it is actually their conative style that is driving their behavior.

Fact-Finder. With this dominant style, research and "fact-finding" is most important. This child asks a lot of questions and wants to deeply understand a subject or project before beginning it. They may *never feel* that they have enough information to either start or complete something. With a Fact-Finder child, you'll have to put on your "patience" hat because they will ask a ton of questions about things. They are trying to get a deep understanding of things and this is how they feel most comfortable in the world. This is how they learn best. And at the same time, you can tell them that it is impossible for them to gather all the information that they *feel* they need. It will never feel like enough. Therefore, you can help them get comfortable with moving forward in the world without having all the answers. You can help them choose thoughts that can hijack that "need to know" and self-doubt. For example: "It's okay not knowing—Hashem isn't giving you all the information at this time. And it is safe to move forward. It is safe to take action. That is Hashem's will." Tell them to allow the questions to flow through them as if they were holding a hose. The questions are the water and there is no end to the flow of questions, but they can choose to turn off the hose and swim. The pool has enough water in it to have fun in.

Implementer. This kind of child can't keep their hands off of things —everything needs to be touched and felt. Words don't mean as much as concrete objects. My husband as a child was always tinkering with watches, cameras, and anything else he could take apart and put back together (and sometimes not!). They may grow up to be an architect, builder, engineer, or inventor.

Follow-Through. If this is your child's dominant style, they love to set up systems. Remember what I said in the self-care section? When I was on a Kolbe coach call once, a woman with a high Follow-Through number (Kathy Kolbe has a conative quiz people can take) said that she loved to organize her *dirty* silverware in the dishwasher basket. The spoons had their section, knives theirs, and forks theirs. Education systems were developed by Follow-Throughs and therefore serve this type of conative style best.

Understanding your child's Kolbe is a gift of relief. You can stop comparing your kids to other kids (even their siblings). It is a wonderful thing to understand how your loved ones operate in the world. This fulfills the Torah teaching "Chanoch Le'Naar Al Pi Darko" (Proverbs): "Educate a child according to his way." We are obligated to understand that each child is very individualistic in their learning style.

continued

The typical educational system is generally based in the Fact-Finder/Follow-Through system with no hands-on learning. This is actually quite painful for a child who has a high Implementer action style because it goes against their nature to learn through books and linear systems.

Education systems need to change to fit the budding needs of our children. The nervous system shuts down and prevents learning when it is in fight, flight, or freeze mode. This can happen in a classroom setting if the teacher is critical or if the child feels stupid and less than.

As a mom, you can help each of your children by being aware of their learning styles as well as their natures. You can be their advocate on their journey through life. I hope these answers give you some insight and enlightenment on your parenting path.

Be that person on your child's team by believing in them, picking out qualities about them that you can emphasize with, and let them know that you see and respect those qualities in them. Add a dose of healthy boundaries, and your child will bloom. Breathe along the way with love and compassion for yourself and your own brave journey as a parent.

Blessings!

Letter 2
Child's School Complaints

Dear Miriam Racquel,

My child comes home from school complaining—either about the kids in his class or the teacher or the amount of work that he has to do. I know that he just wants to vent, but it's hard to listen to. I wish that he liked school and I feel sad and worried that he doesn't. Won't his negative experience at school affect his feelings towards Yiddishkeit?

Dear Awesome Woman,

I'm so sorry that your child's experience at school is challenging. It's heartbreaking for me that children are born with a natural curiosity about life and a love of learning only to be put in schools where the atmosphere and attitude squash that love. As I mentioned in the previous letter, the educational system needs to shift to truly educate children according to their way, to lessen the academic pressure as Rabbi Shimon Russell says, and to bring joy and kindness into the classrooms. As a baalas teshuvah, I have been surprised by the lack of ahavas yisroel (not just between children, but with the adult educators as well) that takes place in Torah observant schools. I agree wholeheartedly with what the Lubavitcher Rebbe says (as quoted by Simon Jacobson, *Toward a Meaningful Life)*:

> "A child's character education should take priority over his academic education. All educational efforts are basically meaningless unless built on the solid foundation of good character."

I know that I didn't become frum because of the academics of Torah, I became frum because of the emphasis on middos and beautiful values. And good character doesn't just include the students, but the educators as well. Sigh.

In his book, *The Ami Letters,* Rabbi Shais Taub shares the following as part of his response to a mother whose child had left Yiddishkeit:

> *To sum this up, let me tell you what I once heard from a young man who had completely left Yiddishkeit as a teenager and then came back in his early twenties. He offered the following piece of advice to the yeshivas: "Treat every talmid as you would the son of a generous, non-observant philanthropist."*

And this goes for girl's education as well.

To answer your question, there is a concern that children will leave Yiddishkeit if they continually have negative experiences in school. Emotional wounding from the educational system is a significant part of the reason why so many children become KIPS—"Kids in Pain"— as expert Avi Fishoff of Twisted Parenting refers to them.

That being said, there are beautiful things you can do as a parent to help your child:

1. **The quote I start this chapter with can be a lighthouse on your journey.** Make your house a haven for them—a safe, loving, and light-hearted space.

2. **Be on your child's team—they need you as their advocate.** I found Mazlish and Faber's book, *How to Talk So Kids Will Listen and Listen So Kids Will Talk,* to be especially helpful in being able to validate my children's emotions and negative experiences, along with Peter Levine's and Maggie Kline's book, *Trauma Proofing Your Kids.* Recognizing your children's emotions is key to giving them a safe space to vent. And you can do the **ROAR! Process** from Chapter 2 with them, as well, so they can release whatever is inside in a productive way—that way they will be less likely to release their frustration and anger all over their siblings or even in class inappropriately. Even young kids can draw pictures or scribble out their frustrations and fears, rip the paper, and have tiny **ROAR!** tantrums to give release to their nervous systems. They can send that negative energy to Hashem for recycling into light when they are done. They can also just put their hands on their tummy and feel the queasiness there or on their faces if they're feeling hot.

> "When children feel understood, their loneliness and hurt diminish. When children are understood, their love for their parent is deepened. A parent's sympathy serves as emotional first aid for bruised feelings. When we genuinely acknowledge a child's plight and

voice her disappointment, she often gathers the strength to face reality.”

—Haim Ginott

3. **Strengthen your child's middos by educating them about respectful ways of speaking and acting to others.** At times, I've been appalled at the way children are allowed to just take seats and grab food at shul kiddushes, interrupt their parents whenever they feel like it by standing in between them and the person they are talking to, and not say please and thank you. Menschlichkeit is so important, and it's important to convey to children that adults are different than them and should be treated as such. Obviously, we don't want just blind subjugation to authority figures (that can be dangerous), but we do want children to know that adults are not just bigger kids—they deserve kibud just for being an adult. And that is an obligation of the parent to teach.

   Parenting is that balancing act of hearing our child's feelings as well as educating them to respect authority. My children have complained about the difficulty of learning in camp and some school classes because the chutzpah makes it impossible to even hear what the teacher is trying to share. That kind of atmosphere is unfair to our teachers and to our children.

4. **A child's nervous system shuts down to learning when it is over-taxed, overwhelmed and in fight, flight, or freeze.** Behavioral Neuroscientist, Stephen Porges shares amazing info about the Polyvagal theory and how the vagus nerve in our bodies affects how we interact in the world around us. Safety is key in the classroom (as well as at home). If a teacher or children are

bullying your child, speak to the authority who can do something about it. Sometimes it's the teacher themselves, or you may need to go to the principal. Switching classrooms may be a possibility or resource rooms.

Again, understand your child's unique learning style and remember that most schools teach favoring Fact-Finders and Follow-Throughs. Many children (and people) are Implementers and Quick Starts. Cookie-cutter style teaching is not for kids—they are more like clay, and you've got to work with the consistency and mold gently and kindly. Also, explain to your child about their nervous system—freeze because of being overwhelmed and constant criticism is a serious thing! By helping them understand their learning style, you can strengthen their abilities as well as compensate for their challenges.

Haim Ginott says so wisely to teachers and to parents: "I can be a tool of torture or an instrument of inspiration. I can humiliate or heal. In all situations, it is my response that decides whether a crisis will be escalated or de-escalated and a child humanized or dehumanized."

5. **Try to see what your child is doing right, and emphasize those middos and learning styles.** Use quality words to share with your children. These words will be the ones they repeat to themselves throughout their lives.

   Some examples:

   "I respect your kindness and generosity."

   "I respect your humor."

   "I see your inner strength."

"I see your respectfulness."

"I see your determination and will power."

"I respect your punctuality."

"I respect your honesty."

"I see your fun imagination."

Doing this on a daily basis is food and fuel for our children's spirits.

6. **Celebrate yourself as a parent for all the wins that you have throughout your day.** It's important to keep your spirit up while you navigate this journey. Process your fears around your child's Yiddishkeit by getting help from a mentor or coach/healer.

I believe that kids today are showing us the necessity to change a system that is not working—the education system as well as the community system. That is why I love the work of Avi Fishoff of Twisted Parenting and Rabbi Shimon Russel—they are trying to fix a system to save our children's souls.

> "Today's children," the Lubavitcher Rebbe said, "do not need to be overly criticized or lectured about their shortcomings. They are their own biggest critics. Instead, they need to hear more about their strengths and incredible potential."

Blessings!

Letter 3
I Always Feel Like I'm Getting My Parenting Wrong

Dear Miriam Racquel,

I always feel like I'm doing parenting wrong! I beat myself up all the time. Is there any escape from mother guilt and feeling lousy? And I know that when I feel lousy I act even worse to my family. Help!

Dear Awesome Mom,

I feel your pain! I've definitely been there myself, and that vicious circle is so unproductive and certainly doesn't get you what you really desire, which is a peaceful, loving and kind home.

So, here are a few suggestions to help you climb out of that pit and parent with more success:

1. First, feel the emotion in your body. If it's sadness or grief, it is heavy in your chest or heart, or if you feel frustrated or annoyed, notice if your jaw is clenched or if your chest is tight. Remove yourself from the scene (your kids) and have a private few moments to release that energy. Imagine G-d taking that energy and recycling it into light, but it's removed from you and your home.

2. Use the guilt to decide on positive changes. How can you right the wrong? Guilt can be used for good if it moves us forward into getting the help and information we need to make changes.

The Rebbe writes:

> "Feeling dissatisfied with oneself is a good sign, for it indicates vitality and an urge to rise and improve oneself, which is accomplished via a two-way method: withdrawal from the present state, and turning to a higher level."
>
> *—From a letter by the Rebbe, dated 16 Adar 5712*

Emotions convey messages to us. Mother guilt can actually be productive; it prompts you to take an honest look at how you are handling your parenting and to make changes.

Ask yourself:

What was my motivation for that behavior? What was the trigger that caused me to react as I did? What can I do to meet my needs in a more productive way?

If you do any of the things that you consider "bad-parenting," allow yourself to say only once: "Oh, no! I messed up again!"

And then that's it.

On many occasions, the Rebbe taught us the important message of: The past is over; don't get lost in regret. There are many letters and teachings with this theme such as this:

> "I advise you from now on to stop weighing and dwelling on things that are of no practical value, and especially the kinds of thoughts that only lead to despondency; rather place ever-increasing efforts on the performance of Torah and mitzvos …."
>
> *Letter of the Rebbe, dated Erev Shavuos, 5716*

Don't allow your inner critic to have a heyday. Don't allow it to get carried away, while you lay on the floor in a puddle of shame. Living in shame and regret for the past does not move you forward, nor does it heal the wounds of others you may have hurt with your mistakes.

Negative habits can be broken and switched up for good ones. Determined action is the key. Make apologies, change your energy and show up differently.

3. Implement positive action. As the driver of your home, take hold of the wheel and ask yourself how can you fix it?

a. Can you take a parenting course that provides support and mentorship?

b. Can you get more help? Getting a mother's helper or babysitter will give you another set of hands.

c. Are you doing enough self-care throughout your busy day? Exercise, connecting with friends, learning Torah, davening, simple creativity and even five-minute nature breaks can make a difference.

4. Do a self-compassion break, and try not to be so hard on yourself. Put a hand on your heart and say:

> *"I'm hurting" or "I'm feeling overwhelmed" or whatever the feeling is.*
>
> *"Other parents have made mistakes, too."*
>
> *"May I give myself comfort and kindness, may I give others comfort and kindness and make amends."*

5. Celebrate yourself for your amazing victories! What are you getting right? G-d sees all your efforts, and it's great if you can, too. Did you feed your kids? Did you hug them and say, "I love you"? Did you get them off to school so they could learn? Did you laugh with them and read with them? All these are wins!

Take moments throughout the day to be grateful for each and every positive thing that you did. Let those be illuminated in your mind and heart.

Since Chanukah comes from the root word chinuch, which means "education," let's take a lesson from the Chanukah candles:

1. On the first night, we light one candle, and slowly work our way up to kindling all eight. When we look at life and especially parenting, there are so many goals, steps and expectations that lie ahead of us. And yet, we would overwhelm ourselves if we actually thought that we could accomplish all those things in one step. Just like we know that each day another candle will be lit, have the belief that you will get things done—that you will follow through on your "To Do" list, your goals, your dreams, your desires. One action at a time.

2. Each menorah can look different from the other; some are silver, others are made from glass or tin in different shapes and sizes. Be sure to grow in your parenting using your own unique style. The key is to respect your way and go at the individual pace that you can handle.

3. As the amount of light from the candles continues to grow, so do you. You are never in the same place as you were before. Though at times it may feel like you have lost your footing, you have not. Keep going!

Each of us has so much light to offer ourselves, our children, and the world. Just like the glow of the Chanukah lights increases day to day, so can yours. Step by step, day by day.

Blessings! 

(Originally published at *TheJewishWoman.org*)

Letter 4

Feeling Drained and Encouraging Children's Independence

Dear Miriam Racquel,

I'm a mom of a few children and work part time. I have aches and pains all over my body and am so tired. I've been to doctors and chiropractors and no one can tell me why my body hurts so much and why I feel so drained. Do you have any ideas?

Dear Awesome Woman,

I'm so sorry that you're feeling drained with body pains. I'd love for you to read the Self-Care chapter and take action on what I mention there! My self-help journey started because I also had those aches and pains, and I was completely empty inside. It was my body's way of saying, "Stop!" And that's exactly what it sounds like to me—your body is saying, "Stop! Something isn't working here!"

> "Since my body is a cherished vessel for my soul, how can I nourish (not ignore) my body today?"
>
> —*Miriam Racquel Feldman*

Homeplay Exercise

To Work or Not to Work?

Having kids and juggling a job is a dance. Hashem did not say to women "thou shall have a career," meaning it is not your financial obligation to support your family while you're raising children. Working and career is not for all. That being said, some women will go insane staying home all day with the kids and some women will go insane trying to work, even part time. Being responsible to others, like a boss or client is a pressure that is hard to manage with the unpredictability of taking care of children. The decision to work is partial to you and your husband, your lifestyle, your location, your values, and so on. For some women, work can give them pleasure, direction, and focus so that they're better moms for it. Some couples have the wife working and the husband staying home with the kids.

"Play" with what works for your family and be open to multiple possibilities with no hard and fast rules.

And whether you are working or not, make sure that you have household help so that you're able to manage your home with as much energy and good mental health as you can. The Lubavitcher Rebbe's recommendation to women was to always get help. And yes, that costs money. But as believing Jews we know that Hashem is in charge of parnossah, sc you and your husband are a team with this. Maybe he is the one making the keli to receive from Hashem by having the job, or maybe it's both of you, but either way, the financial flow is from Hashem.

Homeplay Exercise

Encourage Children's Independence

Having kids set alarm clocks instead of waking them up, make their own lunches, and do something I call "lollipop laundry" are some of my favorites in terms of raising kids into capable, responsible adults. **When people feel competent, they are empowered.** The book *Positive Discipline* by Jane Nelson is a great read in this direction.

A suggestion: Lollipop Laundry

I came up with Lollipop Laundry because having a bunch of boys in a row, all the dark pants and socks, along with the white undershirts and underwear, looked so similar that checking each label for size took too long. This simple and easy laundry solution was very rewarding for my children as well as easy on me as a busy mom.

You can start this as young as age five. I had children of many young ages when I began this system. I gave each of them their own laundry container—the upright mesh ones take up the least space—which was designated for their dirty clothes. When it was halfway filled, they brought it downstairs to the laundry room where it got washed alone (small cycle), dried, and then dumped back in their laundry container.

I did separate out the white shirts from the individual bins and washed those together with bleach because hanging them to dry was a way of easy sorting in and of itself. In terms of the other light clothes, I was fine with washing the dark and lights together in warm water and spraying on stain remover beforehand for the undershirts. For those who want to wash whites and darks separate, just give your child two mesh laundry hampers instead of one. Have them separate the whites and darks which is again, a great skill for them to learn.

The fun part of this system was putting a healthy lollipop on the bottom of each mesh hamper. When they put their clothes away, they discovered the lolly at the bottom of the bin. For the younger ones, the discovery never got old and they kept to the rule—put the clothes away first and then you get the candy. Older than age seven, some of the kids grabbed the lolly first before putting the clothes away, but that was okay with me.

Voila! Happy children, happy mommy! The children were excited to do this task because they loved the special treat hidden among their clothes. I was happy because the clothes were put away without me doing it and without an argument, because the reward makes the task fun. There is also no mix up of clothes because the clothes are washed and dried separately.

In terms of folding, I left that up to my kids. Some liked to fold their clothes, while others just placed them unfolded in the proper drawers—I wasn't particular.

This system is a fun and lighthearted way to do laundry and is very adaptable to each household and children's individual personalities. Many of my children are grown now and can do their own laundry without the candy reward, but they still have fond memories of lollipop laundry.

Homeplay Exercise

Privacy and Mommy Time

It's very important to educate children that adults take time for their own needs; they do not have to be "on" and available 24/7. Again, do this with wisdom and discretion according to safety and your children's ages. But I've seen children interrupt their parents constantly when they're speaking with guests and even stand between the guest and parent. Allowing this is just teaching children to be disrespectful of adults. Having mommy time, or mommy and tatty time, are very important in terms of raising mentchlich children. It's called beautiful boundaries.

Privacy and mommy time: You can put scissors, a glue stick, magazines or catalogs, and a scrapbook in your bedroom or even bathroom. Lock the door to get private time. Use these spaces as pseudo "offices" to collage. Glue whatever pictures or words that cause you to feel joy, an uplift of spirit onto the paper. Spend ten-fifteen minutes doing this and you'll feel like you had "me" time to rejuvenate and head back out to the trenches. You can also keep one of those doodling coloring books in the bathroom with some markers and use your private bathroom time to, again, get some "mommy alone" time. Or just close your eyes and rest a few minutes on your bed.

Of course, if the kids are too young and can't be left unsupervised, please hire a mother's helper. You need help!

Homeplay Exercise

Kid's Creativity

What can you do to encourage your children's creativity and encourage their independence? Ask Hashem for insight—He's a partner in your child's creation. Look online for ideas, ask friends.

Here's one:
Offer the kids chocolate chips for each feather or acorn they collect. This will keep them outside and occupied for at least fifteen minutes. Be outside with them if necessary and close your eyes for a few minutes. Put your feet up. Don't try to "get things done"—minutes of rest time in between doing is so important to restore your energy.

Homeplay Exercise

Make Simple Meals

Crockpots, air fryers, egg timers, rice cookers, instant pots free you from standing over a stove. Find simple, healthy recipes, cut up fruits and vegetables, and plan ahead so the kitchen doesn't become a trap.

When my kids were young, I spent way too much time trying to make very healthy, macrobiotic meals. I look back now and cringe. I got burnt out and it wasn't fair to my children. Children need a happy mom, not a perfect one. What will make you happier?

I hope that I've given you some ideas to free up some of your time, take the load of responsibility off your shoulders and put some of it onto your children. This encourages independence and respect with your children. You're also teaching them empathy instead of self-centeredness.

Blessings!

Letter 5

Traveling with Kids and Shalom Bayis

Dear Miriam Racquel,

Every time my husband and I take a trip with the kids, we wind up fighting. I want a vacation and so does my husband, but obviously the kids need to be taken care of, meals need to be cooked, and plans need to be made for us all to have a good time. I don't want everything to fall on me and sometimes it doesn't seem worth going anywhere.

Dear Awesome Woman,

I hear you! Going away on vacation with kids is a little bit like an oxymoron, a total contradiction in terms.

Homeplay Exercise

What Do You Desire?

To put this simply, it is so important for you to be practical and realistic when it comes to travel plans and vacations. If you've read the Marriage chapter then you know how important it is for a woman to tap into her desires. What kind of vacation do you desire? Take the time to ask yourself that.

continued

If you really want time alone with your husband, can someone watch the kids while you go away? My husband and I were able to do this at times when we had the help of relatives, friends, and babysitters, some who stayed overnight. It can be a short trip within driving distance or a longer one if you have that luxury. This time invested in your marriage is worth every penny and bit of effort to make it happen. It's like putting a gold coin in your marriage bank account and you'll just be able to enjoy being in each other's company.

If you desire to travel with your children, then how can you make it as simple and easy as possible? This kind of vacation requires a few meetings with your husband to get expectations set on how you visualize the vacation for yourselves. Discuss money and spending, discuss what the days can look like, who will take care of which kids on the plane to make the flight as easy as possible, what activities you'd like to do and how to go about the food situation, since traveling kosher takes extra care and thought. Share how you'd like the mornings and bedtime to go. Also discuss giving each other time for self-care. All these nitty-gritties are important. Traveling together in peace and care is the goal. Know your desires and tell your husband what you'd like, and what you may be afraid of.

As your children grow, travel expectations will change. Be realistic and practical. Traveling with younger kids was much different for my husband and I than traveling with teenagers. With teens, the nights are late for them, and in the mornings they tend to sleep in. My husband and I would get up early, go to watch sunrises at the beaches, take walks, and do our davening and writing long before the kids would wake up.

Family activities started later in the afternoon and having those realistic expectations made a huge difference in our travels.

I hope that sharing these tips will provide you with the help you need in creating vacations that are peaceful, fun, and rejuvenating for you and your entire family. Amen!

Blessings! 

Letter 6
Will My Son Ever Remember to Do His Negel Vasser?

Dear Miriam Racquel,

My son knows to do negel vasser and yet, every single morning he forgets. I ask him, "Did you do negel vasser this morning?" and he sheepishly grins and shakes his head. Or after he leaves for school and I'm cleaning up the house, I notice a full negel vasser schussel by his bed. It's right there by his feet when he gets out of bed. How can he forget every morning? I'm so frustrated and annoyed. Shouldn't he know better by now? I've explained to him the importance of getting the tumah of sleep off his hands to start his day—that he shouldn't touch anything until it's done. Why is he not doing it? How can I get him to do it?

Dear Awesome Woman,

I hear how frustrated you are. And this frustration can apply to any part of parenting where we've shared information a dozen times and believe that our kids should know and act on what we've given over.

Here are a few options to dial down your supercharged thoughts and nervous system around this situation:

1. Be careful to stay away from "future tripping," which refers to awfulizing the future. It's like taking a trip with your mind and holding a really negative vision for your child, G-d forbid. This is not productive nor kind nor realistic. Just because your son isn't doing negel vasser does not mean he is irresponsible, rebellious, full of tumah, and will leave Yiddishkeit in the future. We don't know what Hashem has in store for your son. As I mentioned previously, connection and relationship are everything with parenting. You can join up with your son and just do it with him, you can reward him with a chocolate chip (if he's young) when he doesn't do it, you can just prod gently by saying (even whispering in his ear), "Negel vasser," with no judgment.

2. Do the ROAR! Process. Allow yourself to be frustrated and release. No harm done when it's in private and diffuses strong emotions.

3. Be kind. Who knows why he is not doing it, but kindness leads to trust and relationship and this is the most important feature of parenting and one that you have the most control over.

4. Trust that in yeshiva dorming, all the boys will be doing negel vasser and your son will too!

5. Especially if you are a baalas teshuvah, you were taught that negel vasser, as well as other religious practices, is a big deal. "Oh my gosh! Tumah on the hands!" G-d has broad shoulders and can deal with some tumah on a child's hands. **What Hashem may be testing *you* with, though, is "connection before correction."** Be careful when using gevurah with your child and focus on creating an emotionally safe home.

6. You could try using a reward system or chart. Many creative ideas for making charts and types of rewards can be found in parenting books and online.

7. Change your expectations and for sure turn every "should" into a "could." Write down this thought: "He *should* do negel vasser." Feel the internal tension and energy inside you with that. Perhaps your chest is tight and your jaw is clenched with this thought. Now, in contrast, write down this thought: "He *could* do negel vasser... if he remembered, if there was a reward, if it was important to him, if G-d wants me to help him, etc." Notice what this thought feels like in your body.

8. Just remind him by saying the word, "Negel vasser" (with a loving, caring smile on your face). No added languaging needed.

I hope my tips help you feel less frustrated! These options can be used anytime that you are "shoulding" something in parenting, as well as when you're bewildered by the fact that you've said something at least a dozen times, and yet nothing feels like it's changed. What you're doing is shifting the energy around the situation and bringing a greater potential for peace, love, and connection, as well as effectiveness in your interaction with your child.

Blessings!

Letter 7
Teens & KIPS

Dear Miriam Racquel,

My teenage son is having a very difficult time. He was such an "on-the-path" kid—yiras shomayim, loved G-d and Torah. And then he went away to yeshiva and changed. He is depressed, anxious, and rejecting Yiddishkeit. My husband and I are trying to set boundaries with him—no secular music, he has to wear his tzitzis, and get up for morning minyan—but to no avail. Now he is very angry with us and things are getting worse. He also has younger siblings and I'm afraid that they'll be influenced in a negative way. I'm so scared.

Dear Awesome Woman,

I'm so sorry that you are going through this. And I'm so sorry that your son had experiences in Yiddishkeit that have turned him off to the beautiful Torah derech that you and your husband had laid out for him. So many children are suffering nowadays. I love that parenting expert, Avi Fishoff of Twisted Parenting, calls these children KIPS— "Kids in Pain" rather than "off the derech." This helps give us the proper perspective on our children and can literally save lives.

Our children choosing not to follow in the path of Yiddishkeit, especially if one is a baalas teshuvah and have been mesiras nefesh for Torah, is a huge heartbreak. The pain is so deep. And so is our child's.

Avi Fishoff says that our children actually want to do the Torah and mitzvot that they were raised with. However, they are in so much pain it feels to them that not only did Hashem trigger their wounding (if they got wounded by a religious person), but that Hashem doesn't answer them when they call out for help. They feel so hurt by Hashem. Avi Fishoff emphasizes that KIPS are sensitive, sweet Yiddishe souls who have prayed every day for Hashem to help them keep their faith and heal their pain, and yet don't feel that Hashem answers them. I cry every time I think of this.

I will share with you some somatic wellness tips for staying sane through this situation, as well as some advice for keeping your home a loving, peaceful, nurturing, and emotionally safe place for you and your family.

First the Don'ts! This is an emergency situation and we don't want your very precious child to slide further downhill.

The Don'ts

1. Don't do the boundary thing or go down the tough-love, gevurah path. Your child is in pain and hurting! The hard boundaries will only push them further away. This was the biggest shocker for me when I heard this. When a child is acting in a certain way, I thought tough love and boundaries were important, **but in the situation that you're describing, the key is to drop all expectations, including boundaries.** You're not going to try getting them back on the path through gevurah. Watch Avi Fishoff's "Twisted Parenting" videos and see why. The actions you may take will depend on the severity of what you are dealing with; however, the mindset of parenting a Kid in Pain is the key to maintaining a relationship with your child. Supporting this relationship will help your child's wounds heal and will help you keep them safe as they experiment with going outside of some of the values that you raised them with.

2. Don't shame them. Shame clips wings. We may not even realize we're shaming our children, but harsh judgment and even normal expectations result in shaming the struggling child—the KIP. And that is probably how they got their wings clipped in the first place.

Now the Do's!

The Dos

1. Do release the unhealthy belief that you are your child's religious policewoman. If your child is a teenager, then know that you are not their religious police woman anymore. You've done your job. They know the Torah rules—they've lived with them for fifteen-plus years. If they're not doing it, you being their police woman won't help.

The message that is so beneficial to a KIP is: "We love you and we trust you." With this loving energy in the home towards the KIP, the KIP can feel accepted and safe and everyone in the family can relax. "Zero expectations" of the KIP is key. This concept can be hard to digest because it is so unfamiliar; however, we are fortunate in our generation to have someone like Avi Fishoff dedicating his life to our children and educating us on how to face the challenge of a child struggling with the Torah path.

2. Do grieve—your somatic system welcomes grief when necessary. When your dreams of your child being a certain way are broken, there will be tears and pain. For many of us, grief sits around the heart and chest area. Put a loving, gentle hand on that area of your body and bend forward (like a curling over, protective position). Bring into your imagination a Tzaddik, a Tzedakes or even a compassionate angel. Feel that love and comfort. You may even hear a message. Do this as often as needed.

3. Do the ROAR! Process when triggered—which happens less and less when you've changed your mindset to not think of yourself as your child's religious policewoman. Definitely do the **ROAR! Process** if you have anger towards the yeshiva or educational system that triggered their downward spiral and towards whoever hurt them. Do the **ROAR! Process** if you have anger coming up towards your child pushing boundaries or disappointing you. It's okay to feel what you are feeling! You are human and Hashem knows that. Keep giving that energy to Hashem to recycle into love. Emotions and trauma are layered, so this process can be repeated as often as you need to use it.

4. Do change your mindset. We hold limiting beliefs in our mind. The Lubavitcher Rebbe said a word about leaving mitzrayim—*metzar*—which means limiting. It is for us to do our own yetzias mitzrayim every day by moving out of limiting mindsets and deepening our faith in Hashem. We do this by releasing the snake venom of the yetzer hara lies— those about ourselves and others as well as our situations. Hire a coach or get a mentor—this is not a path to walk alone. We all have blind spots and need the hands of others to hold when in crisis.

5. Do praise your child often (as well as your other children) with quality words. This tip comes from Avi Fishoff and parenting coach Devorah Weiss. You can either say these in person or text your child loving, kind, and supportive messages. Find what you admire in them—emphasize their positive qualities. They will repeat these encouraging and kind words to themselves internally, and that will help them build their resiliency as well as trust in themselves as a smart, kind, reliable, trustworthy, wise, responsible person—all great qualities that build the kind of adult you'd like them to be.

Here are some examples:

"I see your determination and perseverance."

"I admire your courage."

"I respect the way that you handled that situation. That shows sensitivity and wisdom."

"I woke up with such pride in you! You've got such a good head on your shoulders. I trust your decision-making abilities and I trust you as a person. I admire your honesty. And I admire the respect you have towards others. I see your determination and perseverance in finding your own voice and values. I see your courage as you walk your very own unique path!"

6. Do remove pressure in any area that you can. Imagine that your child had a broken leg, chas v'shalom. You wouldn't expect them to walk, run, or do anything physically strenuous. It's a similar situation here. Something is feeling broken inside this child. You are on the healing and mending path with them. What may be doable for a "normal" situation (work, school, etc.) may not be doable for them now. If it helps them by giving them structure, or meaning, then by all means encourage that. But above all, do what benefits the child's healing.

7. Do know that your other children will appreciate the kindness that you're showing your KIP. Though you are afraid that your other children will be influenced negatively by being around the KIP sibling's behavior, there's a greater lesson that your children are learning and that is ahavas yisroel. Sure, maybe it's easy to have ahavas yisroel for non-observant Jews who are living outside our homes, but what happens if they live inside your home? Do you kick them out and harshly judge them? Or do you use deep compassion, kindness, and understanding for the Yid in your household? We've all read stories about the level of ahavas yisroel that true Tzaddikim have for all Yidden. Now it's time to practice that, and your other children will not only learn from you and embrace that sibling, but it will make them feel safe that your love has no bounds and will always include them.

8. Do get good somatic healing and/or therapeutic help for yourself. Just like you invest in yourself to care for your body by having a gym pass, invest in your mental and emotional care by having a good therapist, somatic healer, and/or coach. Friends are great, but they can't provide your body and emotions with all the care that you'll need during such a stressful time. I favor integrative approaches that treat the body as well as the mind. Trauma accumulates in the body from difficult situations. The fight or flight responses can be triggered and freeze, dissociation, and numbness are also very real. When you work with the body as well as the mind, you're allowing energy to flow. This promotes healing on a cellular level, as well as neural pathway shifts for the mind.

9. Do get professional guidance from someone specifically in the field of KIP parenting. Avi Fishoff is the expert. There is also the Neshamos Organization run by the very kind and compassionate

Meir New. Rabbi Shimon Russell and his wife are good resources. A mentor or coach is also important—just make sure that they are versed in the approach you've decided upon for your child. If you feel that the "Twisted Parenting" approach is best, then don't pick someone who is unfamiliar with it and tells you to reinforce strict boundaries and make contracts with your child. You'll just be getting conflicting advice which will hurt you and drain your energy. You can't afford that at this time.

10. Do get good support for your child if they request it. Once you're doing the Twisted Parenting, loving-kindness methods, your child may not need outside help. You become their best friend (they are not *your* best friend, but you can be theirs) and trusted confidant because they feel so safe, soothed (a term from Shimon Russell), and loved by you. If they request outside help, it can take trial and error to find a therapist (and sometimes psychiatrist if needed) who is a good fit for your child. Find one that is versed in Twisted Parenting and one they feel safe with and understood by. Vulnerability is key with therapy, coaching, and healing. If your child does not feel safe, their nervous system will not be regulated in order for their mind and body to heal. That's probably how your child got wounded in the first place—by a teacher or someone with a yarmulke or sheitel who criticized or who was too harsh on them. Their nervous system went into freeze mode like a deer in the headlights—especially if they are a sensitive child—and when and if it unfreezes, they just want to take flight (leave Yiddishkeit) or fight (rebel). That's the way the body works. So, in looking for a therapist, find one that your child wants to go to. Pets can also be a great support. If your child requests one, consider it. Though they are an expense and another living being to care for, your child may feel very soothed by their presence.

11. Do make a "Never take anything for granted" board. I have a whiteboard with different colored dry erase markers. In the mornings, I choose a color and write "Never take anything for granted" on the top of the board. Then I jot down a few things that come to mind when I say this phrase. When you say this phrase, you realize the blessings you have, the things that *are going right*, the things that you may take for granted but shouldn't, like the physical abilities you have. Can you see? Hear? Move? Breathe? Some people can't, so don't take what you can do for granted in any area of life—including what you feel blessed by with your children. This ups your emotional and energetic vibration. It feels great in your body, in your mind, and in your soul!

This does not mean that we ignore real emotions that come up for us—for this we have the **ROAR! Process** or just plain feeling the physical sensation in the body. That's being honest. But it is just as honest recognizing that we have wonderful blessings that Hashem is giving to us all the time. Let's take time to notice those as well!

As Jews, we live in a dichotomy. We know that Hashem is good and brings only good to us, yet it doesn't always feel good. We know that there are challenges as well as blessings. We are souls in bodies and we are bringing the world to complete geulah, the ultimate fixing. We are creating a dwelling place for Hashem here on this very physical planet. It was for this purpose that we were created. Let's fulfill our purpose! That includes integrating our humanness—imperfections and all—with our holy souls and recognizing our blessings and Hashem's goodness to us.

A final note on this:

We think that Hashem wants us to raise a child in the way of Torah and Mitzvot. Especially for a baalas teshuvah, my goodness, didn't we turn our worlds upside down to do so? To become more observant of Judaism is a huge transition and transformation!

If Hashem triggers our child with a painful situation, G-d forbid, and our child is rejecting Torah because of experiencing wounding from someone religious (and sometimes that includes us) it is difficult. It is painful that Hashem seems to have other plans for our child than being frum. Part of our Torah heritage is the belief that our job is to bring light to the world through Torah and mitzvos. Part of that belief is to pass on this incredible knowledge and holiness to our children. If we have a child who rejects this heritage for whatever reason, we may feel that we have failed. We thought there was a linear path of Torah observance and bringing light to a dark world, but with a child who is a KIP, there is a different light to bring to the darkness of the world, and you and your child's path together will illuminate that. Deep compassion, self-care, prayers, and finding gratitude where you can are what you need as you walk this journey. I wish you only success and brachas for your family.

Geulah now!

Blessings!

Letter 8

PANDAS

Dear Miriam Racquel,

My thirteen-year-old son is acting very odd. He used to not have any trouble going to school, sometimes even liking it. Now he just wants to stay home. He claims that others are looking at him weird. He sounds paranoid, but that was never an issue before in his life. He also has become incredibly anxious and makes strange movements, almost like tics. In addition, he developed an aversion to certain foods that he used to like. I brought him to his pediatrician and the doctor thinks that he may be developing an anxiety disorder and that we should start with therapy before trying meds. Help! I'm so frightened over his changes and I just don't understand where this sudden change of behavior is coming from.

Dear Awesome Woman,

I'm so sorry that your son is not well and I understand your intense fear. Though I am not a doctor, I'd like to bring to your attention a condition called PANDAS—**P**ediatric **A**utoimmune **N**europsychiatric **D**isorders **A**ssociated with **S**trep. This is an autoimmune encephalitis (inflammation of the brain). It is basically undetected strep antibodies in the blood that affect the brain. Many doctors don't know of this disease and neither do parents, but it is essential that if a child or teenager presents with tics, OCD, depression, anxiety, strange moods, aggression, hallucinations, eating disorders, paranoia, or clinginess to get a strep-antibody blood test to check for it. Regular therapy and medicines for anxiety, OCD, or other neurological disorders will not treat this autoimmune disorder—parents and children may suffer for years. An early detection is extremely important because the younger the patient, the more successful the recovery.

There are some experts and doctors who treat this illness—Dr. Susan Schulman, a frum doctor in Brooklyn, for example. In her book, *Understanding Your Child's Health,* she includes a chapter to make parents aware of this condition. She has a protocol with important information that may be obtained from her office. Since your pediatrician may not have heard of PANDAS or even worse, may not believe in it (yes, there are fools out there even in the medical field), find a doctor who will at least do the blood test. But again, it should be one of the first things any pediatrician tests for when these symptoms show up. The child may not have even had a sore throat or suffered from detected strep, but for some children the strep antibodies cross the blood-brain barrier and it makes them feel mentally off-balance. Adults may have it as well.

Antibiotics, tonsillectomy, and adenoid surgery, homeopathy (on Facebook, see Homeopathy for PANS & PANDAS), IVIGs, supplements, and diet (specifically Dr. Eric Bakker's naturopathic protocol), along with other treatments may be used to treat this horrific disease. Wendy Nawara (*https://wendynawara.com/*) is an angel in getting treatment to those diagnosed with PANDAS. A trained social worker, board certified patient advocate and expert PANDAS consultant, she had her own journey through this illness when three of her children had it. She, along with another mom, pushed legislature through in Illinois for insurance to cover the cost of treatment, and she works tirelessly in the field of PANDAS to assist parents through this hell. She knows of all the doctors and treatments available worldwide. She has personally been a saving grace for my soul and sanity on this journey, and I am grateful that Hashem sent her to me.

It is also smart to test (do the Western blot assay) for Lyme disease which can cause havoc in the body as well as psychological and psychiatric symptoms.

I share the story of my son's journey with PANDAS and Lyme disease on a Neshamos podcast. Perhaps if this is your son's journey, it will be a support for you. May Hashem heal.

Blessings! 

Letter 9
Miscarriages

Dear Miriam Racquel,

My heart is breaking. I've been fortunate enough to have a wonderful child so I don't mean to complain, but I've had two miscarriages this past year, and I'm in despair of having more children. The doctors haven't found anything wrong—one was a blighted ovum and the other, they're not really sure why it happened. But they are encouraging me to try again.

Still, the unknown feels so scary. I'm trying to trust G-d and tap into my faith, but every time I see a pregnant woman, I feel happy for her and yet sad for me. What should I do? How can I recover, and not stay stuck in my disappointment and grief?

Dear Awesome Woman,

I'm so sorry for your loss. I understand how painful that can be; I suffered four miscarriages. Like you, I was grateful to have what I had, and I also found the pain, grief and disappointment very intense.

Now that time has passed, I am older, hopefully a bit wiser, and have developed tools for processing emotions. Here are some suggestions that would have given comfort to my grieving self back then. I hope they will help you as well.

1. Give yourself compassion. Although we know that everything comes from a loving G-d and happens for a reason, Judaism has a healthy foundation of compassion as well.

I want to share with you a beautiful, telling story that illustrates this:

When Rabbi Sholom DovBer Schneersohn, the fifth Chabad Rebbe, was 5 years old, he played a game with his older brother, Zalman Aharon. The game was called "Rebbe and Chassid." Zalman Aharon sat in a chair with a hat, pretending to be a Rebbe, and Sholom DovBer sat opposite him, playing the chassid. Sholom DovBer brought up the subject of a mistake he had made and asked for a rectification (a *tikkun*). Zalman Aharon swiftly responded with advice: "Begin praying with a *siddur* (a prayer book), not by heart. This is your *tikkun*."

"You are not acting like a real Rebbe," Sholom DovBer retorted.

Puzzled, Zalman Aharon asked, "Why? I gave you good advice."

Already very wise at the tender age of 5, Sholom DovBer answered:

> "A Rebbe first lets out a sigh of commiseration and only then he gives advice. You didn't show me any compassion—and therefore, you are not a Rebbe, and your advice is useless."

What can we learn from this story? Compassion is key to any advice you may receive, including the advice you may try to give yourself—to move on, and not feel sad or disappointed. It's perfectly OK to make space for the emotions of grief, disappointment and sadness from your losses. And it's OK to comfort yourself as someone else would comfort you.

Just like you would nurse a bruised or broken leg, you can nurse a \ hurting heart. Take a few moments when your sadness feels intense and your mind wanders to your disappointment and to validate that you're hurting. Even saying the words "I'm hurting" (in the compassionate tone a friend may use to say, "I'm sorry that you're hurting") will help that physical sensation of sadness move on. This tiny act of self-compassion will help you move on and become a vessel for new life instead of remaining stuck ruminating in the pain of loss.

2. Review the laws of Family Purity, whether in a class or a one-on-one setting. The Rebbe emphasized the importance of this review, particularly when a couple needs blessings in the area of fertility. Many miracles occur through Divine channels, and you definitely want to be on the receiving end, welcoming those with open arms.

3. Speak to a compassionate rebbetzin or mentor so your mind can be in a state of kindness to yourself. Our minds can run afoul and ruminate with so many thoughts that are hurtful to us. The Rebbe taught us that a Jew is never stuck, so we don't want to feel stuck in a grieving cycle of despair or depression, G-d forbid. When you open up to a wise mentor, your mind will be more at ease. She can help you have more nourishing thoughts, making way for the possibility of more births.

4. Understand that there was a purpose to these miscarriages, though the "why" remains a mystery. Even when there is pain, our faith encourages us to know that there is a purpose to everything. To help settle this knowledge into your being, say these words to yourself in a soothing tone: "I'm so sorry for what has happened to you. I know how much you would have loved to have carried these pregnancies to completion and be holding healthy babies in your arms. You're such a nurturing and compassionate being, and you love to love and give. I don't know why the opposite has happened or what G-d's reasons are. What I do know is that it is important for you to give yourself love and care during this time."

5. Practice gratitude whenever possible, by never taking anything for granted. Jot down your blessings, and G-d willing, He will grant you many more.

All these proactive yet compassionate steps will be helpful. You are opening up Divine spiritual channels, as well physical, emotional and mental ones. You are shining rays of light upon the brokenness of your spirit.

Blessings!

(Originally published at *TheJewishWoman.org*)

Letter 10
Shidduchim

Dear Miriam Racquel,

My daughter is ready to date. I'm not really sure where to begin and the task seems so overwhelming! Though I'm excited, it does feel like a huge to-do on my already full to-do list. The thought of spending hours on the phone calling shadchanim and then researching the guys feels so daunting. Help! Any suggestions to make the process easier?

Dear Awesome Woman,

I hear you! The process of shidduchim is definitely something to navigate, and we have to try our best not to get overwhelmed. We don't want to overtax our bodies and compromise our health in trying to find our child's bashert. Your body may be revved up for "getting the task done," but that is most likely coming from your mind, which can be a slave driver in trying to make things happen. Looking for a shidduch for your child can just be like the process you want them on, which is slow and steady, using their body as well as their mind to navigate this territory. Being in touch with your intuition, your body's wisdom, and your wise mind is a way to stay safe and grounded.

Here are some additional tips for navigating this process:

- Do you have any mentors who already have children married and have gone through the process to sit with and ask questions? My husband and I did this and the advice was phenomenal.

- Do just one or two things in the direction of shidduchim a day so you don't get overwhelmed. Remember, your mind might be saying, "I have to get this done," or "I should do more!" but that is most likely your yetzer hara. Instead, try saying this to yourself: "I choose to do two things today in moving forward for my daughter's shidduch—I'll call two shadchanim." Or "I choose to call two references on the resume I was given." Using the word "choose" instead of "have to" or "should" dials down tension in the body. Take a few moments to see what each word feels like in your body. You'll know that you're on the right track when you can breathe and it feels more expansive, more exciting, rather than overwhelming and tense.

- Decide what tasks you'd like your husband to do on this journey and then ask him. Sometimes it was my husband who made the calls and sometimes it was me. We acted like a team, which is the best way to go about parenting.

- Please read and have your daughter read Chapter 5: Dating.

- Make wedding collages (or a few!) with feel-good words and pictures (chuppahs, etc.). Where your attention goes, your energy flows. And we want our energy to be focused on abundance, blessings, and goodwill as we navigate the shadchanim, the mazal process, and your daughter finding a kind bashert in good timing.

- Keep steady on the path practicing emunah and faith, knowing that Hashem has your daughter's soulmate picked out for her —he is already in the world and present. The effort is focused on finding him.

Blessings!

Letter 11

Being a Great Mother-in-Law

Dear Miriam Racquel,

My oldest is getting married! I'm very excited and at the same time, very nervous. I've heard all kinds of stories, some good and some scary, about becoming a mother-in-law. I'd like to hear some suggestions from a professional. What kind of advice do you have that will help me be a great mother-in-law?

Dear Awesome Woman,

First of all, mazel tov to you! That's such beautiful news, and what a milestone it is. You're asking a great question. I was fortunate to have wise people share some very smart advice with me when a child of mine got married, and I hope it will help you too:

- It's really true what they say about shutting your mouth and opening up your wallet. Be as generous with your money as possible in helping the new couple set up a home and life for themselves. At the same time, recognize that they have their own way of doing things. They are creating a bayis ne'eman with their own style, flair, and derech. Give them space and yet, let them know that you are there for them.

- Know that the couple is on their own journey and will have challenges like we all have. Try your best to be a compassionate presence in their lives and not an overbearing one with tons of "shoulds." You can always be a sounding board and help where you can. If they ask for advice, for sure give it, though sometimes advice is not appreciated unless you have that kind of relationship with your child.

- Be grateful and appreciative of this new addition to your family. Look for the good in him or her! Jot down the sentence "Never take anything for granted," and then see the wisdom and gratitude that flows from that. Mentioning some of these appreciations and positive things out loud is a great idea.

- If strong emotions come up around anything, do the Shadow Work Homeplay Exercise (from Chapter 6—shadow work is not just about your spouse—you can do this exercise about a judgment you have on anyone) and the **ROAR! Process** to release tension. And by all means get help if you need to—a mentor or coach can be very supportive on your journey to have a beautiful relationship with new family members. You want your child's spouse to feel loved, appreciated, and cared for just like I'm sure you did when you married and entered into your husband's family.

Celebrate that your child has entered a new and exciting stage of life where they have moved from your nest and are creating their own.

Blessings! 

Parnossah, Work, and Career

Every person has a preference
for a particular occupation
or business over any other,
as G-d has implanted within his nature
love and affection for it.

—Rabbeinu Bachya ibn Pekuda

Letter 1

Job Burnout and What to Do About It

Dear Miriam Racquel,

I really dislike my job and find it very draining. I come home exhausted and in a bad mood every day. I feel like I can't leave because my husband and I need the money. I'd love to find something else to do, but I'm not sure I could make the same salary. What should I do?

Dear Awesome Woman,

I'm so sorry to hear that you dislike your job so much. And being drained is not a recipe for good health—not for our physical, spiritual, emotional or relationship health! Take to heart these words from the wise Torah sage, Rabbeinu Bachya ibn Pekuda:

> *Every person has a preference for a particular occupation or business over any other, as G-d has implanted within his nature love and affection for it. The same is the case with other living creatures. He has implanted within the cat the instinct to catch mice, within the hawk the instinct to hunt the birds that are fit for it; similarly, you will find among human beings that different personalities and physiques are predisposed toward certain trades and occupations. Whoever discovers within his personality*

and nature an attraction to a particular trade, and his body is fit for it and can endure its difficulty, should pursue it and make it his means of earning a livelihood, accepting its sweetness and its bitterness. Let him not be discouraged if his income is denied him on occasion; rather, let him trust in G-d, that He will provide him with his livelihood all his life.

As you can see, G-d does not want us to be miserable earning an income. In particular, G-d has instilled in us, as our Creator, a certain attraction to a particular trade. Each job may have parts that we don't enjoy—and accepting the sweetness and bitterness is part of our journey—however, having an affinity for the profession you're in is extremely important.

Being in a job that we don't enjoy affects our nervous system, and that, in turn, affects our health. It is a mitzvah to take care of our bodies because the body is a vessel for our soul. A sick and drained body is a poor vessel for the soul.

Judaism teaches that it is important to work to earn money, but also teaches that G-d is the true source of our income. If G-d is the one telling us to take care of our health and have a job that is attractive to our personality and nature, who are we to argue?

To create a new reality for yourself where you have a job that you love and one that energizes you rather than drains you, here are a few steps you can take:

Notice What Lights You Up

What situations, people and activities uplift your spirit, and fill you with a sense of energy and purpose? What kind of jobs do you feel attracted to? Right now, we're not taking the big step of deciding what new profession or job to move into. With this "noticing," you're taking little steps to just explore what affects your body in a positive way. What learning style do you have? Are you an extrovert or an introvert? Tap into your body's wisdom by becoming aware over the next few weeks of what brings a sense of expansion and lightness as opposed to what brings heaviness and dread.

1. **Jot this awareness down in a journal.**

2. **What tiny steps can you take to explore the possibility of a new opportunity?** Are there people to reach out to? Is part time an option? What is the reality of working in that position? Perhaps throw out some questions on a group chat. Women are usually willing to give their opinions, and you may get some great information this way.

3. **Have a heart-to-heart with your husband by starting with your desire:** "I'd love to find a new job. I can't keep working at one that depletes my energy and one that I dislike so much. I'm exploring first by gathering information and seeing what opportunities there are in positions that may be healthier for me. And I'm aware of the money concern so I will do my best in keeping that in mind, also knowing that G-d is involved in this process."

4. **All big steps start with little ones.** Have patience, trust in G-d (eyes wide open for synchronicities and possibilities) and kindness towards yourself.

Put Your Trust in G-d

Everything starts from within and radiates outward. Saying these affirmations (even if you don't feel that they are true at the moment) will help you create positive movement in the direction you'd like to go, which is to find a new job that you enjoy: "G-d is the One who provides. G-d gives me a job I love."

Money is given to us directly from G-d, just like manna was given directly to the Jews in the desert after they escaped Egypt. Our sustenance comes from Above and is connected to our faith. In fact, the Lubavitcher Rebbe recommends learning Shaar Habitachon ("Gate of Trust") from Rabbeinu Bachya ibn Pekuda in order to solidify our faith, which in turn opens the channels for our livelihood.

The Jews in the desert had to trust that G-d would provide for them every day. Leftover manna had to be discarded, or it would become wormy. And yet, they also had to go out of their tents to collect it; they had to put in some effort. What a balancing act—taking action yet having faith that G-d will provide! G-d expects us to walk this spiritual tightrope. In fact, for those who believed, their portion would fall right by their tents, while those who didn't have such faith had to travel farther to collect theirs.

Words have a powerful effect on our emotions; they can even create our emotions. As you walk this tightrope, play in your head the mantra of empowering words. You will feel that effect in your body, and it will help you feel strong and brave as you explore new territory.

Recognize That Challenges Are Tests to Make us Stronger

In a letter to someone having financial challenges, the Rebbe explains:

> *When G-d said to Abraham lech lecha, ordering him to leave his land, his birthplace and father's house, it was very difficult for him to do so. Even to separate himself from one of the three attachments was difficult, not to mention all three together! Then Abraham was told to go to an unknown (to him) land (Canaan,*

> *later to become the Land of Israel), where, he was promised, he would become great, and a source of blessing for all. Yet, no sooner did he arrive there, a famine broke out with such severity that he had to leave at once and go to Egypt, which undoubtedly was with G-d's approval. Under these circumstances, one might have expected that Abraham could very seriously question Divine Providence, which seemed so inconsistent and contradictory. All the more so in view of what is written in Pirkei d'Rabbi Elazar that the famine affected only the land of Canaan and did not extend to any other land, which was clearly intended to test him. Yet not only did Abraham not complain, he did everything with joy and gladness of heart. Of course, it all turned out only as a test of his bitachon ('trust') in G-d, for soon afterward, he was richly rewarded, and he returned to Canaan richly laden with cattle, silver and gold, as the Torah tells us. In reference to this experience of Abraham, the Midrash states that everything experienced by Abraham also happened to his children.*

Look how confusing it must have been for Abraham! And yet, it was only a test of Abraham's trust in G-d, and he soon returned back with riches.

Tests don't make sense to us because there is a spiritual realm from which these tests emerge, a world completely beyond the rational. We do, however, have the Torah's wisdom to guide us.

The test in earning money is to make us stronger—to test our faith. When we earn money or get a stable paycheck every week, do we recognize that it is truly G-d giving us that income? Or do we believe that it is our employee, a client or just our own efforts providing for us? It can certainly look so.

Right now, you are being tested. You have a job that earns you a good income and yet your body is affected. You are drained. How will you move forward? Can you rise to the challenge of leaning into G-d by saying, "G-d, I know you provide my family with money. I am miserable in the job I have now and would like to make a change. I am scared. Please guide me to a new job that I love—one that is healthier for me and one that earns a good income at the same time. Thank you." Trust and faith, plus action, is a powerful formula.

I wish you much success in finding a job that fills you with energy. These steps of tapping into your creative potential and knowing that the same G-d who provides the finances is the same G-d desiring you to do something you love with the personality and talents you have will give you the strength to forge a new path.

Blessings!

(Originally published at *TheJewishWoman.org*)

Chovot Halevavot (*The Gate of Trust*), ch. 3.

Letter 2

Unpleasant Co-Workers

Dear Miriam Racquel,

I love my job, but some of my co-workers are really catty and unpleasant to work with. How can I stay at my job but not get so affected by the negative energy of the environment?

Dear Awesome Woman,

Ooh—that's tough. I suggest four approaches that can help you with this one:

1. **Use the BRAKES Method** from Chapter 4 which will help bring wise discernment in interactions with these co-workers. See them for how they're choosing to show up.

2. **When you're triggered, use the ROAR! Process** in Chapter 2 to get emotional flow going in your body. You don't want energy to get stuck in your system.

3. **After doing the ROAR! Process** you can then do the Owning Your Shadow Parts exercise Chapter 6. On one hand, we need to discern how people are showing up. On the other hand, we need to recognize our judgments of them and own those parts within ourselves. It's a fine line to walk, yet doing the Shadow exercise

will dissolve some ego-residue. Humility shifts energy. And as your energy shifts, G-d willing, theirs will too.

4. **Say affirmations** such as these twice a day to help create a more loving atmosphere for yourself. Your vibration will rise and people's energy will shift for the better, or they may leave your life because you are not open to receiving negative energy anymore:

"Hashem surrounds me with kind, caring people."

And the following affirmation is one of my favorites. I have memorized it and I say it on behalf of myself and my older children, because it includes all positive aspects of a job.

"I have a job I love, I work with and for people I truly like, and I earn good money."

—Louise Hay

Blessings! 

Letter 3

Overwhelmed

Dear Miriam Racquel,

I have a two-year-old toddler and am pregnant again. I'd love to be a stay at home mom, but my husband and I both agree that we need more income and I have to get a job. I'm looking for a part-time one, but my heart is not in it. Right now, my toddler goes to a small playgroup three times a week for half the day. I love having the mornings to myself because when my toddler is around, my head just buzzes with all the energy he has! It's hard to keep up. When the apartment is quiet and it's just me, I get to rest, daven, meditate, clean up, and just go at my own pace. I can't imagine having another baby to take care of along with my super active toddler AND going to work. Having to be responsible to others when I can barely be responsible to my growing family makes me very nervous. I know that Hashem provides, but don't I have to make a keli for that by getting a job in spite of my fear of being able to manage?

Dear Awesome Woman,

I hear your dilemma loud and clear.

As a Jewish woman, you are the akeres habayis. The atmosphere of the home is created through you and the importance of your role as a mother cannot be underestimated. I love what Mindy Chazan writes in the December 2020 N'shei Newsletter:

> *The mother is the one who creates this warm, inviting, safe, and loving atmosphere in her home. Through her efforts, the home becomes a mikdash me'at and a refuge from the world. A place where everyone can comfortably be and live and learn and discover themselves with no judgment.* (Chazan, 2020)

Mindy continues, as wives and mothers,

> "We are the CEOs of our priceless company—our family!"

Such a big job rests on our shoulders! We need strength, joy, and calmness of mind to create a nurturing atmosphere in our homes.

Now, some women, in addition to being moms, want to work outside the home. They enjoy the outside stimulation and responsibilities. They become depressed being home full time. A friend of mine once asked the Lubavitcher Rebbe about becoming a physical therapist because she wanted to work, she did not want to stay home all day. The Rebbe told her to work part time and emphasized that her husband, children, and home were still a priority. But since she enjoyed working, then she had a blessing to do so.

And let's not ever make the mistake of believing that we are what we do for a living. It may be part of our divine purpose, but it is not our worth even if society mistakes it as such. As Yidden, we know differently. I love this anecdote from Robert Kremnizer: "There was a

Chassid of the Previous Lubavitcher Rebbe who was asked whether he was a lawyer. 'Certainly not,' he replied, 'I am a Jew whose parnossah comes to me through the vehicle of the legal profession.'"

Regarding your situation, you are yearning to be a stay-at-home mom. How can we practically help make this happen for you?

Homeplay Exercise

Have to vs. Choose to

You mention in your letter that you "have to get a job." Let's take a look at the phrase "have to." There is nothing that we "have to" do. Sure, we face consequences when we neglect to do some things, like laundry, pay bills, shower, etc. The consequences will be unpleasant. But the phrase "have to" is a bit misleading—the real truth of the matter is we are choosing to do things because we either want positive results or want to avoid the negative results because we neglected to do something.

1. **From a somatic perspective, when you say "I have to...," what do you feel as physical sensations in your body?** Write out a few sentences of your "have-tos" and just notice what happens in your body. Personally when I use the phrase "have to...," I experience a clenching of my jaw, a holding of my breath, and a slight constriction in my chest.

2. **Now replace the phrase, "I have to" with "I choose to."** For example:

   "I choose to do the laundry because I want clean clothes."

"I choose to go to the doctor because my health is important to me."

3. **Notice the sensations that come up for you.**

When I do this replacement, I notice an expansion in my chest and a felt sense of freedom in my body. I am choosing to do less-than-favorite tasks but the tenseness and pressure are relieved. From this state of expansion in my body, my mind feels more open to receiving intuition, googling creative possibilities of how to better these actions.

For example, when my children were younger and I self-coached myself with the thought "I choose to do the laundry," I became aware of options of how and when to do this task so it didn't feel so draining. I even came up with a fun way to involve my children (see Lollipop Laundry in Letter #4 of Chapter 7: Parenting). It was a far cry from "I have to" with the weight of the world on my shoulders and a grumbling attitude.

4. **Now let's replace "I have to go to work" with "I choose to work." But is this true? Do you choose to work outside the home?** It sounds like you don't. The truth you shared is more like this: "I don't choose to work outside the home because the pressure will be too great on me, and my health and family life will suffer." Your letter conveys that you may have more of an introverted, quiet nature—needing some solitude and peace in your environment rather than being a juggle-everything kind of gal.

Our natures and sensitivities make a difference in choosing not only which job we take, but whether we can manage the responsibilities of a job in addition to our responsibilities as a wife and mom. Even working from home requires responsibilities, and not all women can juggle that without breaking

continued

under the pressure. As mentioned earlier, some women who have children feel strengthened having a job outside the home, while for other women this feels overwhelming. Each has to decide for themselves.

Homeplay Exercise

Blessings for Parnossah

The Lubavitcher Rebbe says, "Money is soul-energy, it represents the very energy of life itself; depending how you use it can either free you or enslave you."

Scholar Simon Jacobson illustrates this idea so well:

> *Some people feel that they and they alone are responsible for their success, that their intelligence and abilities made it so. This is the serious challenge of wealth: to not be deceived by your own ego but to remember that it is G-d who gives us the power to become prosperous.*
>
> *This is not to say that your success is not a result of your efforts; of course it is. And you must do everything possible to ensure success, not just sit back and wait for money to come your way. But you must acknowledge that it is G-d's blessing, and not your effort alone, that creates wealth.* (Jacobson, 1995)

Considering that Hashem is the true source of finances, and that it is not a mitzvah that a woman has a job, what creative ideas do you have that can help the parnossah situation? After sitting down with your husband and sharing with him,

"I'd like to be a stay-at-home mom," how can you, as an akeres habayis, make a keli for parnossah without taking a job? Can you learn some Torah together once a week in the merit of strengthening Hashem's blessing for parnossah? Can each of you be more careful with certain mitzvos to expand your receiving vessels for money?

For about twenty years, while raising my children, I was a stay-at-home mom. I did help my husband a little bit in the office, but my responsibilities were mainly at home. This was a decision that my husband and I made from the beginning of our marriage. Were there ups and downs regarding parnossah? Totally! But we had decided that the kind of stress and toll an outside job would have on me, our marriage, and the children would just not make it worth it. We trusted that Hashem could provide plenty of money through the kelim my husband made. And Hashem did.

So hatzlacha on your decision! And remember to reach out for help if you need—that's what coaches, mentors, healers, and therapists are here for.

I have confidence that with sensitivity, care, a healthy mindset, and yiras shomayim, knowing that Hashem is the true source of money, that you, your husband, and growing family will prosper.

Blessings!

Letter 4:

The Guarding of Touch in the Workplace

I Can't Hug You

Dear Miriam Racquel,

I work in the non-Jewish sector and sometimes it's so awkward to explain that as an Orthodox woman, I don't shake hands with men. At times, I feel so different, like I stick out like a sore thumb. And I'm an introvert so I prefer not drawing attention to myself! Any chizuk you can share?

Dear Awesome Woman,

I understand! As a Modest Goddess, we truly are different! And in the world today, we do stand out. I believe you can look at this as a type of shlichus, an opportunity to represent Hashem and Torah-true Judaism in a beautiful way.

Judge Ruchie Freier shares some very funny examples in her speeches including one time, a colleague knew not to shake her hand, but thought it was okay to give her a big hug. And he did!

Please read on as I share a funny story that happened to me. I originally published it for TheJewishWoman.org to give a large audience chizuk in the observance of the guarding and sacredness of touch for the Torah observant woman. My experience was so out-of-the ordinary and humorous that it could only have been concocted by the One above, the ultimate Master of Creativity.

I Can't Hug You

I quietly entered the conference room as it was filling up with people. The coaching seminar was well attended, with "a group of 19 women and one man. As an introvert, I was trying to make my entrance with the least amount of attention possible.

"Wow! Your hair is beautiful!" I heard shouted towards me as I made my way to the far end of the gigantic table.

I turned, looking for where the voice came from. "Thank you! It's a wig," I announced. "I'm a Torah observant Jew, and as a married woman, I cover my hair." So much for my efforts at staying low profile.

I can break out of my comfort zone when necessary, and in this case, I decided I would. I've learned from my spiritual guide, the Rebbe, that educating others about the Jewish way of life—even if they're not of the Jewish faith—is important.

A beautiful conversation ensued, as I took a few moments to explain why married, Torah-observant women cover their hair, focusing on the mystical meaning. I kept it short and simple, and explained that after a woman marries, her hair can attract a type of negative spiritual force if left uncovered. At home, I cover it with a scarf, while outside the home with a wig. It was an interesting discussion considering none of the people there were Jewish.

We settled into our seats and time flew by as we shared and learned, honing our coaching craft. But my spot in the limelight was not over, and soon, the next wondrous hiccup occurred. We each took turns standing in front of the room and telling others a bit about ourselves and what kind of coaching we specialized in.

The one man present began his personal story. He was only in his early 30s but had already had more than his share of painful experiences. He was covered with tattoos with no bare skin showing except for his very kind face. He had the full attention of all the compassionate women in the audience as he shared the difficult and challenging hand life had dealt him.

He had been a serious drug dealer before getting help for himself and then becoming a coach. Many of the women clutched their hearts, tears in their eyes as he described his path to recovery. And then one of the women enthusiastically suggested: "Please walk around the room so we can each show you some love and give you a hug!"

Uh, oh. I can't believe it! G-d has an interesting sense of humor! No way out of this one. It's going to be necessary to draw attention to myself again because I'll be the one woman in the room who will not hug this man.

It wasn't that I was missing a compassionate heart; it was just that according to my faith, men and women who are not married or closely related can't touch. So there's no shaking hands, let alone hugging.

This was going to be awkward.

As this man made his way around the table, with each woman rising to embrace him, my mind quickly searched for what I could tactfully and kindly say to at least lessen the blow of my upcoming rejection. He had openly shared his story with us and was in quite a vulnerable position. Now I could become another cause of sorrow in his already difficult life!

I turned towards him as he stood in front of me expecting the same hug everyone else had given him. Fully aware that all eyes were on me, I said: "I'm so sorry. I can't hug you because I'm a Torah-observant Jewish woman, and the only men we touch are our husbands and close family members. But I was touched by your story, and thank you so much for sharing."

He was very respectful, nodded and moved on. When it was break time, I went over to speak to him just to make sure that there were no hard feelings. Many people have had negative experiences with religion or religious people—and have felt judged, rejected or cast off. It was important to me to be a good representative of my religion by showing kindness and compassion even amid the restrictions I chose to follow. Thankfully, he was fine, and we ended up chatting about our religious beliefs and how we serve our coaching clients from a place of strength.

Before G-d gave the Jewish people the Torah, He approached the other nations and offered it to them (Rashi, Deuteronomy 33:2). Each had one reason or another for rejecting G-d's gift, but the common denominator was that taking on G-d's mitzvot and living according with His will was too uncomfortable. They were not willing to make the necessary personal and communal sacrifices.

So the Jewish nation received the Torah with the charge of spreading G-d's message to every person in every corner of the world. And ironically, it is specifically through standing up for our convictions, as uncomfortable as it may be, that this is done in the most beautiful way.

Fast-forward more than 3,000 years to a small conference in Portland, Oregon. A simple Jew respectfully and humbly stood up for her differences. People were intrigued and curious, not judgmental or unkind. They were respectful and wanted to know more, not less. Those uncomfortable moments become opportunities for connection, not separation.

I'm aware that in every situation where one needs to do something different according to their practices, it will not always "be accepted with such grace. At the same time, acting with confidence and pride is how to serve your Creator, popular or as unpopular as it may be, as that is being in alignment with your soul and G-d's will.

May our ways be blessed, and may we serve as a light unto the nations.

Blessings!

Afterword

Dear Awesome Woman,

Thank you for coming along this somatic wellness journey with me. May your path be filled with kindness and may your body, mind, and spirit be healthy as you keep your faith with joy of heart.

Love and Blessings,
Miriam Racquel (Meryl) Feldman

Visit me at
www.MiriamRacquel.com
www.YourMarriageMagic.com

Acknowledgments

I'd like to thank my husband for schlepping me on this Torah journey. Without you who knows where I may have landed up in my life. I was definitely a tough customer. Thank you for believing in me and for continuing to believe in me—in my dreams and hopes of writing this book to help other women walk the path that we have taken with less bumps and potholes by sharing wisdom gained over the years.

Thank you to my beautiful children, daughter-in-laws, and grandchildren for being in my life. I love you dearly.

Thank you to my parents, Blossom and Melvin Cook, for being in our lives even though you may not have always understood the path that we chose to take. Thank you to my sisters, Ellen and Audrey, for being respectful and including us in your lives though our paths diverged in many ways. Thank you to all my extended family for the same.

Special thanks to my grandmother, Handel bas Avraham, Grandma T., for bringing the old country to your new home in America. You brought your Shabbos candles and that was a touching stone for me on my journey back to the Torah tradition that you were raised with so lovingly in Hungary. Your faith in Hashem and your gratitude to your Creator—your "Tanks Gott"—no matter how many years you lived alone without Grandpa and with your feet swollen, still rings in my ears till today.

Thank you for all those wonderful teachers, mashpi'im, rabbis, and rebbetzins who opened their doors, their minds, their hearts to me and my family as we walked the Torah path.

Thank you, Hashem, for bringing me Emma Danbury—a gifted, kind editor who has walked the journey of my books with me—I couldn't have asked for anyone better. Emma—you've been such a blessing walking this journey with me. Your support, skills, and gentleness are truly appreciated.

Thank you, Deborah Meister, my finishing editor who really helped birth this book into the world! I am especially grateful that you saved my sanity by fixing all the commas. You are the Comma Queen! What an amazing friend and professional you have been on this journey! It's been a joy and delight to work with you.

And a big thank you and hug to Dovid and Sharone for your feedback, insight, and editing that has contributed greatly to this project.

Thank you, Rebecca Finkel, for the wonderful design on this project. You're a pleasure and gift to work with.

Thank you, Rebbe, the Lubavitcher Rebbe, for your tremendous faith in me and wise guidance. For your belief that this world can be a better place and that each one of us can light our soul candles and create a Dirah Betachtonim, a place for Hashem revealed here on earth.

Thank you, Hashem, for bringing me the gift of healing.

And Hashem, one more thing. May you hear the cries and pleas of your people and reveal Moshiach on earth. May all suffering end. May we truly open our eyes and hearts and awaken to the complete Geulah.

Amen.

Glossary

Ahavas Yisroel: Love of a fellow Jew; Jews are considered One.

Akeres Habayis: Hebrew for foundation of the home; refers to the wife.

Arizal: Kabbalist Rabbi Isaac Luria (1534-1572); his name is an acronym for "The G-dly Rabbi Isaac of Blessed Memory."

B'simcha: With joy.

Baal Shem Tov: Rabbi Yisroel ben Eliezer, a Jewish scholar who lived in Eastern Europe during the 18th century and revealed many secrets and mystical explanations of the Torah. Changed the face of Judaism; founder of the Hasidic movement. In a deep meditation during Rosh Hashanah in 1746, the Baal Shem Tov met the soul of Moshiach. He posed the question, "When will the Master come?" and the Moshiach answered, "By this you shall know: In the time when your teaching will become public and revealed in the world, and your wellsprings will burst forth to the farthest extremes…."

Baal Teshuvah: A Jewish man who becomes more observant in the practice and laws of Judaism.

Baalas Teshuvah: A Jewish woman who becomes more observant in the practice and laws of Judaism.

Baruch Hashem (Boruch Hashem): Blessed be G-d; term of gratitude.

Bashert: Yiddish for "predestined." Often refers to a soulmate.

Bayis Ne'eman: A home built on faith.

Binah: Understanding an idea. One of the Sefirot, the spiritual-energetic flows of the world and of individuals.

Bitachon: Trust; refers to trust in G-d.

Bochur: Young unmarried man.

Bubby: Yiddish for Grandma.

Chassidische: Following the ways of Chassidus.

Chassidus (Hasidus): The teachings of the Jewish movement first founded by the Baal Shem Tov in the 1700s, with emphasis on the mystical aspects of the Torah.

Chas v'shalom: G-d forbid.

Chesed: Love, kindness.

Chizuk: Strengthening.

Cholov Yisroel: Dairy products under Jewish supervision.

Chuppah: Jewish marriage canopy; means covering, protection. A chuppah symbolizes the groom's home and the bride's new domain.

Daas: A deep knowing.

Derech: Hebrew for path or way.

Dirah Betachtonim: a dwelling in the lower realms. G-d's desire for Divine Presence to manifest and be integrated fully in a revealed way in the physical world. This is accomplished through the act of doing physical mitzvahs.

Farbrengen: An inspirational gathering.

Frum: Yiddish for religious.

Geulah: (geula) Redemption. Refers to an everlasting time of world peace and abundance, prophesied in Jewish sources.

Gevurah: Strictness, discipline.

Gilgul *(pl gilgulim):* Hebrew for "cycle" or "wheel." Refers to the Jewish mystical concept of reincarnation.

Golus: Exile. Refers to the era immediately after the destruction of the 2nd Temple (70 AD) until the present moment. During this time, the Jewish nation is scattered around the globe, and there is a lack of world-peace and unity.

Great yeshiva bochur: Refers to an excellent academic young man.

G-d: The word for God written with a dash out of respect for the holy name of G-d, which shouldn't be disposed of improperly. Many Orthodox/Hasidic Jews prefer to write G-d rather than the name in full.

Hachnasat Orchim: The mitzvah of inviting guests.

Halacha (*pl* halachas): Jewish law(s).

Hamshochas halev: Attraction of the heart.

Hashem: Hebrew for "The Name." Refers to G-d.

Hashkafa: Worldview, outlook.

Kabbalah: Jewish mysticism traced back to Moses and even earlier. Reveals the secrets of the universe.

Kallah: Bride.

Kashrus, kashrut: Kosher; strict Torah dietary laws.

Kedusha: Holiness.

Keli: Vessel, spiritual container.

Kibud: To honor.

Kiddush Hashem: Sanctification of G-d's name. Being a good role model.

Kiddusha: Holiness.

Lashon hora: Evil speech; gossip. Forbidden according to Jewish law.

Manna: Special nourishment G-d provided to the Jews in their wandering in the desert.

Mashpia (*pl* mashpi'im): Spiritual mentor, person of influence, giver.

Mekabel: receiver; in the context of marriage and even anatomically, the wife.

Mekarev: To bring another Jew close to Torah observance.

Menschlich: A Yiddish term to behave with kindness and be honorable.

Menschlichkeit: Behaving with integrity.

Mesiras nefesh: Self-sacrifice.

Metzar: Limitation.

Middah (*pl* middos; middot): Character trait.

Mikdash me'at: Small temple.

Mikvah: See Taharas Hamishpacha.

Minyan: Prayer service consisting of 10 men (13 years and older).

Mitzrayim: Egypt, from the root word "limitations."

Mitzvah (*pl* mitzvot, mitzvahs): Commonly translated as a "command" or "good deed." Sourced from the Aramaic word "tzavta" which means "connection" or "attachment"; refers to a connection with the Infinite Light, the source of the mitzvah, in Chassidus.

Moshiach: Hebrew for Jewish Messiah, literally meaning "anointed one."

Negel vasser schussel: Yiddish for "nail water bowl." Chassidim wash spiritual impurity from their hands by leaving a cup and bowl of water by their beds. They lean over their bed in the morning to do this before placing their feet on the floor.

Neshama: Soul.

Niddah: See Taharas Hamishpacha.

Parsha: Hebrew for a section of Torah. Also can refer to being in the time period of dating.

Parnossah: Hebrew for "financial sustenance."

Rabbi: A Jewish scholar or teacher, especially one who studies or teaches Jewish law. Usually referred to as a title for a Jewish man with rabbinic ordination.

Rebbe: A holy man and leader of a Chassidic sect. In this book, "the Rebbe" refers to the Lubavitcher Rebbe, Rabbi M.M. Schneerson.

Redemption: *See* Geulah.

Redt a shidduch: Suggest a date for marriage.

Rosh Chodesh: Head of the month; celebration of the new moon.

Shabbos: Yiddish for "Sabbath." Refers to the seventh day of creation (Friday night to Saturday night), when G-d created rest. The Jewish nation observes this day by refraining from doing any Torah-prohibited work.

Shadchan (*pl* shadchanim): Yiddish for "Matchmaker." One who facilitates between men and women while dating.

Shidduch: A matchmaking system in which Jewish singles are introduced to one another in Orthodox Jewish communities by a third party for the sake of marriage. Also, a term to mean a "match" or "fit."

Schmatta: A rag; can also mean being treated unwell, like a doormat.

Sechel: Intellect.

Shalom: Peace.

Shalom Bayis: Peace in the home.

Shechinah: Used when referring to the feminine aspect of G-d. Comes from the root word, *shochen,* "to dwell within." Also means the Divine Presence.

Sheitel (*pl* sheitels): Wig.

Sheva brachos: Seven blessings recited over wine at a marital ceremony; refers to 7 nights of formal dinners to celebrate with the newlyweds.

Taharas Hamishpacha: Refers to the laws of family purity. These are complex laws of the Torah prohibiting husband and wife from sharing intimacy during her time of menses or other uterine bleeding (*niddah*). The following is an excellent explanation from Maurice Lamm of *Chabad.org*: "Jewish law forbids a husband to approach his wife during the time of her menses, generally from five to seven days, and extends the prohibition of any physical contact beyond this period for another seven days, known as the 'seven clean days.' (That is why one will always find, in observant Jewish homes, two beds for husband and wife, never a double bed.) During this time husband and wife are expected to act towards each other with respect and affection but without any physical expression of love: excellent training for that time, later in their lives, when husband and wife will have to discover bonds other than physical intimacy to link them one to another. At the end of this twelve to fourteen day period (depending upon the individual woman), the menstruant (known as *niddah*) must immerse herself in a body of water known as a *mikvah* and recite a special blessing in which she praises G-d for sanctifying us with His commandments and commanding us concerning immersion (*tevillah).*"

Taiva (*pl* taivos): Lust, greed, desire, following base instincts.

Teshuva: Repentence. Refers to returning to the path of Torah observance.

Tiferes: Harmony.

Tikkun: Hebrew for "improve, fix, prepare, rectify." Often referring to a process of spiritual correction to repair and elevate the world, as per G-d's command.

Tumah: Spiritual impurity. Ex: In sleep, a part of the soul leaves the body through the nails when a person is asleep. Since an absence of life is associated with spiritual impurity, washing negel vasser in the morning removes that state.

Tzaddik, Tzaddikim *female* Tzaddakis: From the Hebrew root word for "just" and "righteous." Refers to a righteous individual or spiritual master.

Tzitzis: (Tzitzit) White strings on a four-cornered garment. An external reminder for men of the 613 mitzvahs because of the Gematria of the word and the number of knots and strings.

Tznius: Hebrew word for "modesty" or "privacy." As the Rebbe has said, "Our Sages explain that *Tznius* and *Kedushah* (holiness) must be observed in every aspect of Jewish life, including speech and thought, and certainly in dress and general conduct."

Yeshiva: Orthodox Jewish school.

Yetzer hara: Evil inclination. Ex: Jew's desire to do something opposite of Torah. For example, gossip or steal.

Yiddishkeit: Yiddish for "Jewish way of life."

Yiras Shomayim: Fear of (G-d) heaven.

Yetzias Mitzrayim: Leaving Egypt; leaving limitations.

Bibliography

Beck, Martha Nibley. *Steering by Starlight: Find Your Right Life, No Matter What!* New York: Rodale : Distributed to the trade by Macmillan, 2008.

Bluth, Rachel. *Jewish Press: Life Chronicles,* (as shared by Florida mom), January 23, 2015.

Braiker, Harriet. *The Disease To Please: Curing the People-Pleasing Syndrome.* New York: McGraw-Hill, 2002.

Brown, Brené. *Braving the Wilderness: The Quest for True Belonging and the Courage to Stand Alone.* New York: Random House, 2017.

COLlive. "Marriage According to the Rebbe," August 11, 2014. https://collive.com/marriage-according-to-the-rebbe/.

Derher, "Merit of the Women," Shevat 5779.

Doyle, Laura. *The Surrendered Single: A Practical Guide to Attracting and Marrying the Man Who's Right for You.* New York: Fireside, 2002.

Eden, Donna, and David Feinstein. *Energy Medicine for Women: Aligning Your Body's Energies to Boost Your Health and Vitality.* New York: Jeremy P. Tarcher/Penguin, 2008.

Fishoff, Avi. *Avi Fishoff TWiSTED PARENTiNG.* Youtube channel. https://www.youtube.com/c/AviFishoffTWiSTEDPARENTiNG.

Forward, Susan and Donna Frazier. *Emotional Blackmail: When the People in Your Life Use Fear, Obligation and Guilt to Manipulate You.* New York: HarperCollins, 1997.

Freeman, Tzvi. "The Myth of Chabad Outreach." Chabad.org. Chabad-Lubavitch Media Center. Accessed June 15, 2021. https://www.chabad.org/therebbe/article_cdo/aid/260455/jewish/The-Myth-of-Chabad-Outreach.htm.

Friedman, Avraham Peretz. *Marital Intimacy.* Linden, New Jersey: Compass Books, 2005.

Global Medical Response, Polyvagal Theory and Emergency Responders: How Our Nervous Systems Impact Our Lives; GMR Life October 2023.

Jacobson, Simon, and Menachem Mendel Schneerson. *Toward a Meaningful Life: The Wisdom of the Rebbe Menachem Schneerson.* New York, NY: Perennial Currents, 2004.

Kalmenson, Mendel. *Seeds of Wisdom: Based on personal encounters with the Rebbe, Rabbi Menachem M. Schneerson, of righteous memory.* New York: Jewish Educational Media, 2013.

Kalmenson, Mendel. "A Model of Love: Lessons from the Marriage of the Rebbe and Rebbetzin." Chabad.org. Chabad-Lubavitch Media Center. Accessed June 15, 2021. https://www.chabad.org/library/article_cdo/aid/1694020/jewish/A-Model-of-Love.htm.

Kohanov, Linda. *The Power of the Herd: A Nonpredatory Approach to Social Intelligence, Leadership, and Innovation.* Novato, California: New World Library, 2013.

Koval, Ruchi. "Parenting Regrets." Out of the Ortho Box. May 17, 2019. https://outoftheorthobox.com/parenting-regrets/?v=f003c44deab6.

Kremnizer, Robert. *The Ladder Up: Secret Steps to Jewish Happiness.* New York: Sichos in English, 2005.

McLaren, Karla. "Grief: The deep river of the soul." KarlaMcLaren.com. Accessed June 15, 2021. https://karlamclaren.com/grief-the-deep-river-of-the-soul/.

McLaren, Karla. *The Language of Emotions: What Your Feelings Are Trying to Tell You*. Boulder, Colo: Sounds True, 2010.

Posner, Menachem. "15 Facts About Reb Zusha of Anipoli." Chabad.org. Chabad-Lubavitch Media Center. Accessed June 15, 2021. https://www.chabad.org/library/article_cdo/aid/4285539/jewish/15-Facts-About-Reb-Zusha-of-Anipoli.htm.

Rosenfeld, Jennie, and David S. Ribner. *The Newlywed's Guide to Physical Intimacy*. New York: Gefen, 2011.

Schneerson, Menachem M. Compiled and Adapted by Rabbi Chaim Miller. *Kol Menachem Haggadah,* p. 85, quoting from Likkutei Sichot, vol. 20, p. 218. New York: Kol Menachem, 2008

Schneerson, Menachem M. Compiled by Rabbi Sholom B. Wineberg. *Healthy in Body Mind and Spirit - Volume 1: General Themes and Subjects Relating to Health.* New York: Sichos in English.

Schneerson, Menachem M. Compiled by Rabbi Sholom B. Wineberg. *Healthy in Body Mind and Spirit - Volume 3: Mental Health.* New York: Sichos in English.

Schneerson, Menachem M. *Letters from the Rebbe: Rabbi Menachem Mendel Schneerson.* New York: Otsar Sifrei Lubavitch, 1997.

Schneerson, Menachem M. Translated by Eliyahu Touger. *Likkutei Sichos: An Anthology of talks by the Lubavitcher Rebbe, Rabbi Menachem M. Schneerson.* New York: Sichos in English.

Schneerson, Menachem M. "Obstacles and Challenges." Chabad.org. Chabad-Lubavitch Media Center. Accessed June 15, 2021. https://www.chabad.org/library/article_cdo/aid/826624/jewish/Obstacles-and-Challenges.htm.

Schneersohn, Rabbi Yosef Yitzchak. Translation/adaptation by Yanki Tauber. *From the Writings and Talks of Rabbi Yosef Yizchak of Lubavitch.* Chabad.org. https://www.chabad.org/library/article_cdo/aid/2529/jewish/Baal-Shem-Tovs-16th-Birthday.htm

Shurpin, Yehuda. "What Was the Manna?" Chabad.org. Chabad-Lubavitch Media Center. Accessed June 15, 2021. https://www.chabad.org/library/article_cdo/aid/4463795/jewish/What-Was-the-Manna.htm.

Tuttle, Carol. *The Child Whisperer: The Ultimate Handbook for Raising Happy, Successful, and Cooperative Children.* Live Your Truth Press, 2012.

Tuttle, Carol. *It's Just My Nature! A Guide to Knowing and Living Your True Nature.* Live Your Truth Press, 2012.

Twerski, Rabbi Abraham J. Jewish Action. "Mirror Image," March 20, 1996. https://jewishaction.com/jewish-living/mirror-image/.

Wisnefsky, Rabbi Moshe Y. *Torah Bereishit, The Book of Genesis.* Chabad House Publications, 2008-2015.

About Miriam Racquel

Miriam Racquel (Meryl) Feldman is a wife, mom, somatic healer, marriage coach, anxiety & trauma specialist, and award-winning author. She helps empower women to trust themselves through the wisdom of their bodies, emotions, and intuition. As an international coach, prolific writer, keynote speaker, and popular podcast guest, her unique somatic modalities have helped bring healing to thousands of women. Marriage magic, dating guidance, narcissist relationship detox, emotional/physical pain relief, and career clarity are her specialties. Her award-winning memoir, *God Said What?! #MyOrthodoxLife,* has received international fame.

Go to: **www.MiriamRacquel.com** and **www.YourMarriageMagic.com** to download free e-guides, listen to podcasts, schedule a Clarity Call, and join thousands of women receiving monthly somatic healing and marriage magic tips.

Miriam Racquel also works together with her husband, Dovid Feldman, L.P.C., to help husbands and wives restore intimacy, trust, and connection. For more information, go to **www.DovidFeldman.com.**

Follow on Facebook.com/MiriamRFeldman

Great Gifts!

Share the light
by giving to friends and family.

Sold on Amazon

Positive reviews
are greatly appreciated.
Thank you!